Photographs Taken In Transit

By Bakthi Ross

Copyright © 2018
Bakthi Ross

Published by Waxwing.

No part of this book may be reproduced or transmitted in any form or by any means, electronic or mechanical, including photocopying, recording, or by any information storage and retrieval system without permission in writing from the author.

Author Bakthi Ross © 2017.08.17

For information or to order additional books, please write to

Waxwing
PO Box 373
MORAYFIELD 4506
AUSTRALIA
OR PHONE 07-54987214

ISBN   978 1 922220 46 2

Photographs of plants and flowers taken using a moving camera

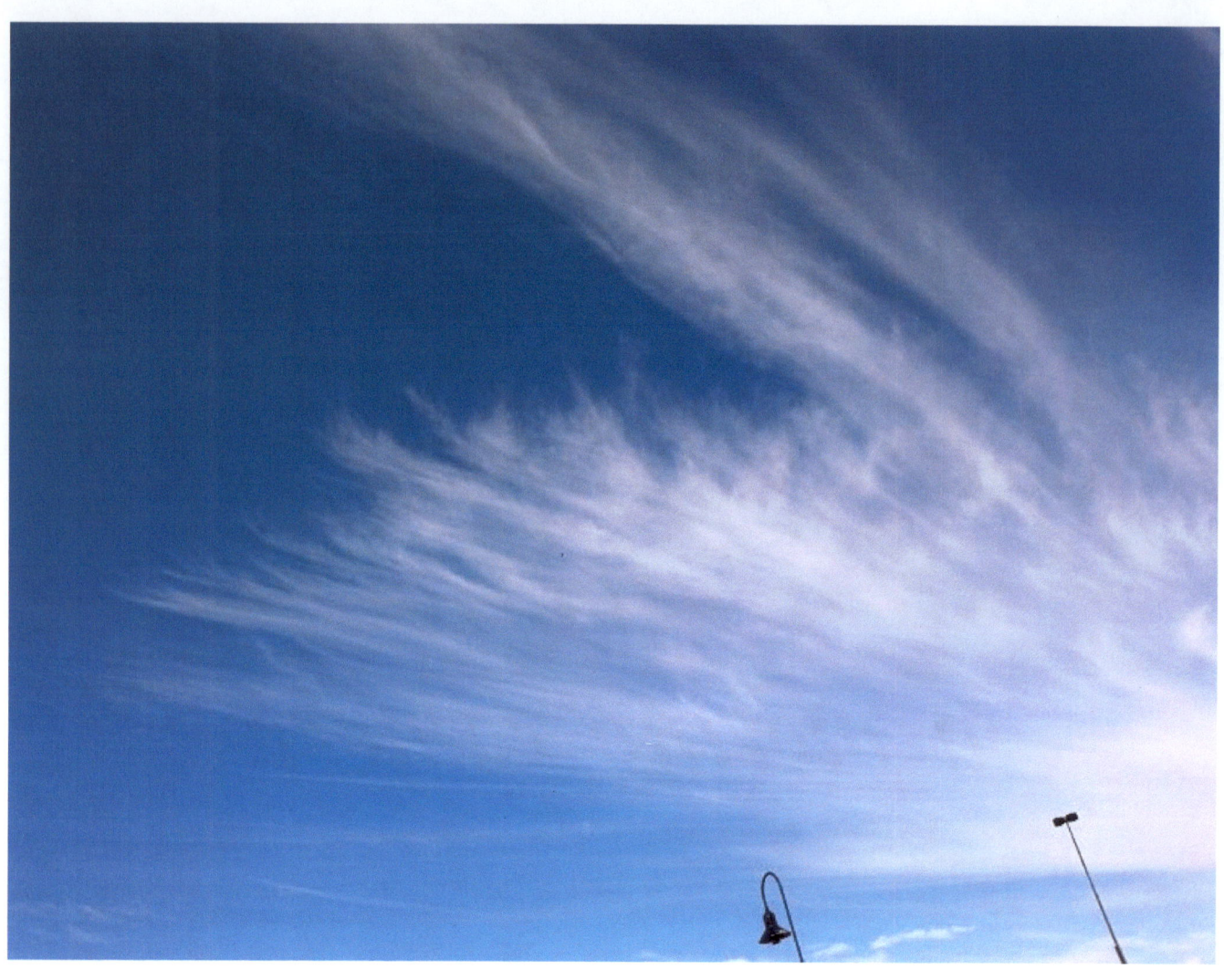

A movements of cloud. This is not a photograph taken while the camera in movement. This is a still picture.

This is a photograph while the camera in movement and lost the features of the things and become red with light.

Another photograph clouded the things and over powered by light.

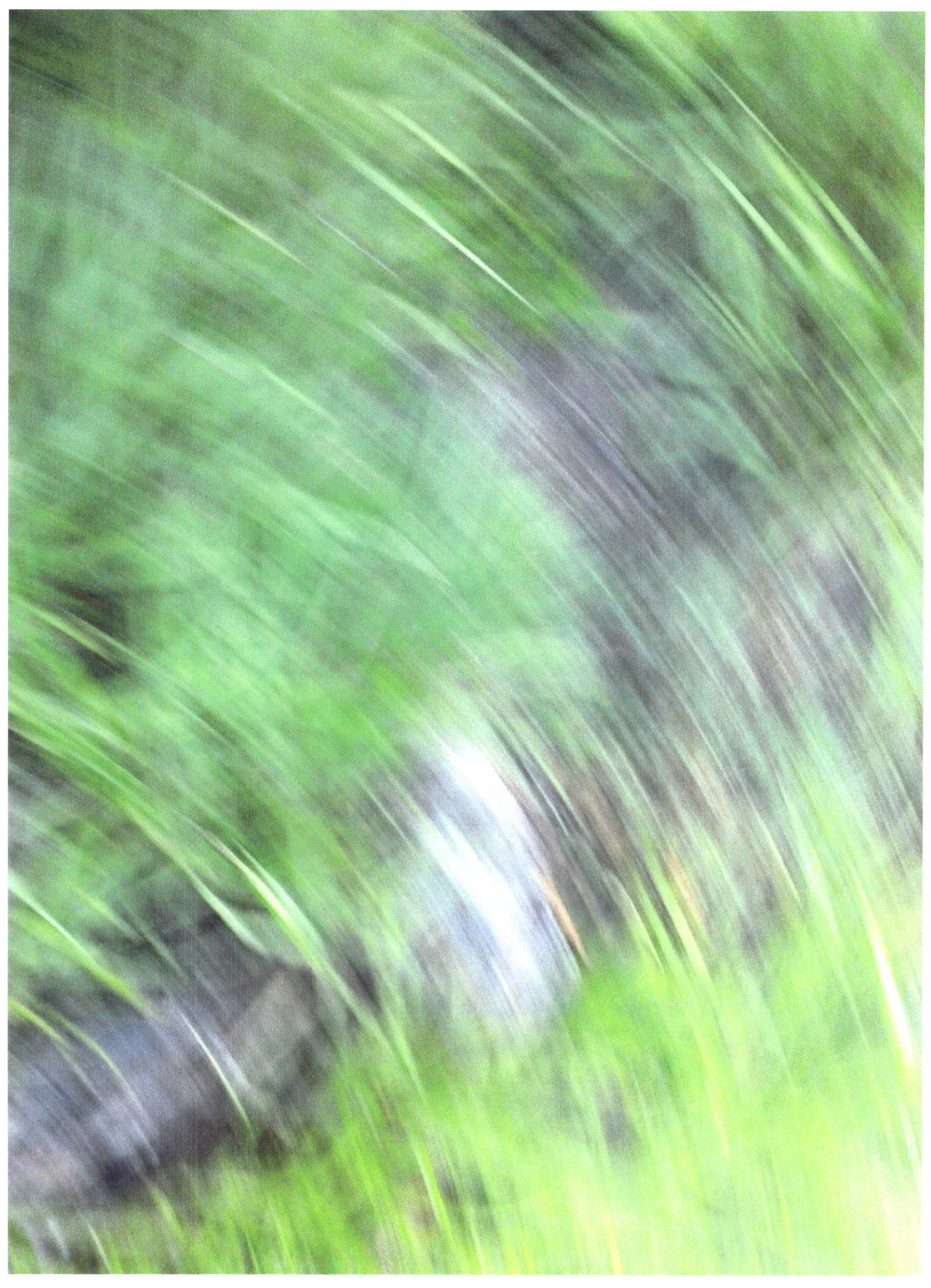

Movements of grass.

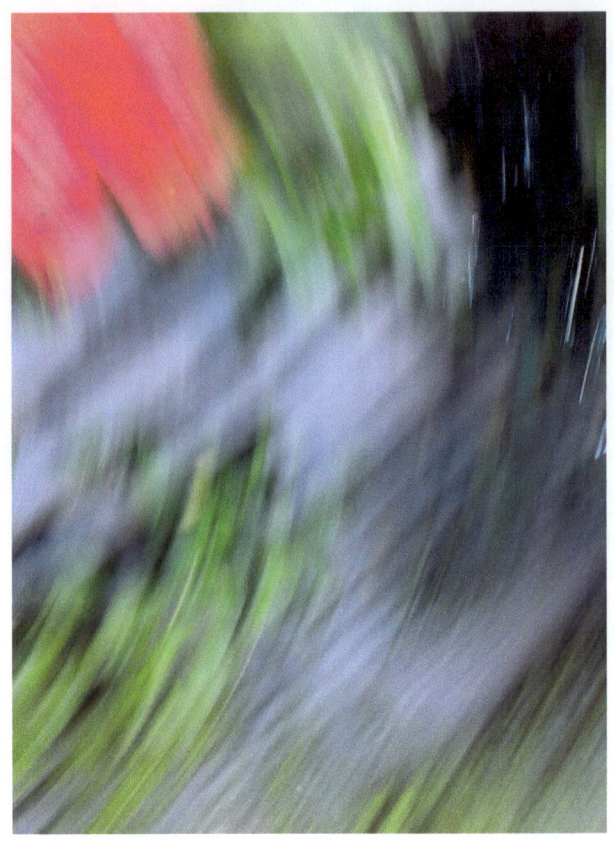

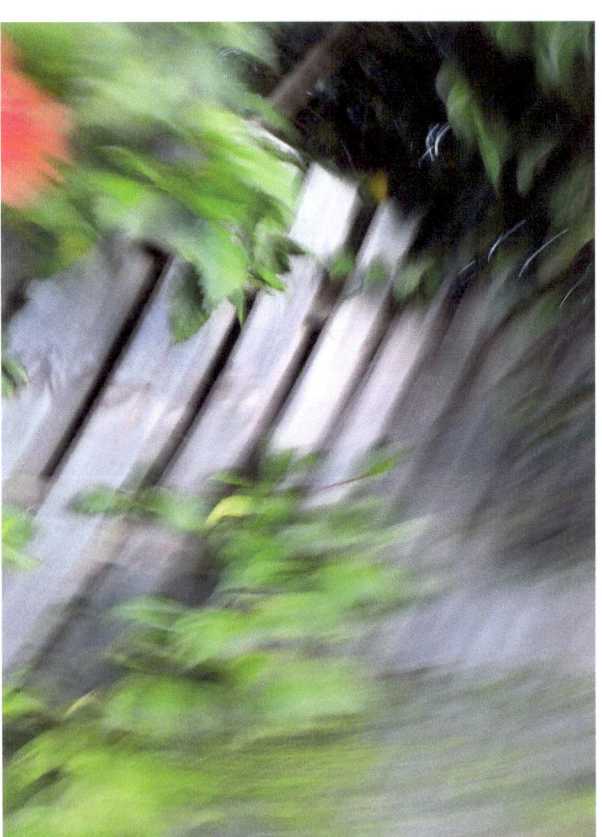

Photographs of plants when camera was in transit.

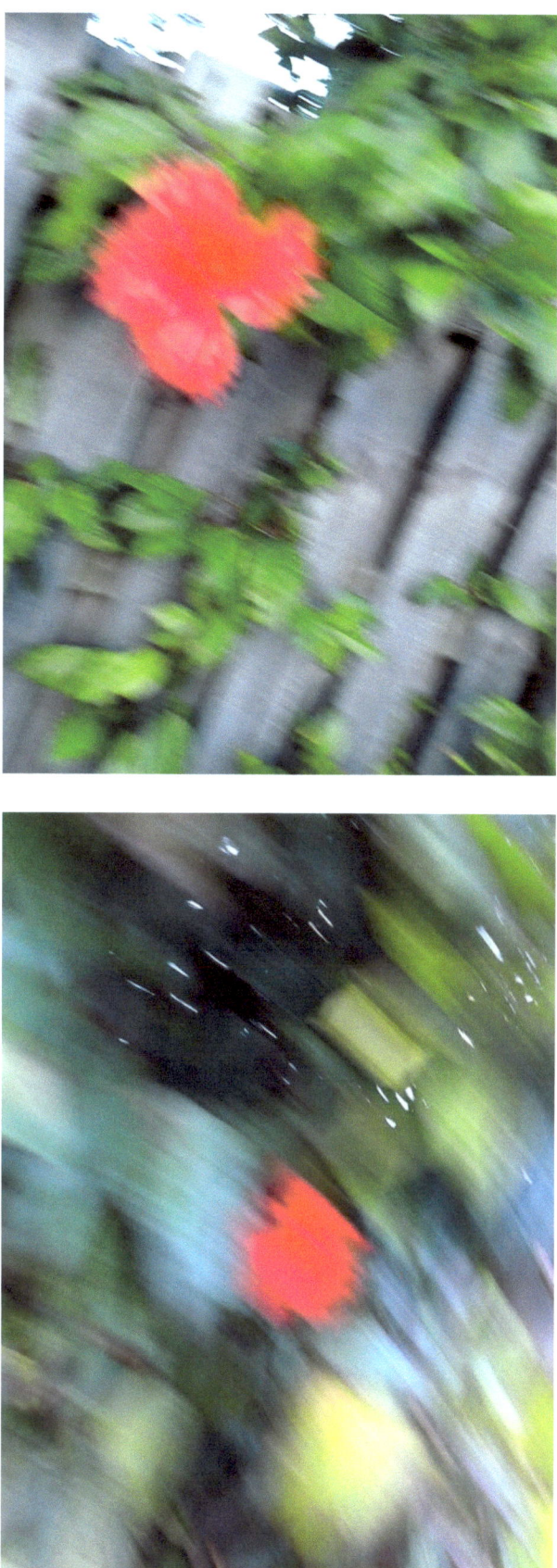

Photographs of plants when camera was in transit.

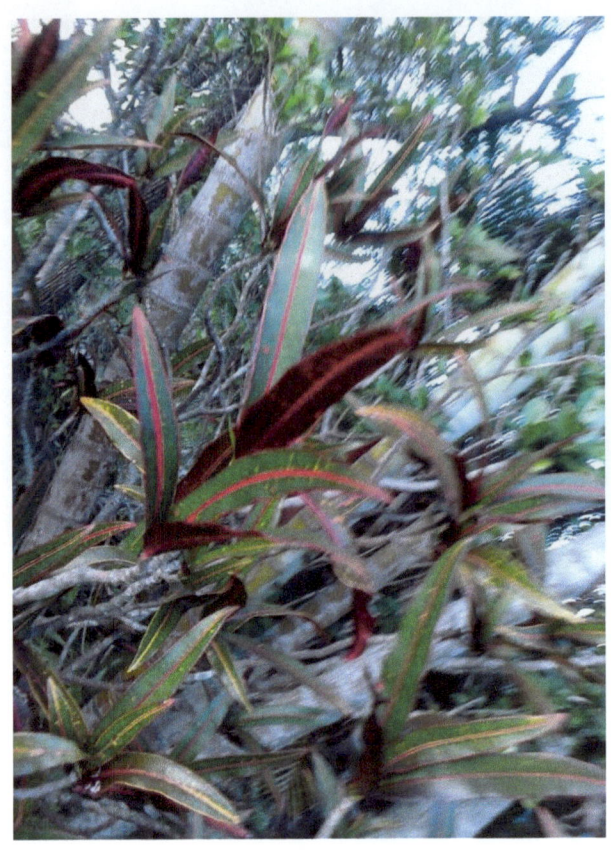

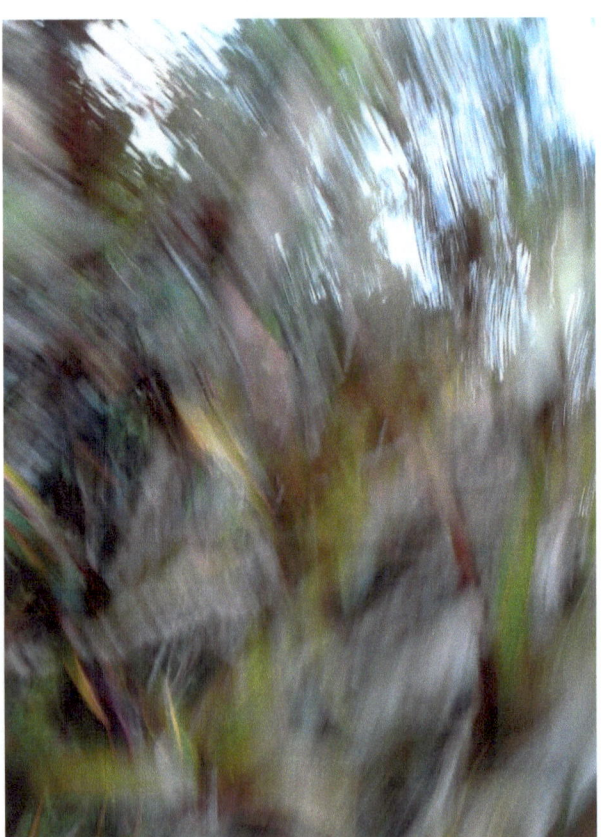

Original plant photograph and the camera in transit made the plant blur.

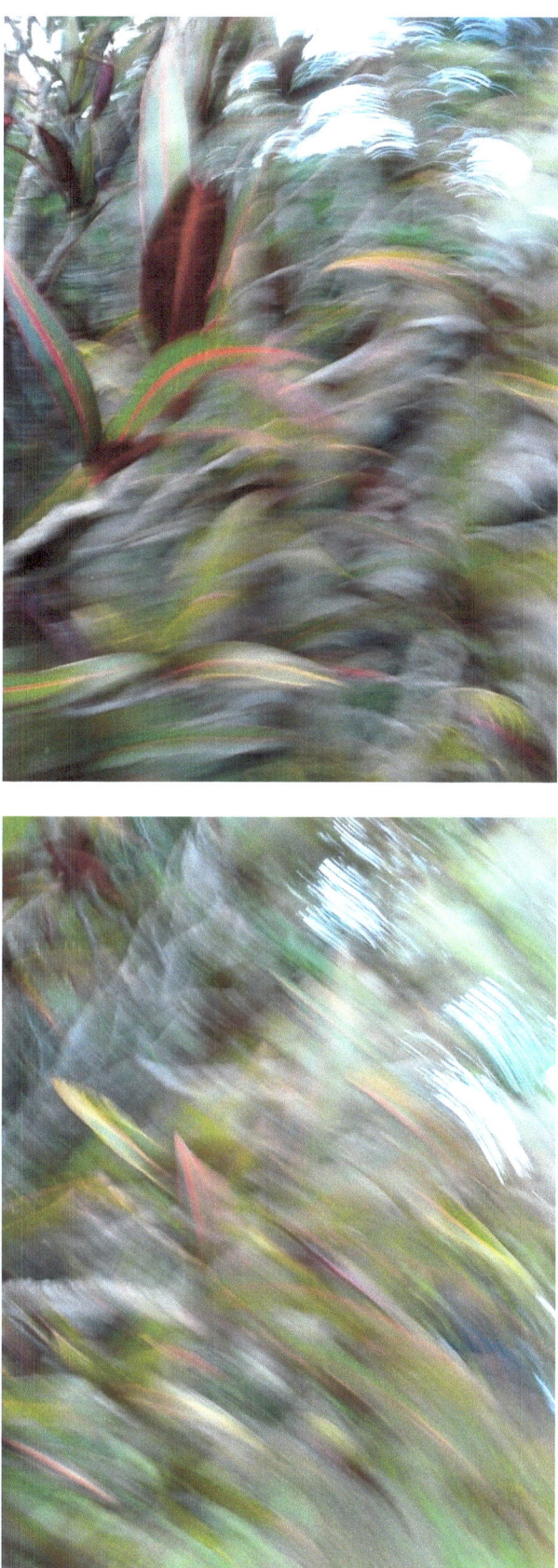

More movements of the same plant on the previous page.

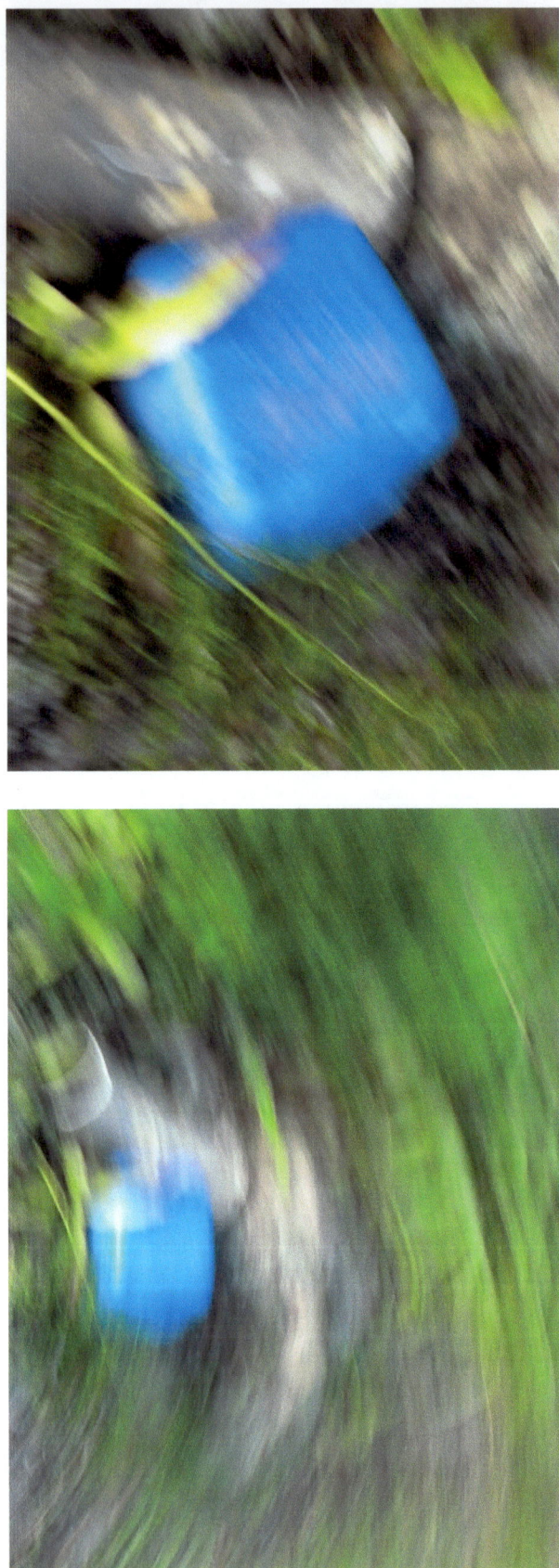

An ice cream container expands the colour when camera was in transit.

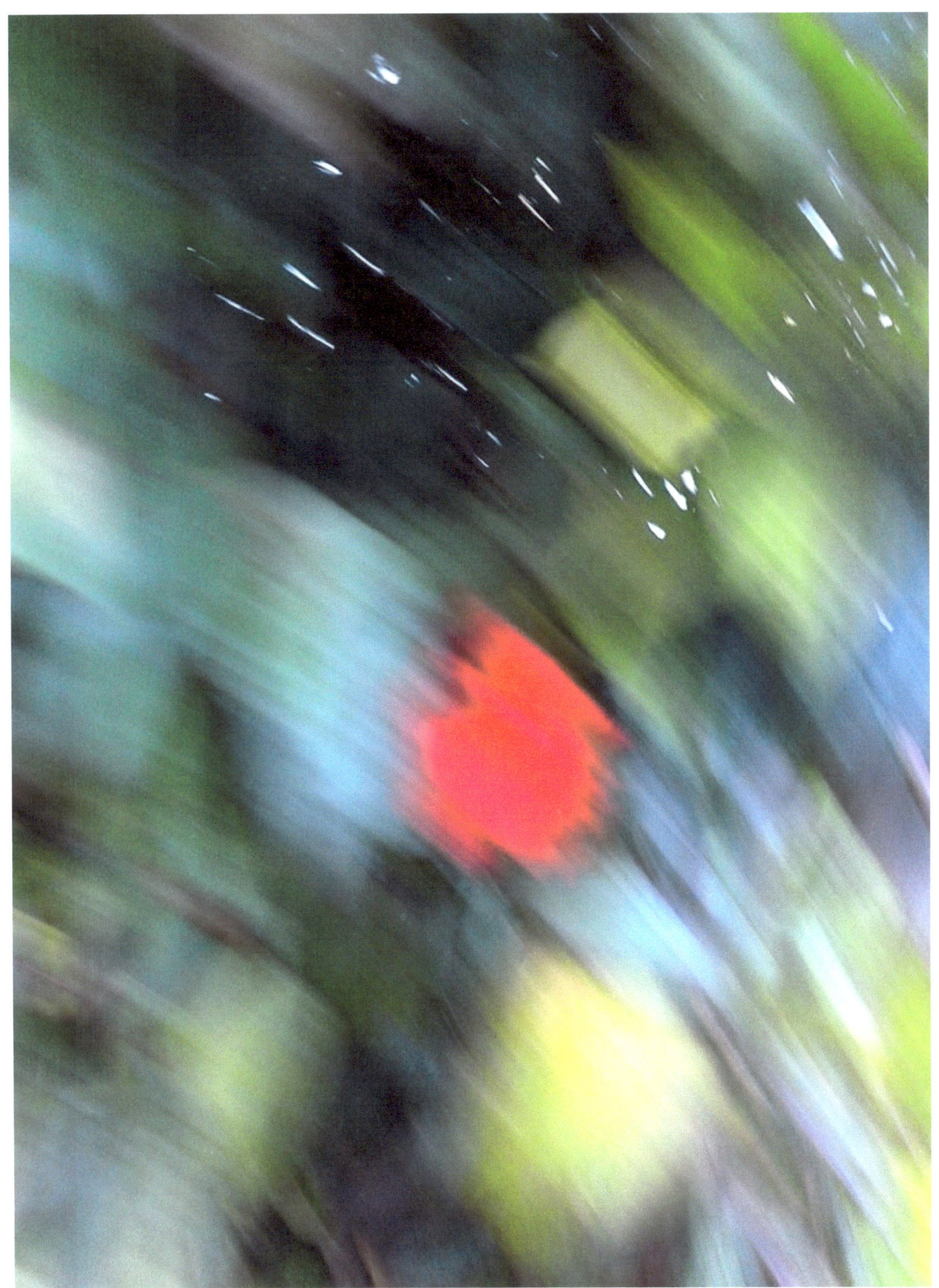
You can see light separating itself and moving as white lines.

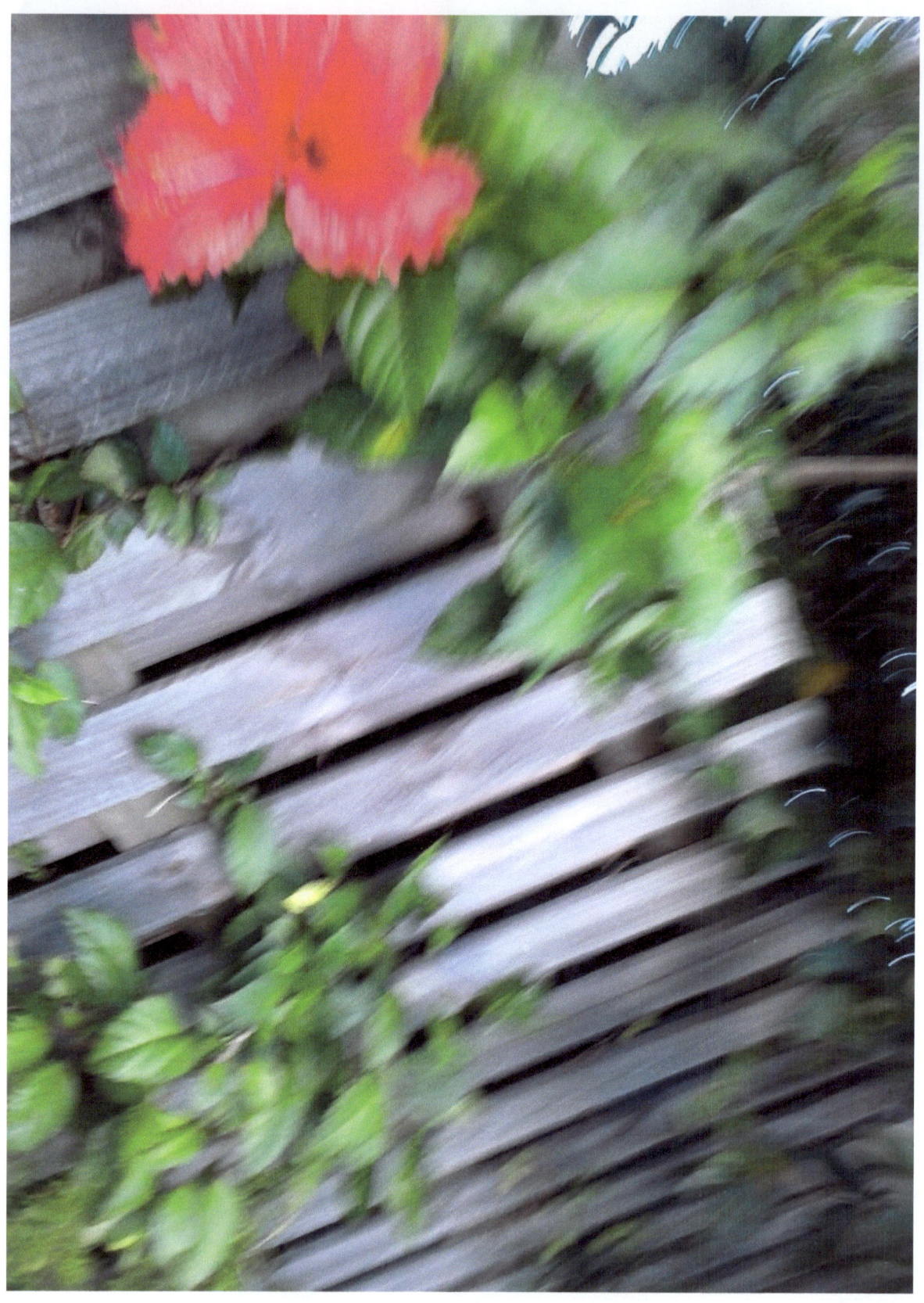

You see can light moving in white lines.

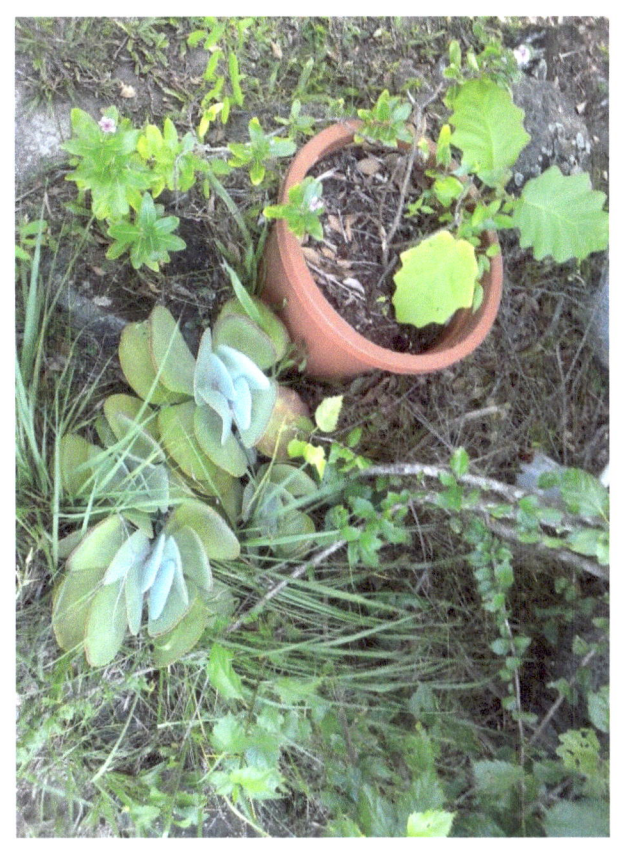

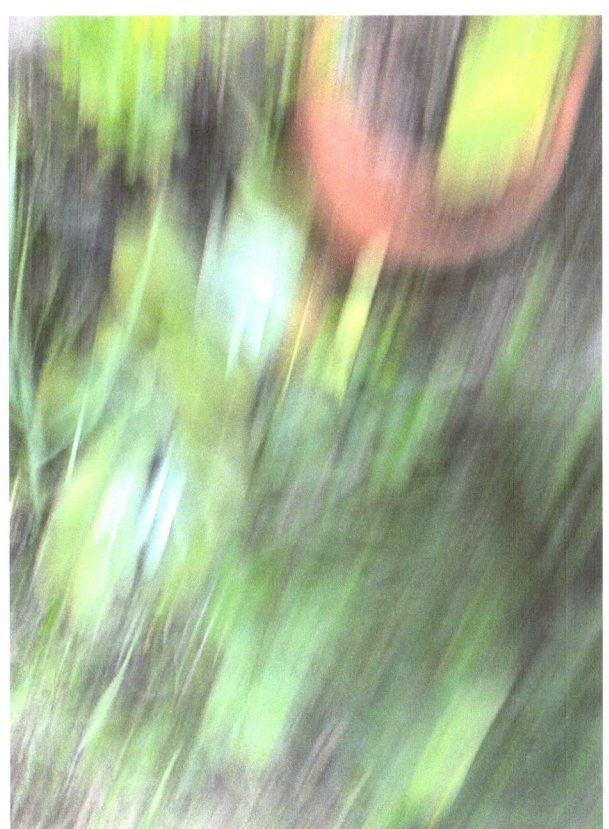

Pot plant taken when camera was in transit.

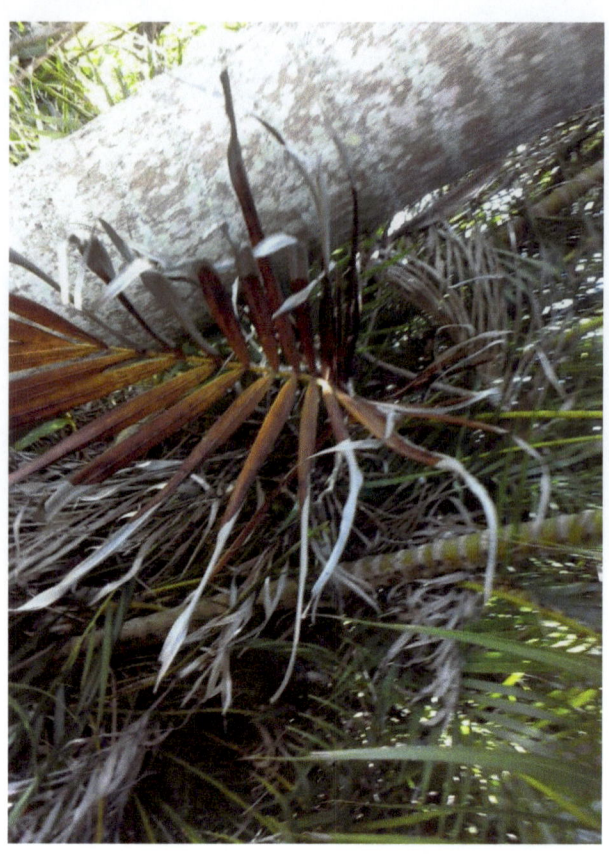

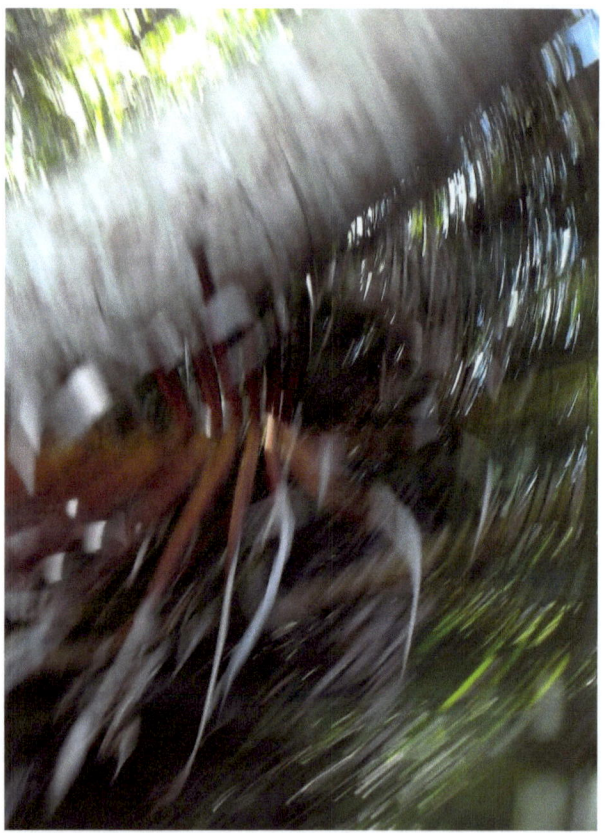

Palm leaf photograph when camera was in transit.

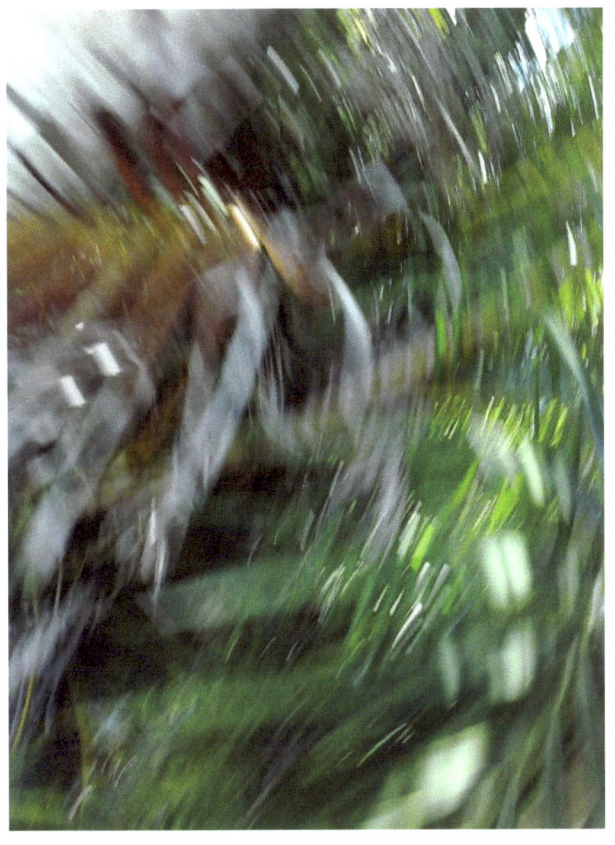

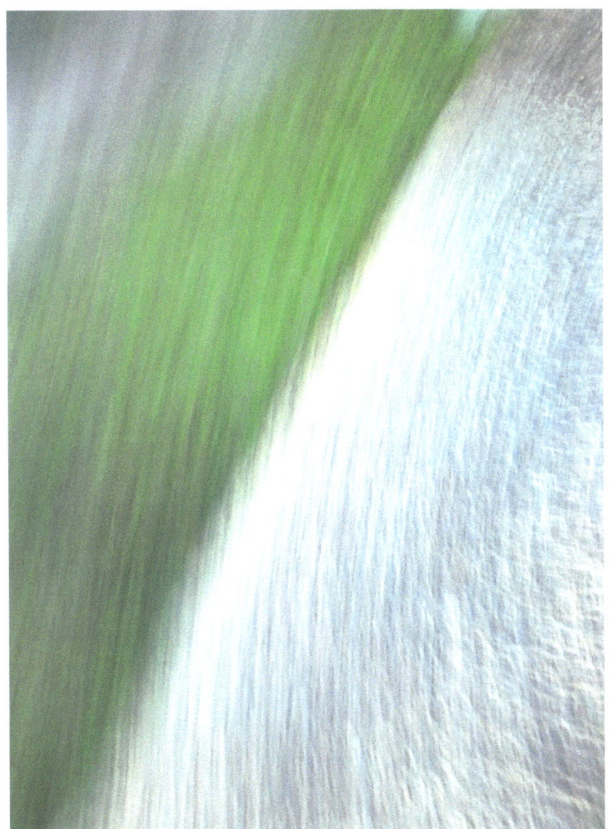

Even the concrete next to the grass forming a rotational pattern.

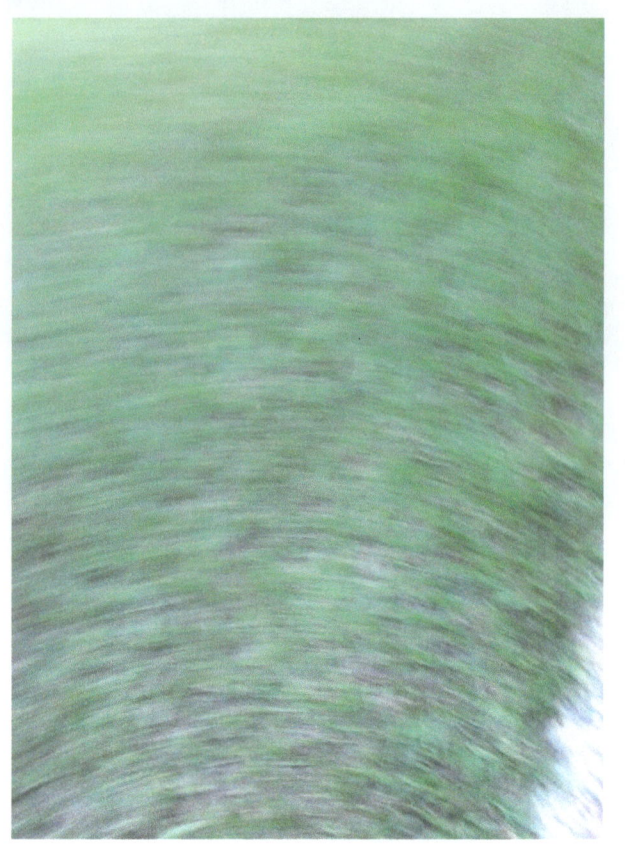

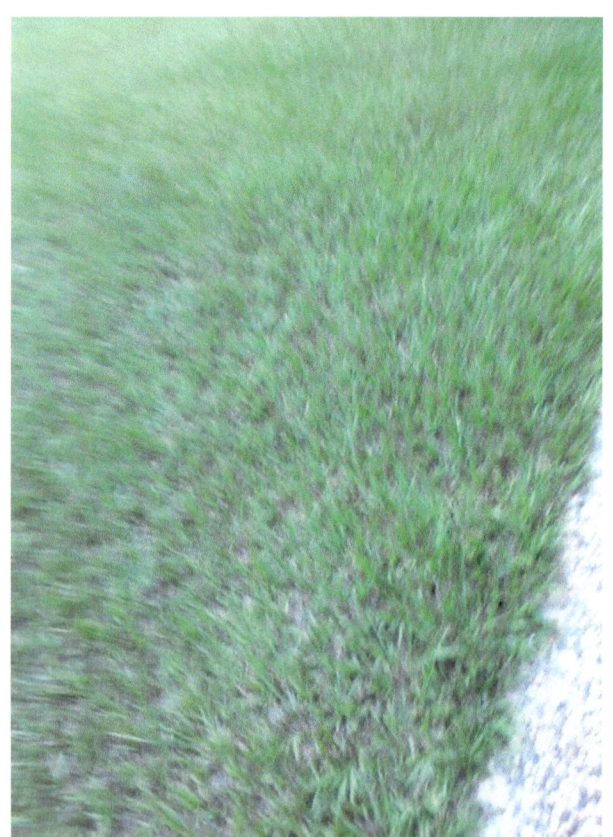

Grass.

Photograph of grass and earth when camera was in transit.

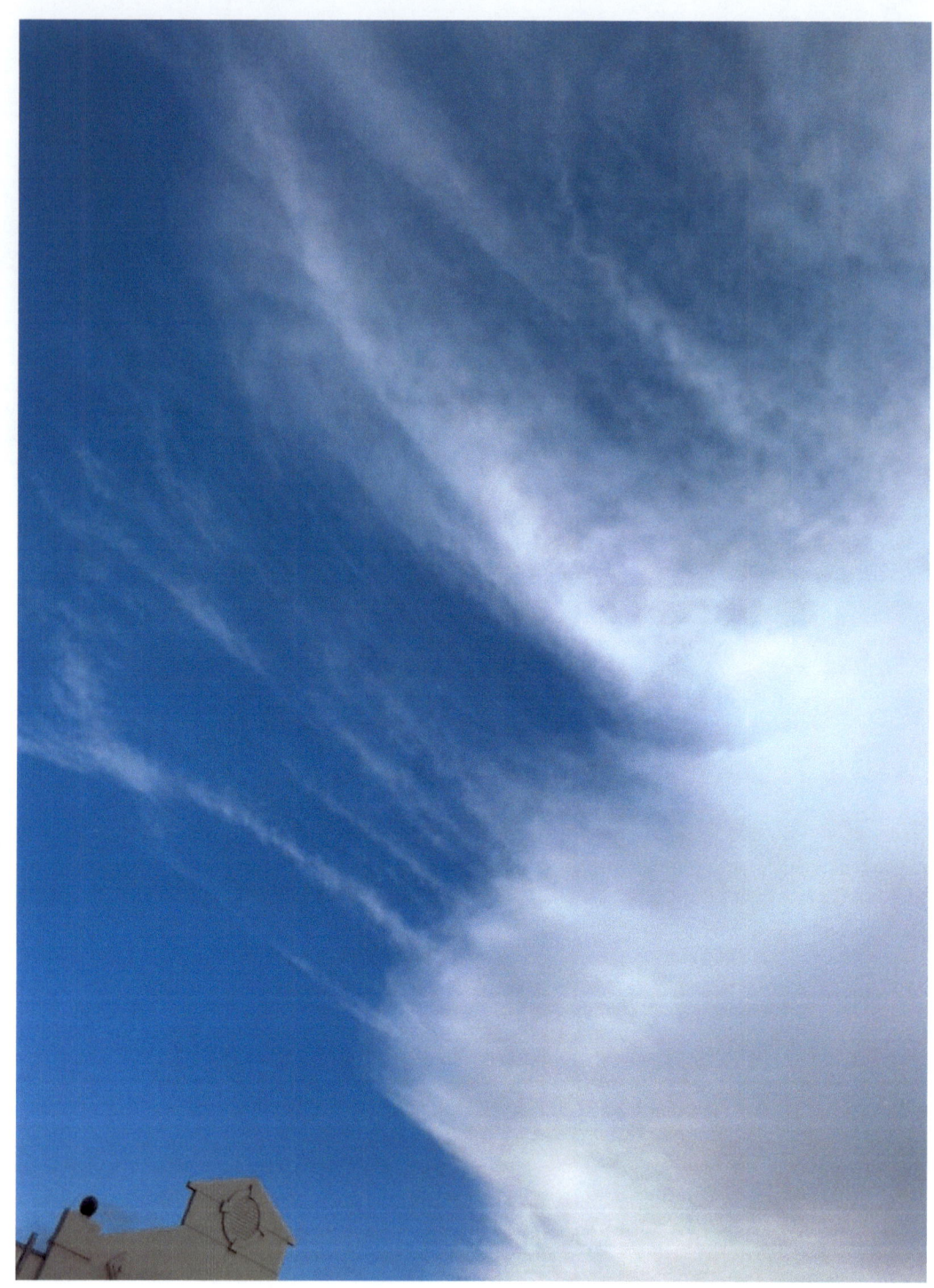

A movements of cloud.

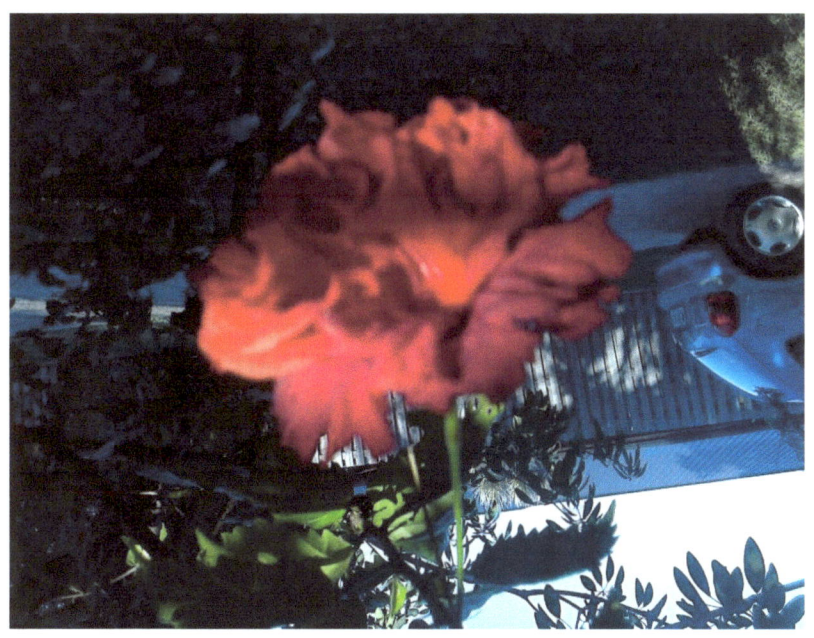

A Hibiscus flower.

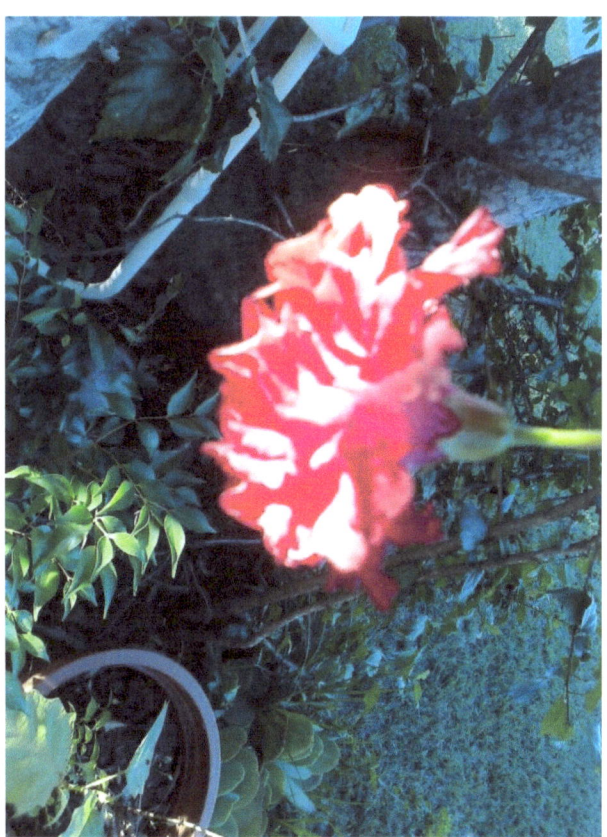

Same flower in different light

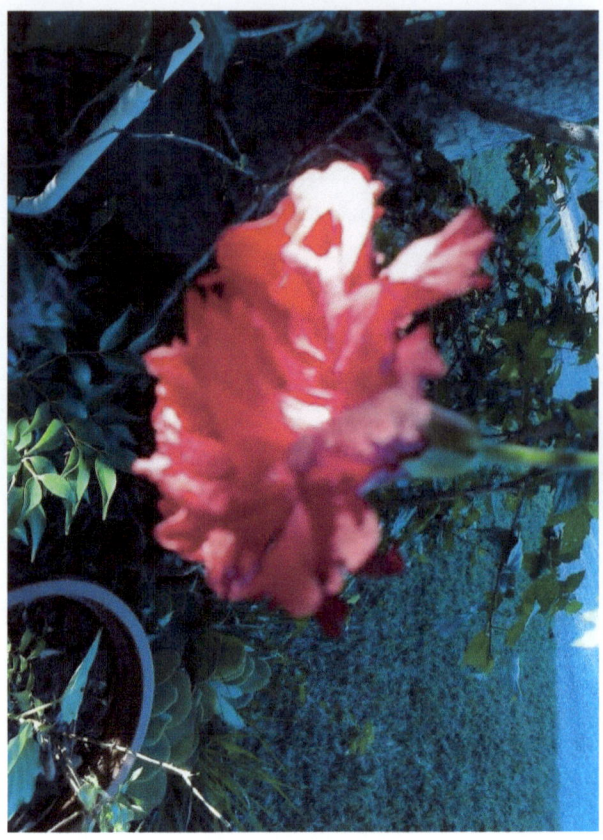

Same Hibiscus flower in a different light.

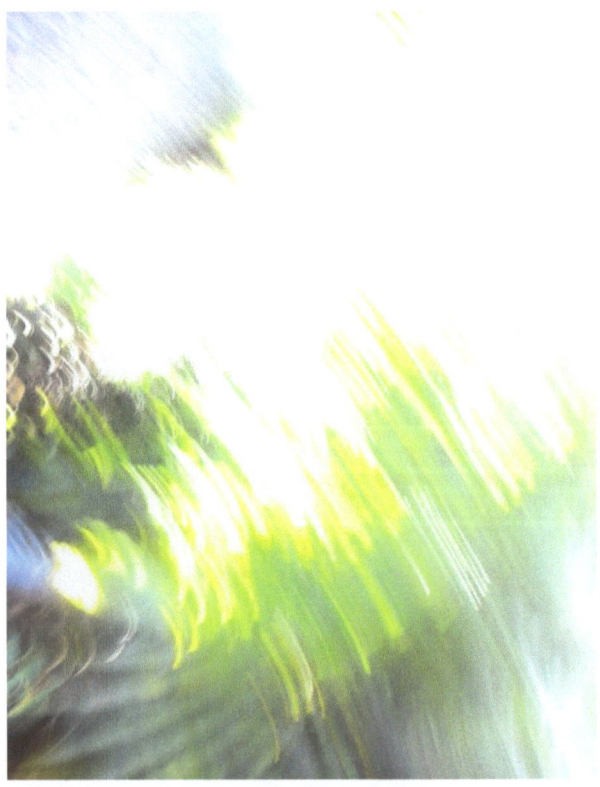

Photograph of plants when the camera was in transit.

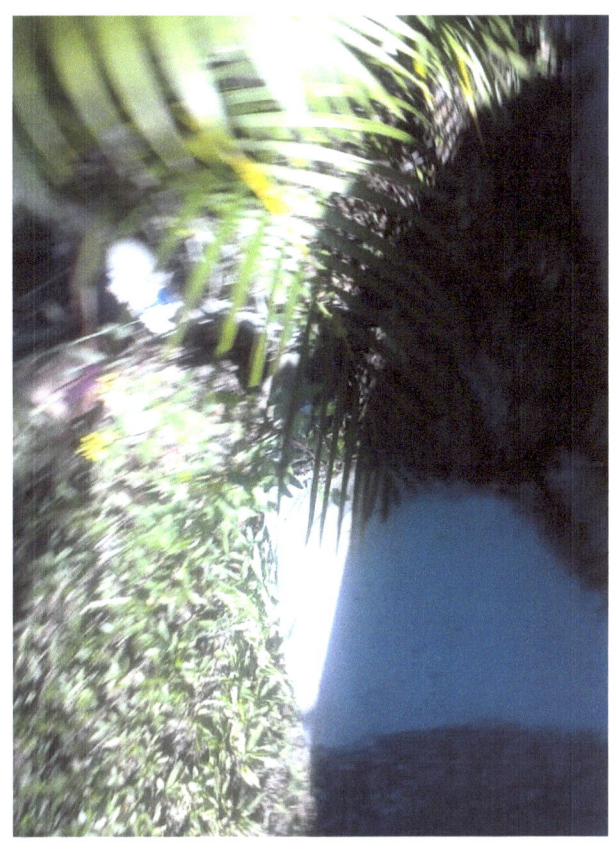

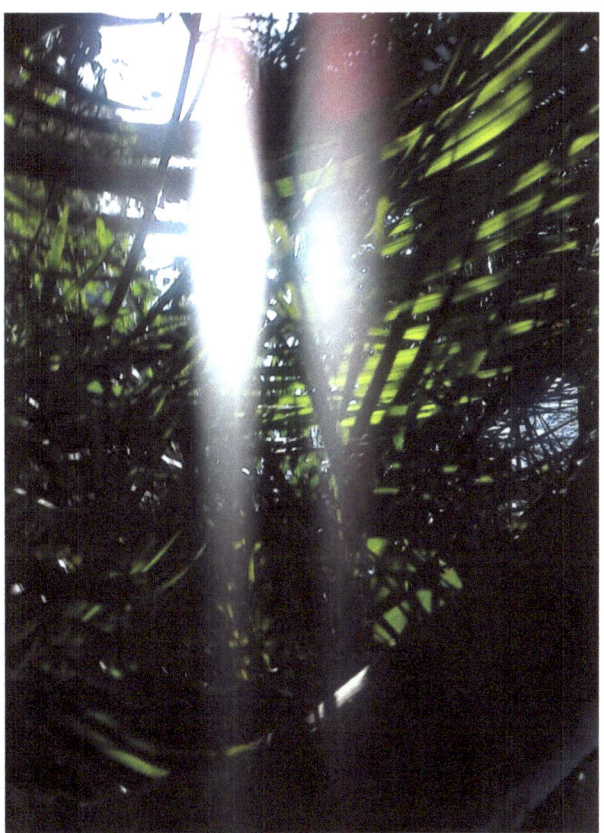

Sun's reflective lights moved with the camera lenses.

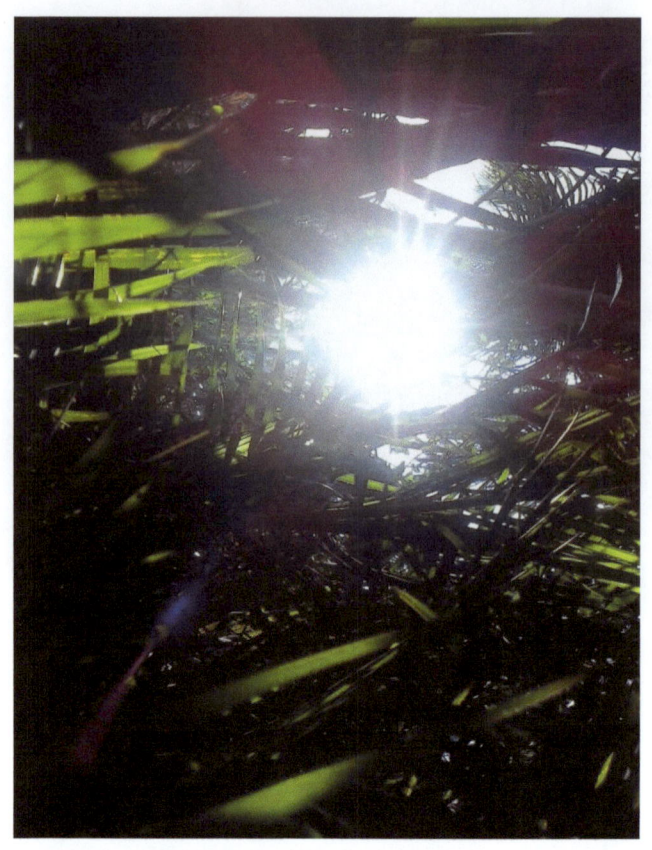

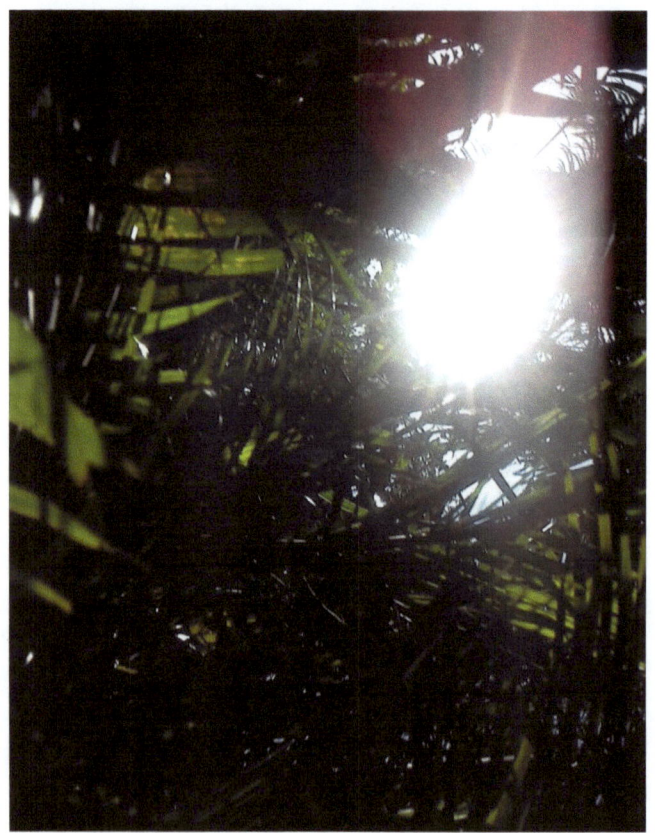

We can play with sun light.

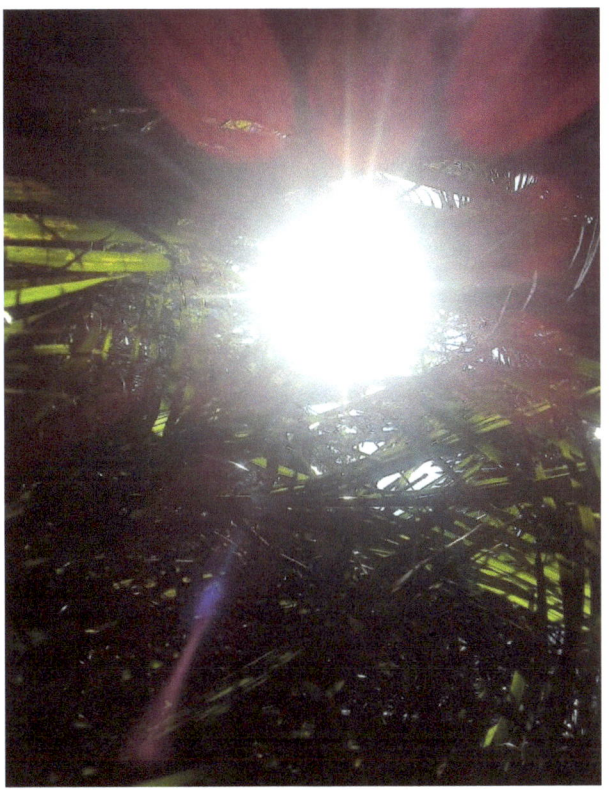

Reflective lights forming red discs.

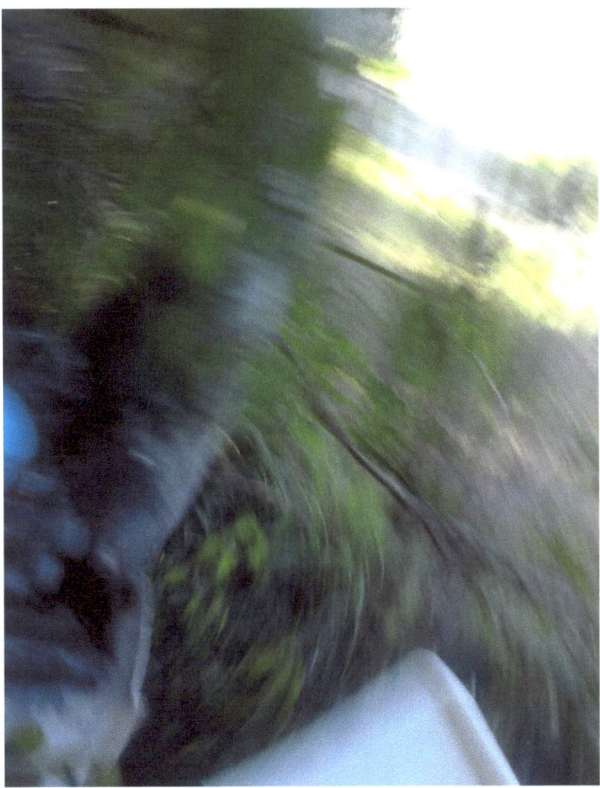

Movements of plants when camera was in transit.

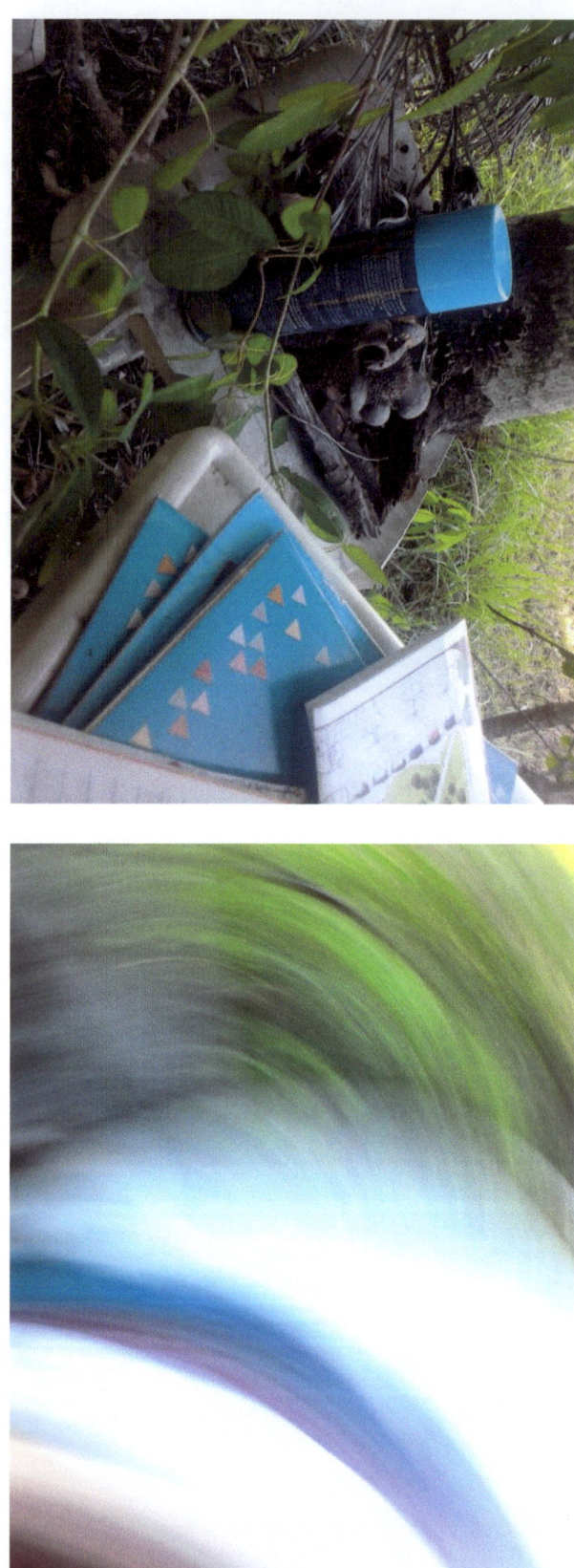

The above exercise books, photographed when camera was in transit makes a nice abstract art.

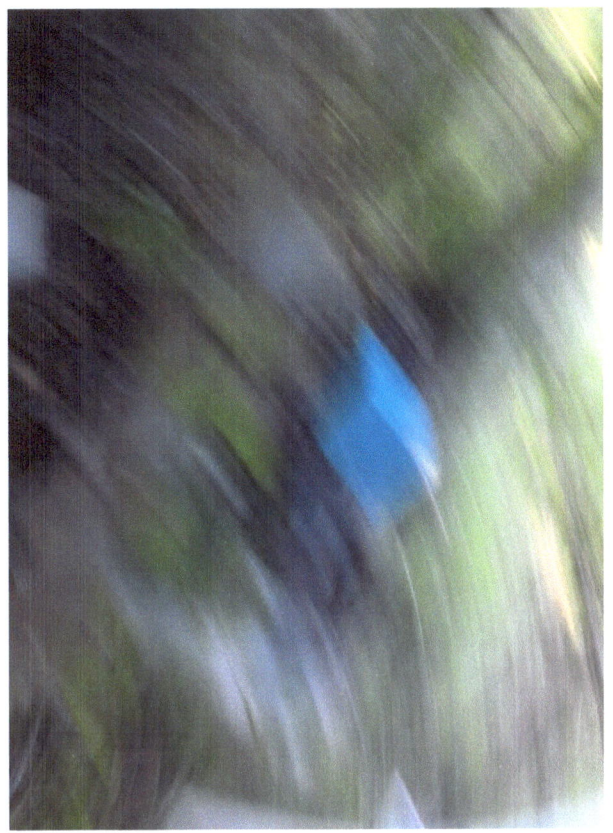

An image in transit.

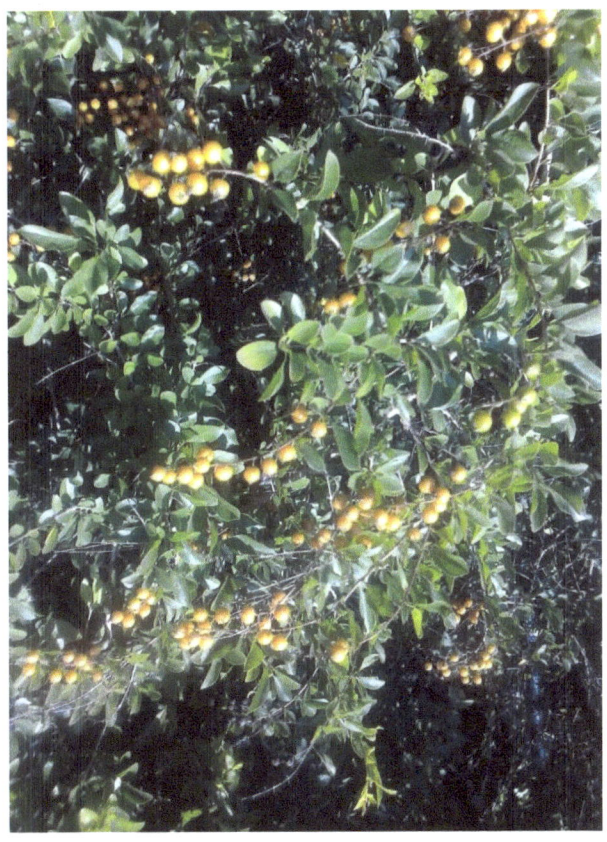

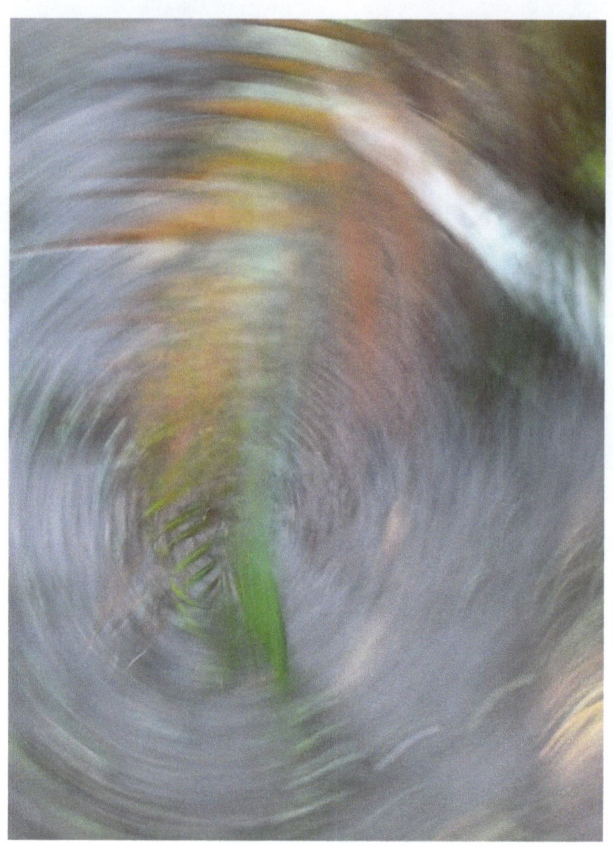

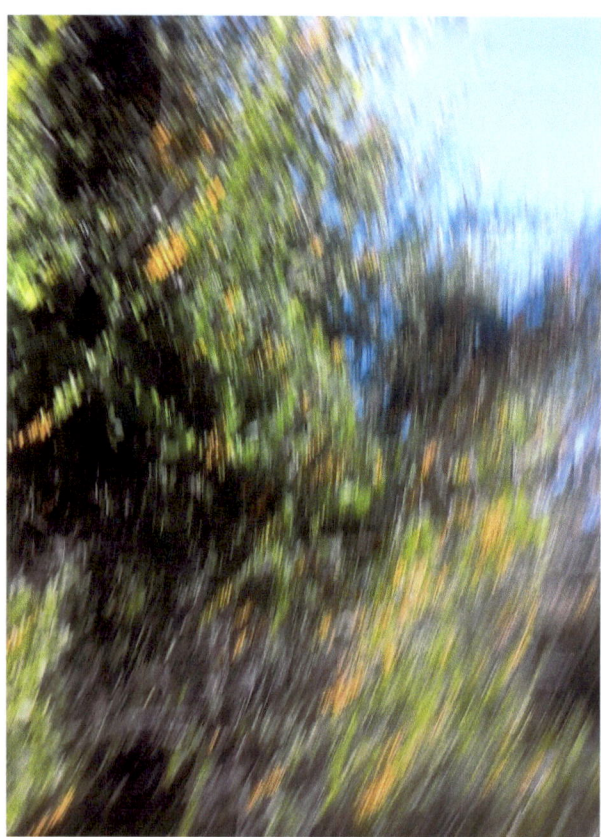

Palm leaves and yellow fruits photographed when camera was in transit.

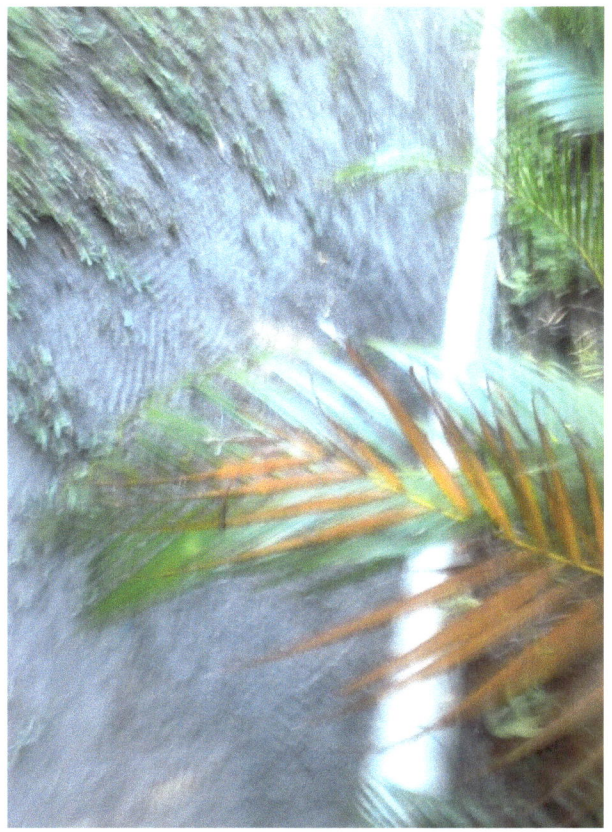

Compare the two photos and see the colour movements.

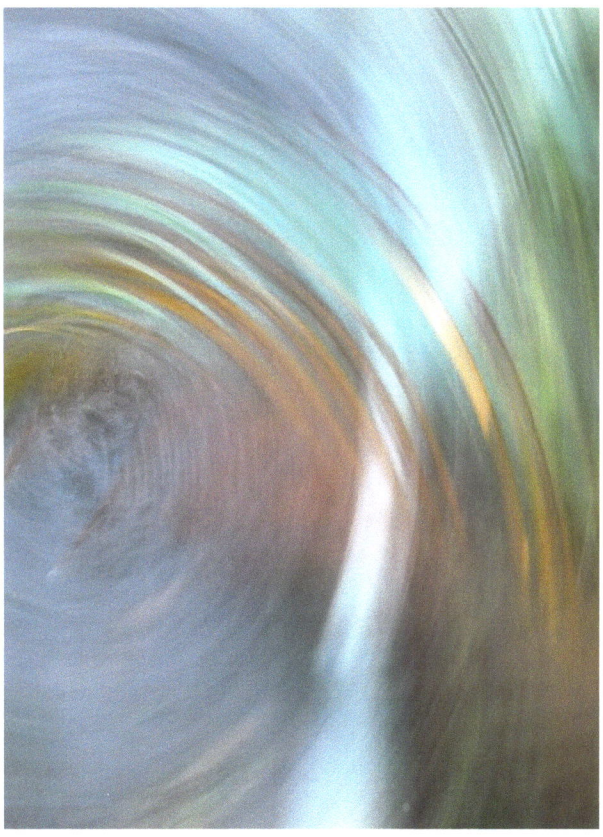

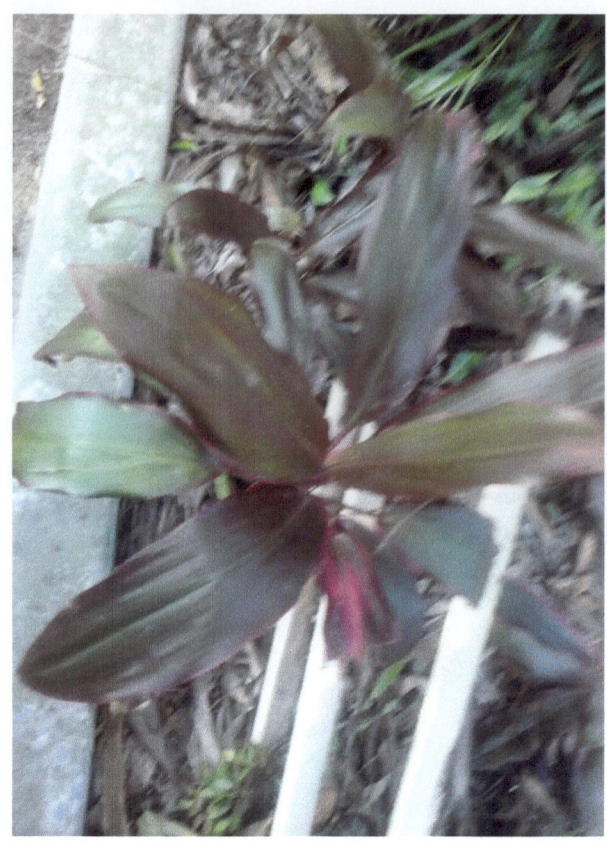

Real plant photograph and photograph of the same plant when the camera was in transit.

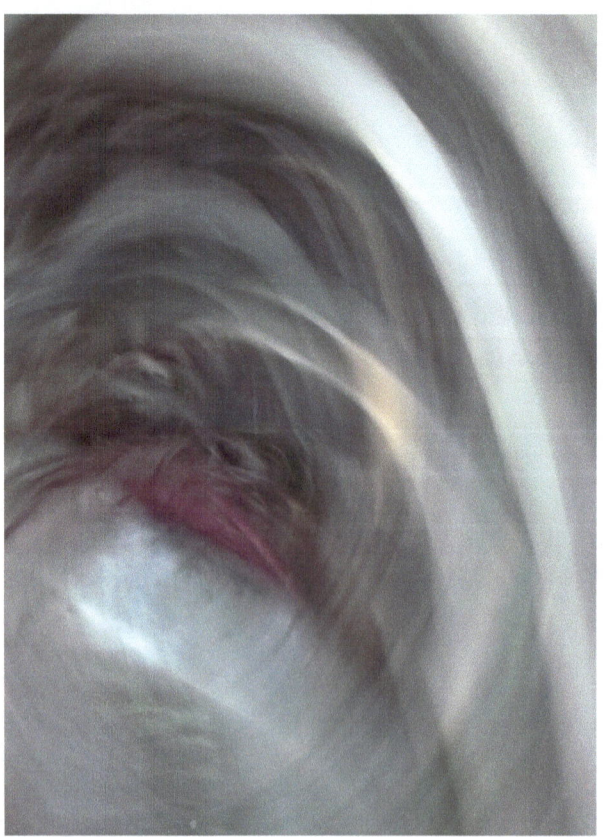

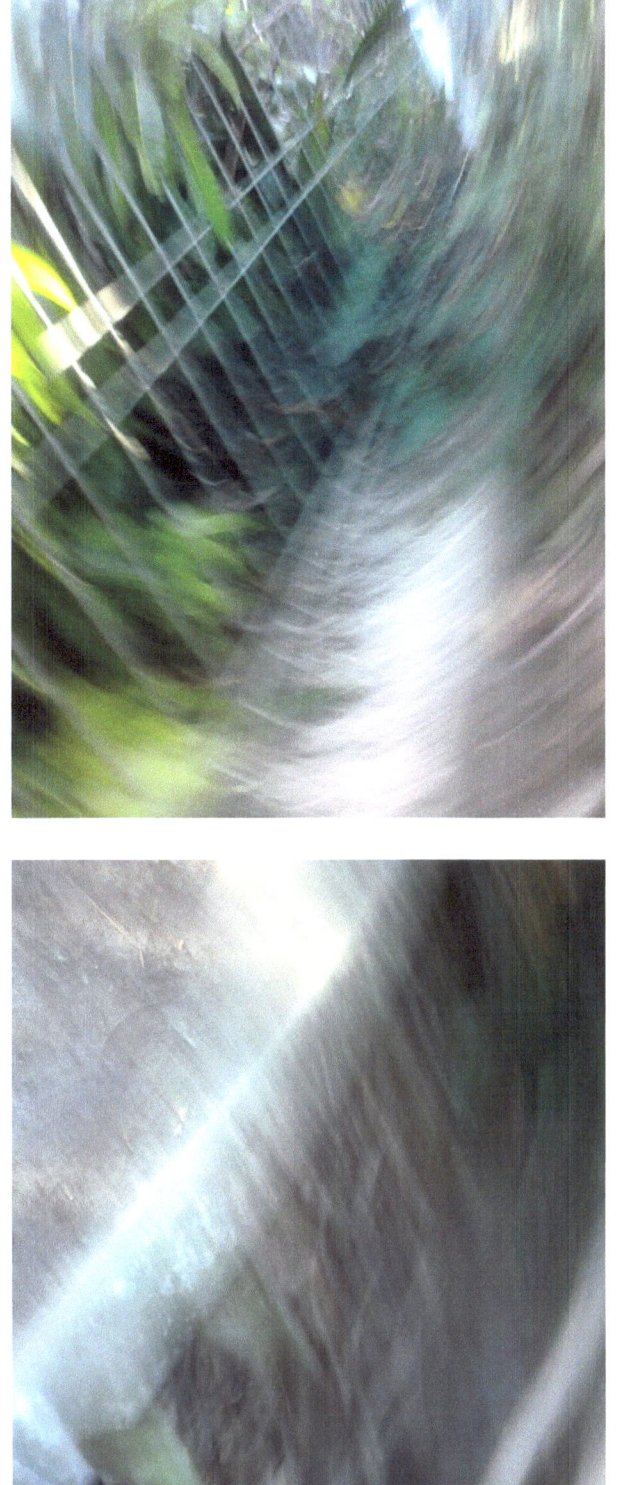

Light in rotation making landscapes like features.

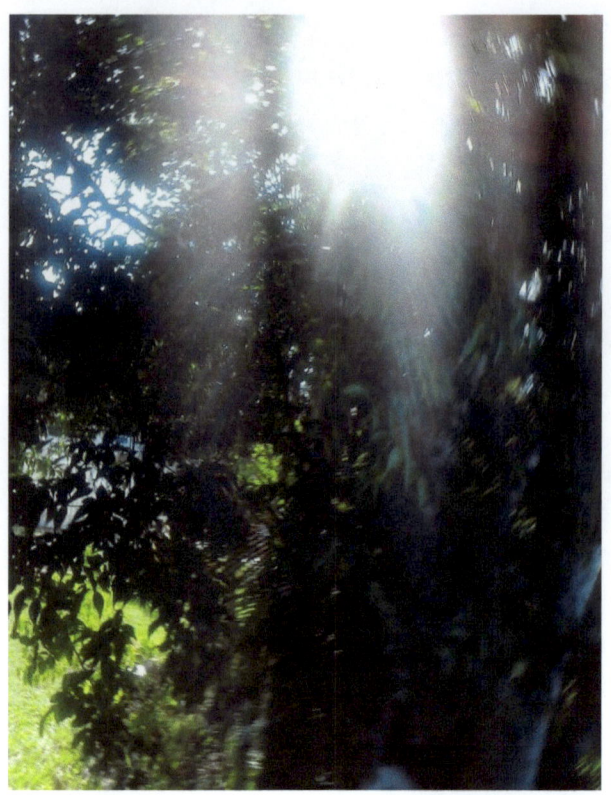

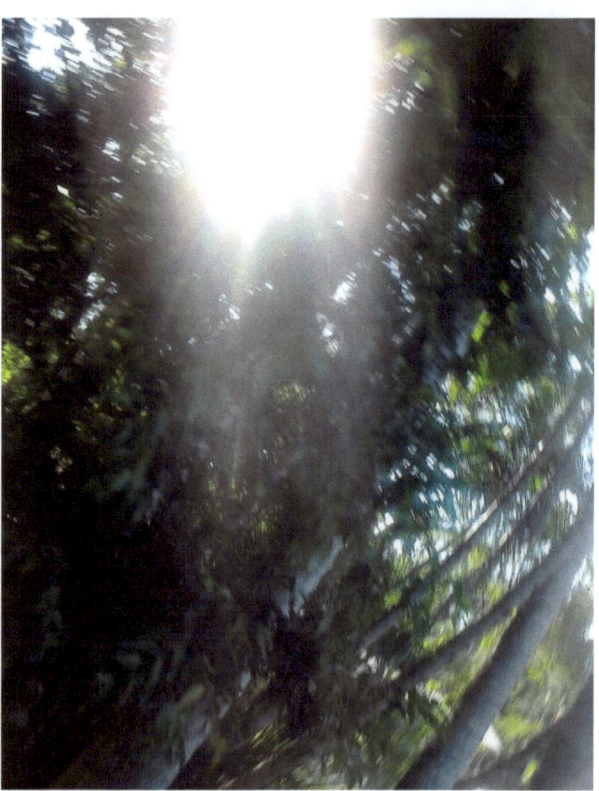

Photographs of light coming in and reflecting off plants. Every reflection off the sun is a sun and it behaves like a sun and spreads the rays and beams like the sun. Sun's disc like reflections behaves like the sun. That was why we do not see the real sun in the sky its light blocks the real features of the sun. The above photographs shows that the sun's light moved forward to reflect off the leaves.

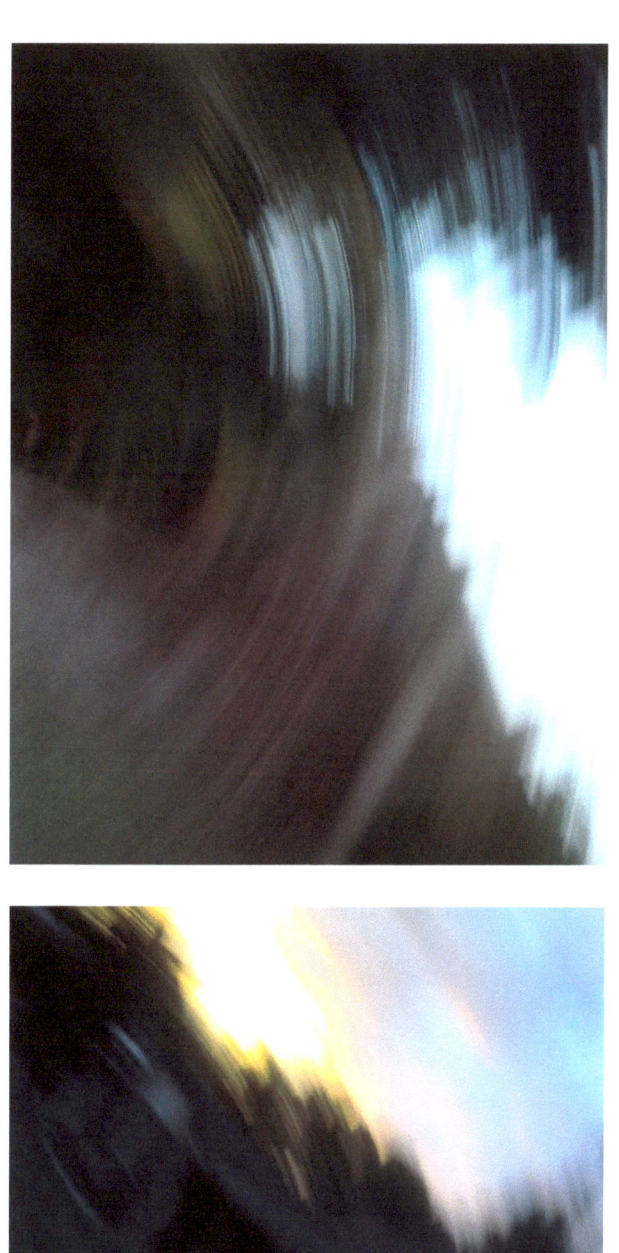

I could even move the cloud and the sun by rotating the camera.

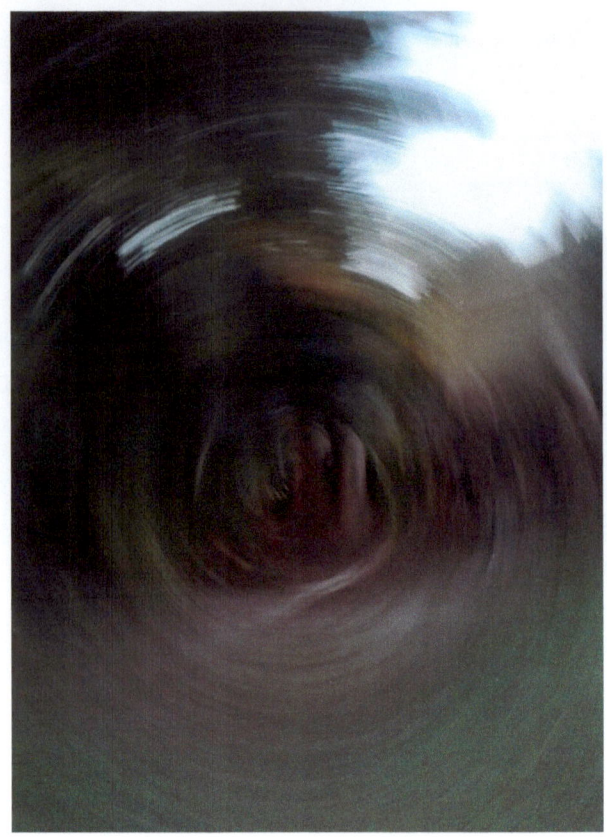

Full rotation of the camera.

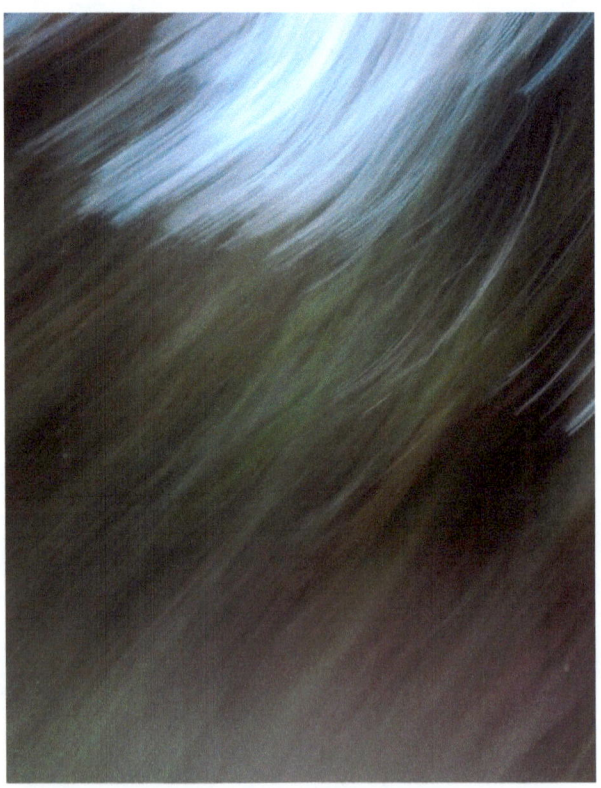

Patterns of waves made by moving the camera over plants.

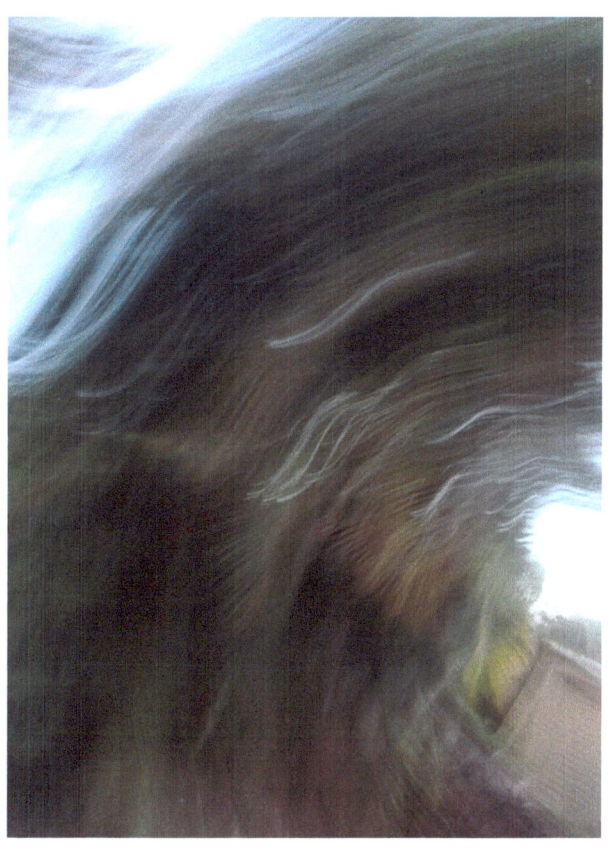

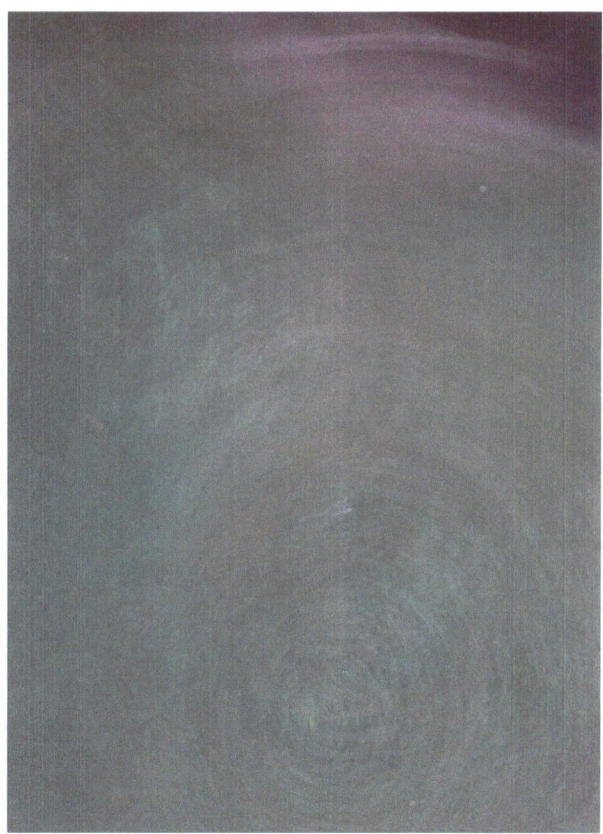

Partial rotation of the camera created rotations of plants.

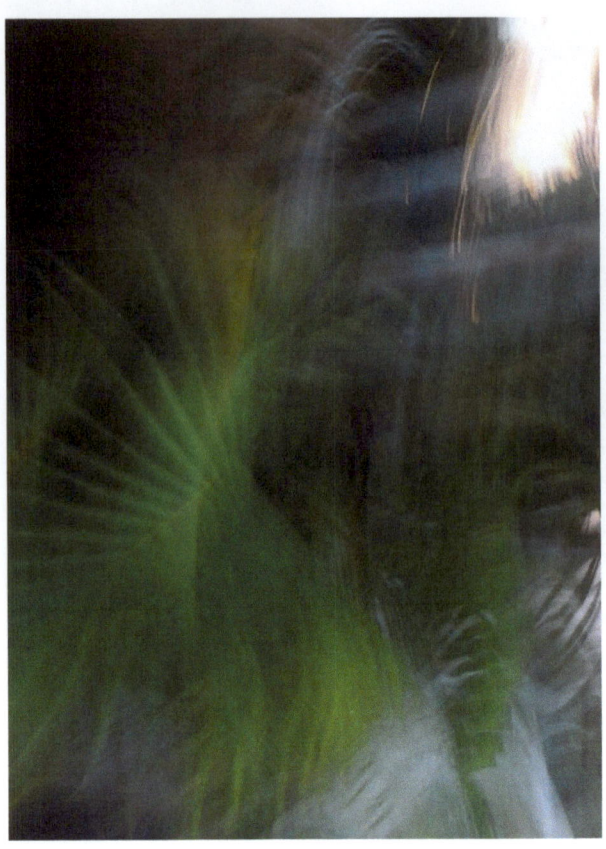

Yellow sunlight flickering in the movements of camera.

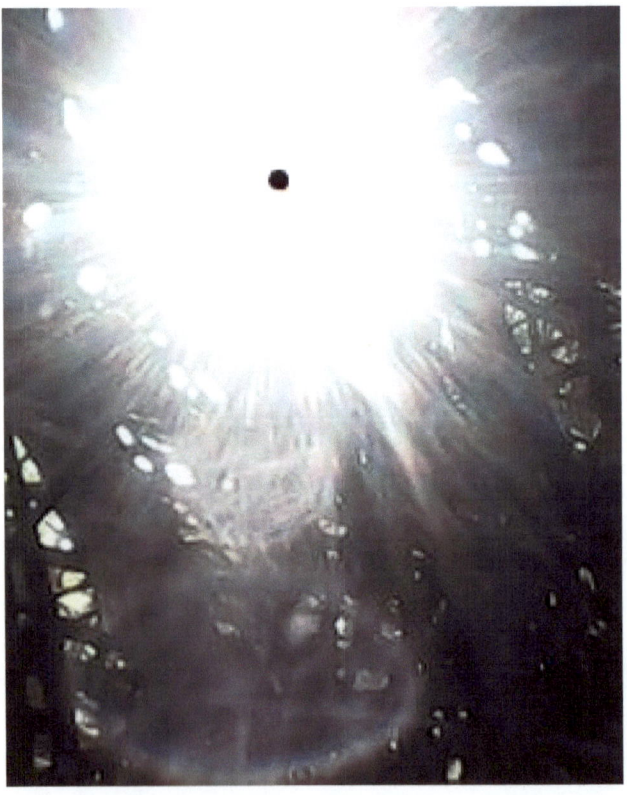

Stellar patterns on the reflective ring from the sun.

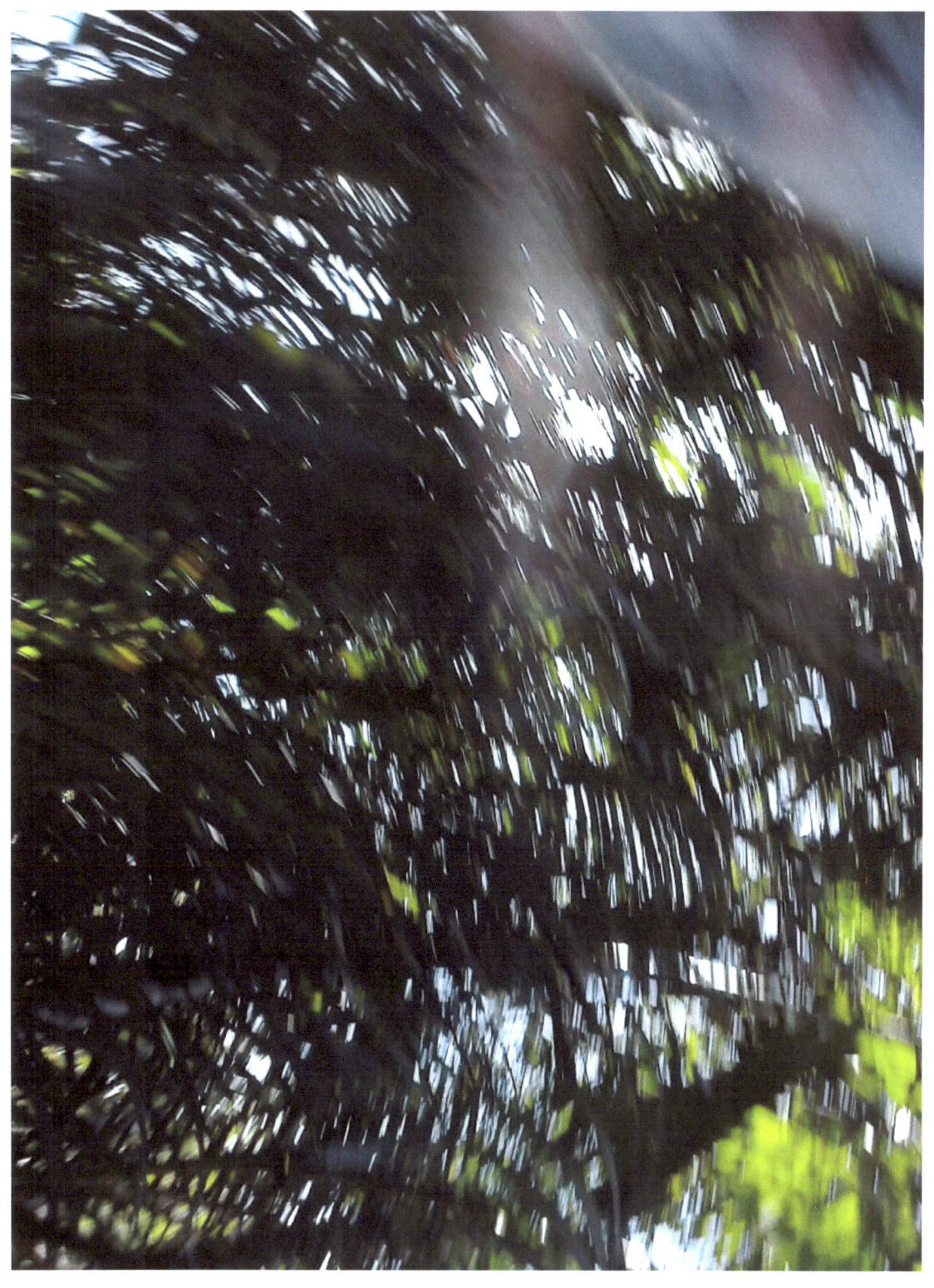

Movements of light and plants.

An abstract illusion when camera was in transit.

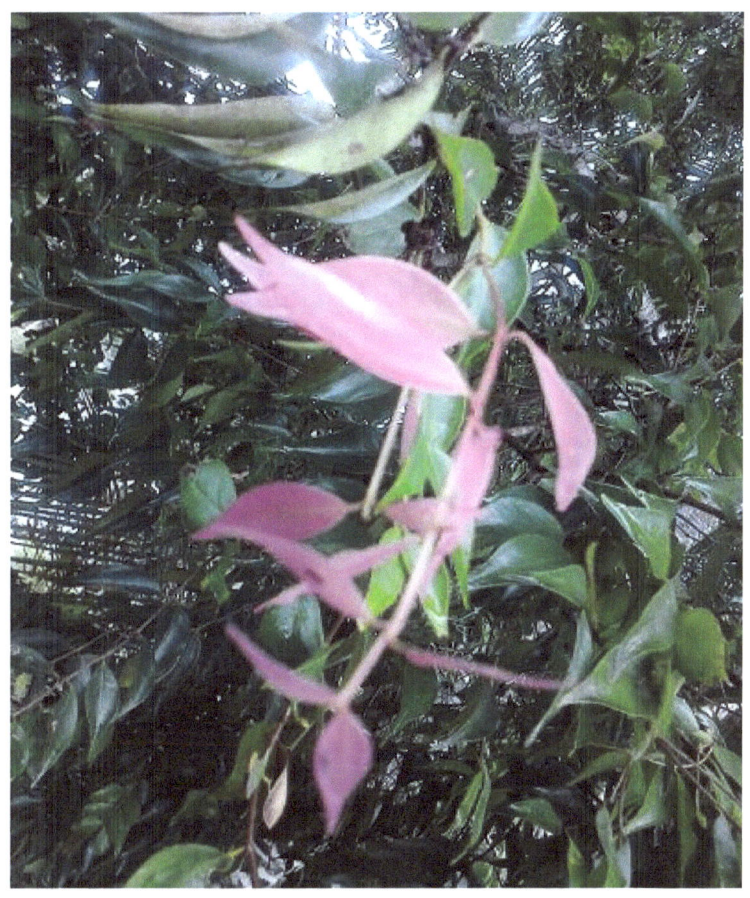

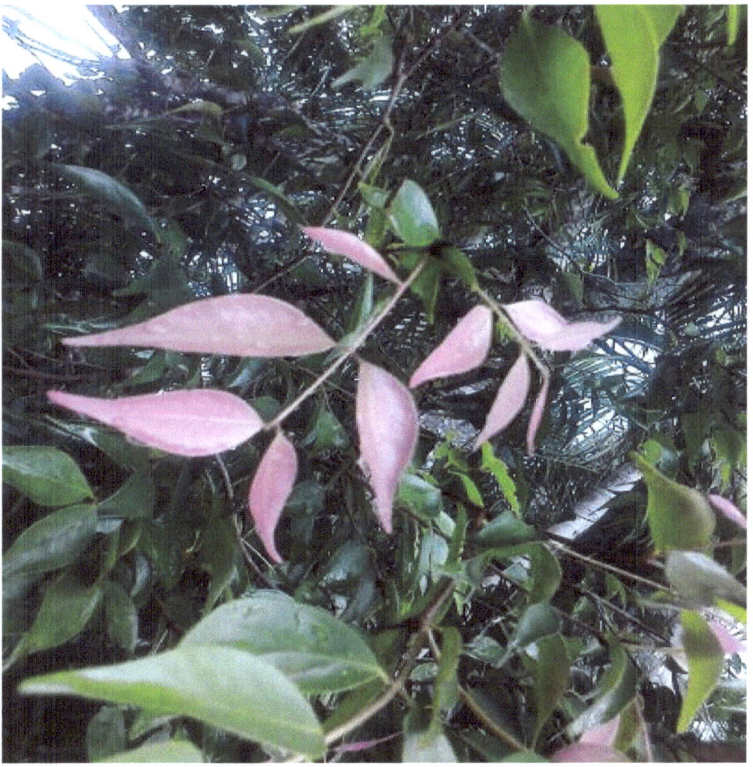

Two real photographs of plants above and the same plants used to photograph while camera was in transit. Photographs are on the next two pages.

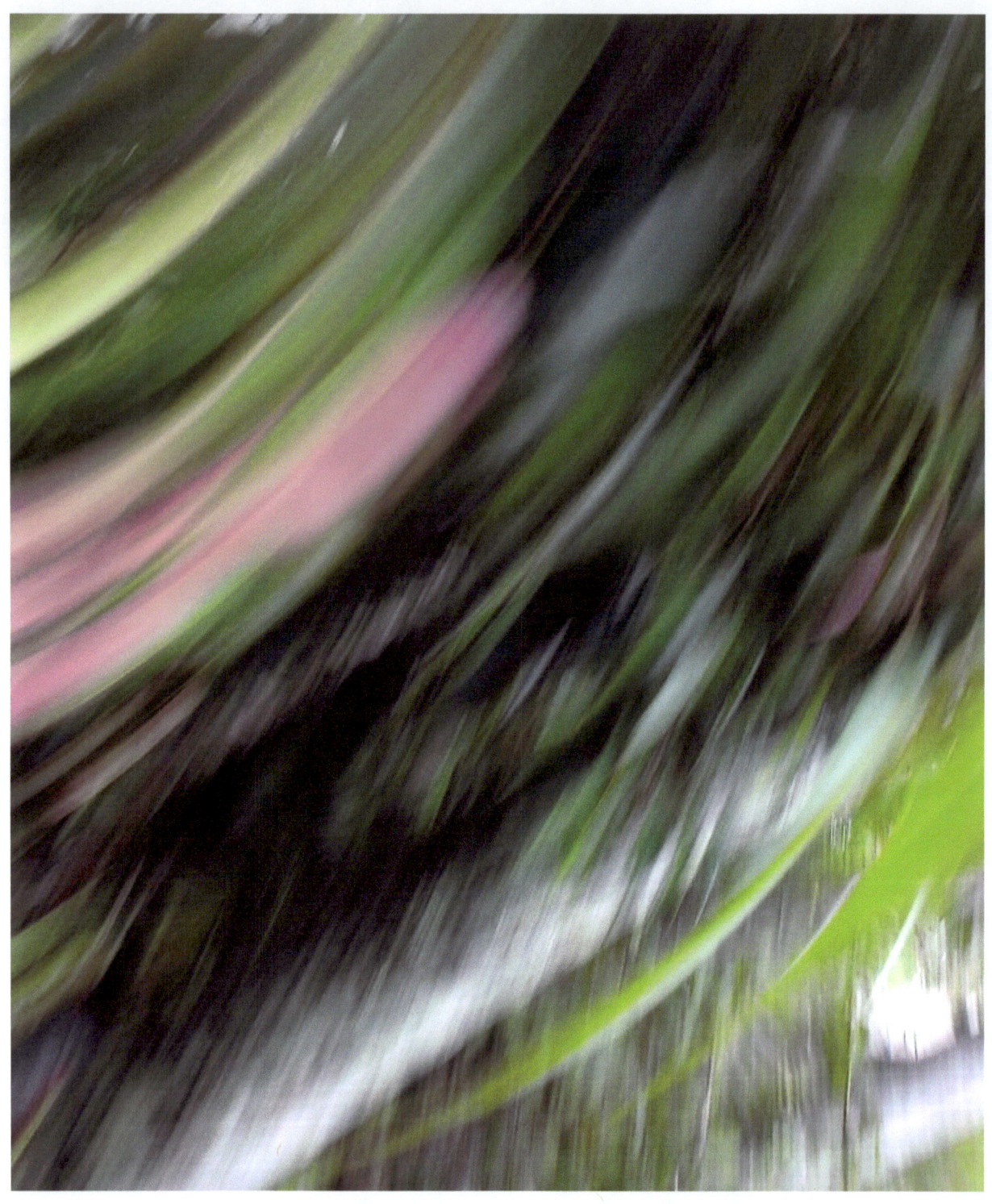

Photographs of plants in the previous page taken when camera was in transit produced this image.

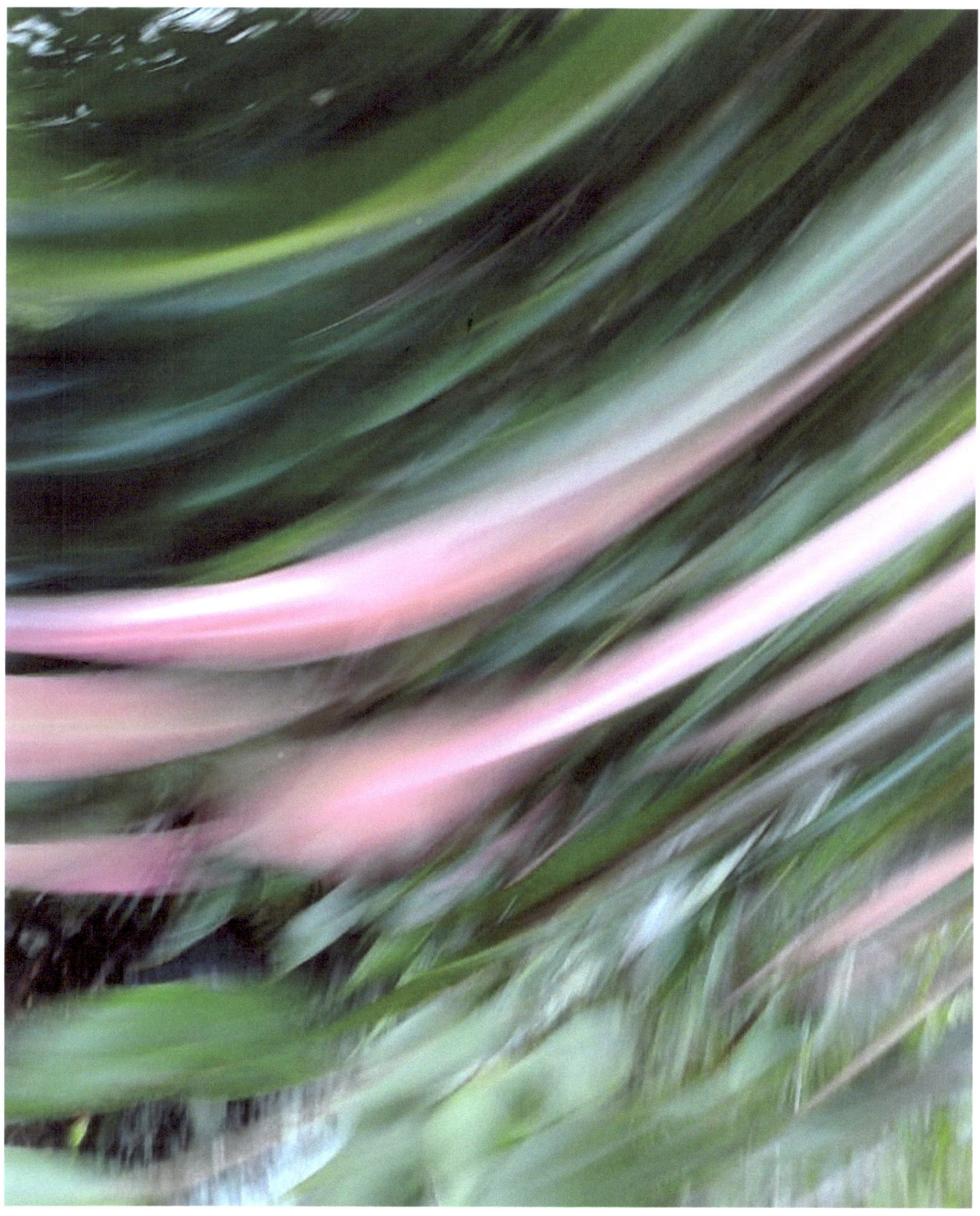

The second abstract photograph of the same plant on page 38 taken when camera was in transit.

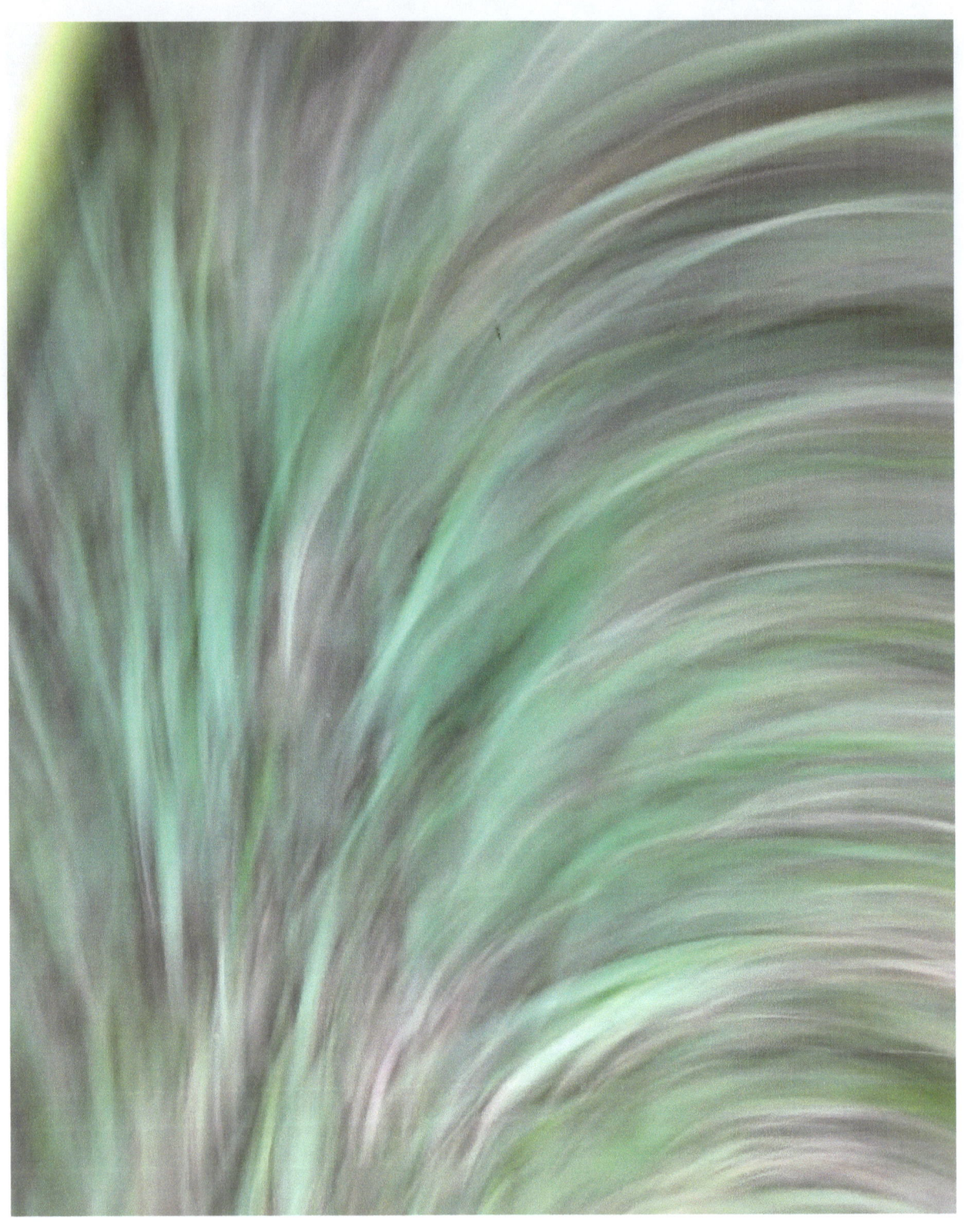

Movements of grass in abstract form.

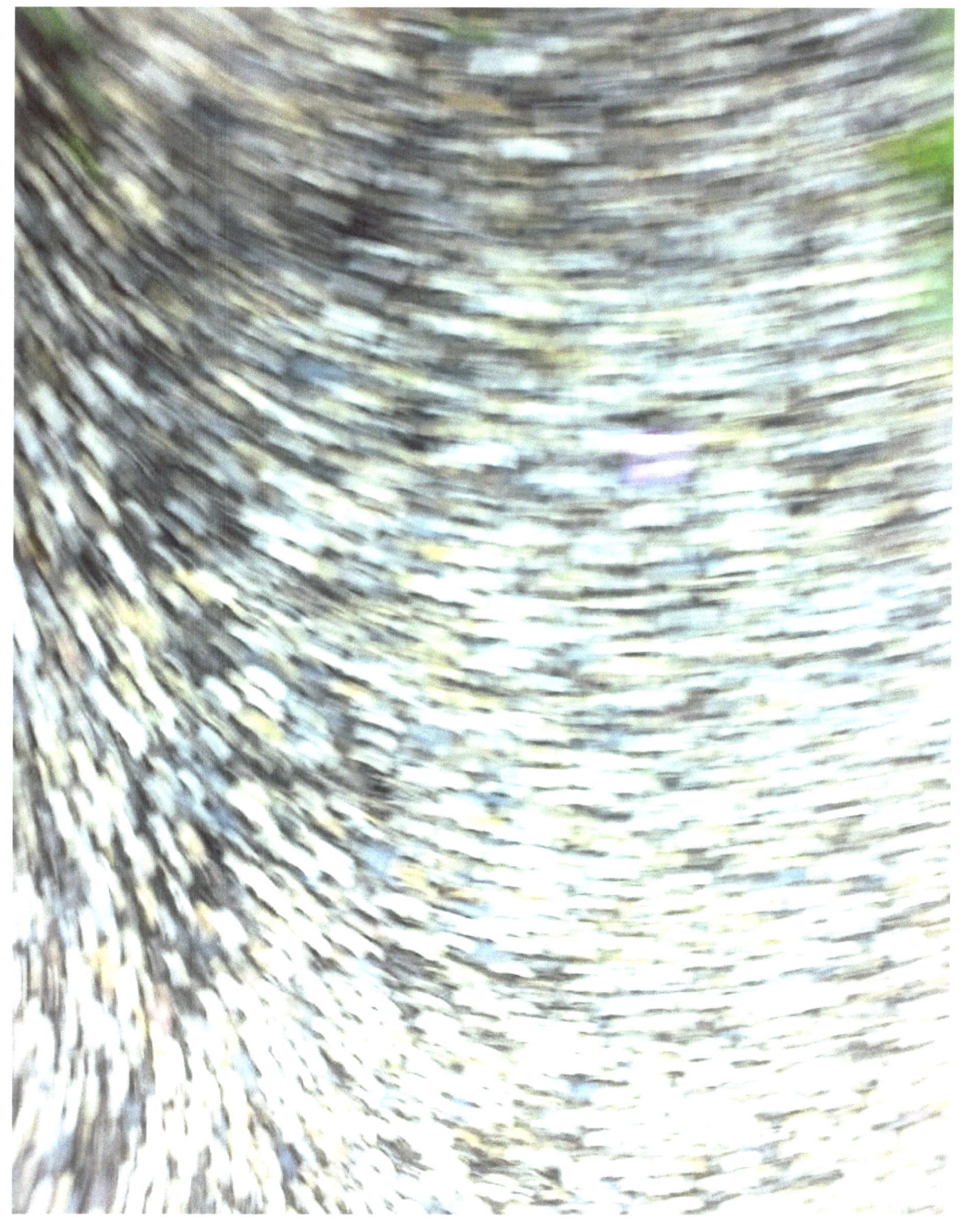

Photographs of pebbles on the concrete when camera was in transit made rectangle patterns. Circles can become squares in rotations.

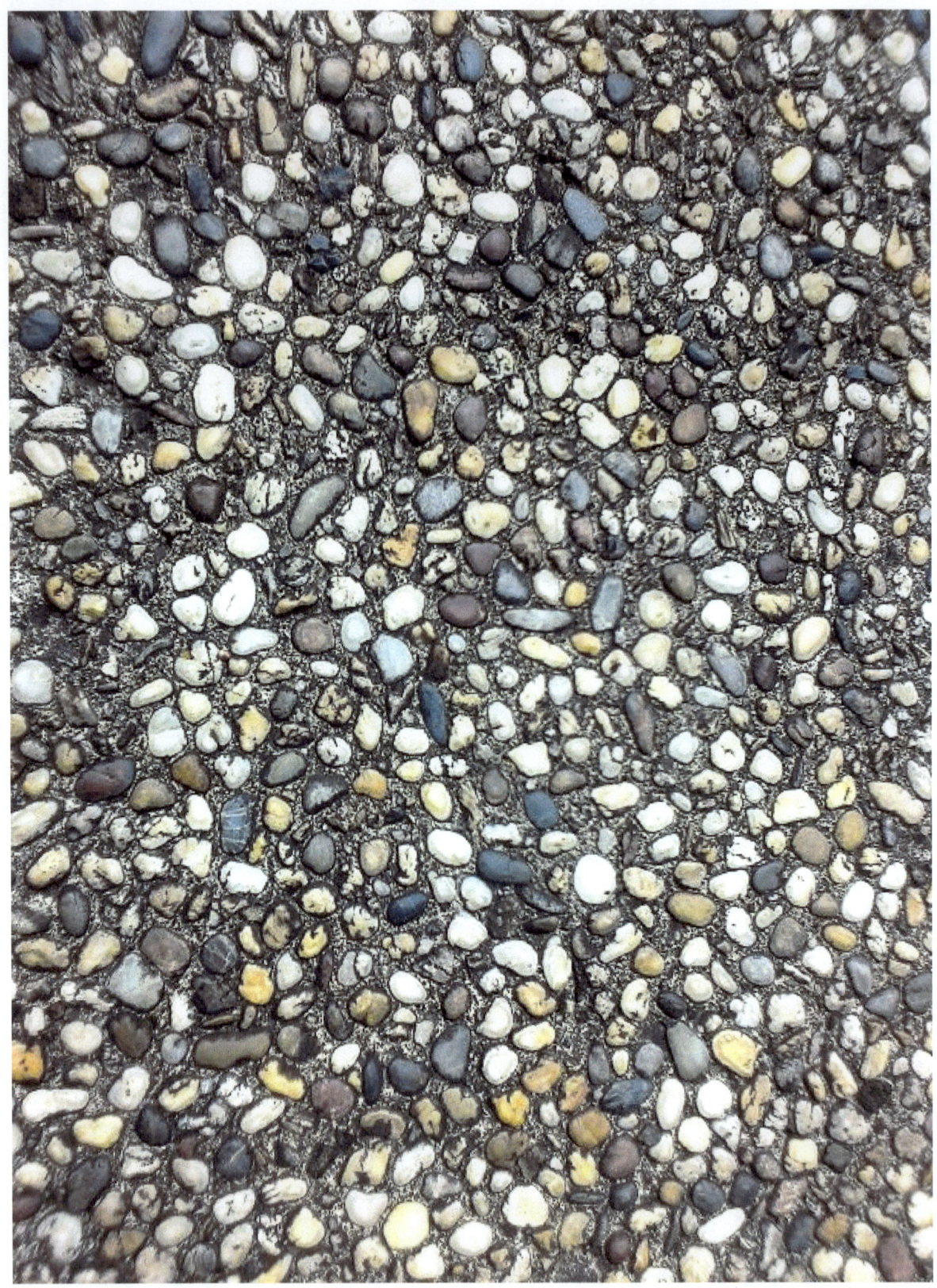

Real pebbles on the concrete looks like the photograph above.

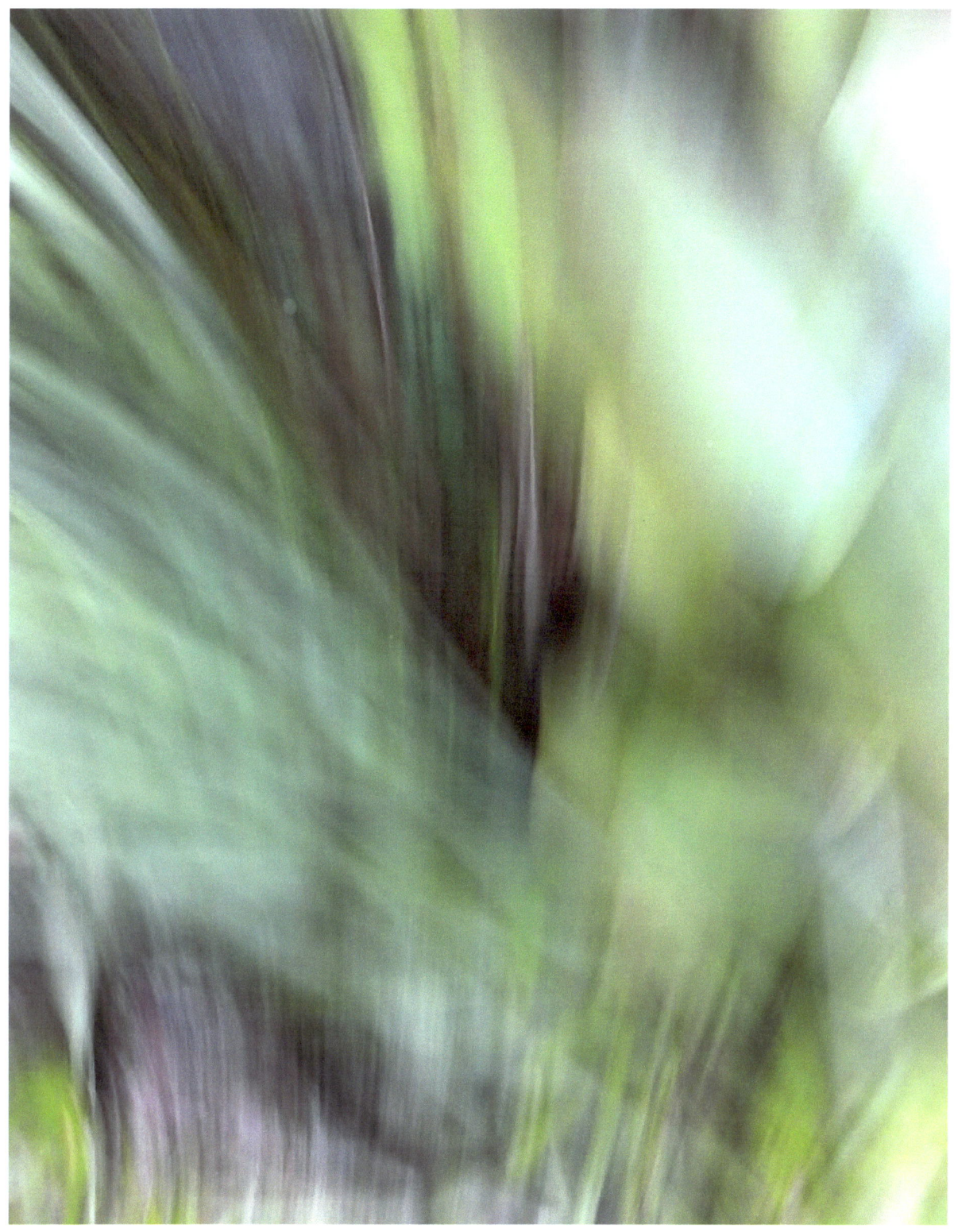

Photograph of leaves taken in transit produced an abstract of leaves.

Grass in transit.

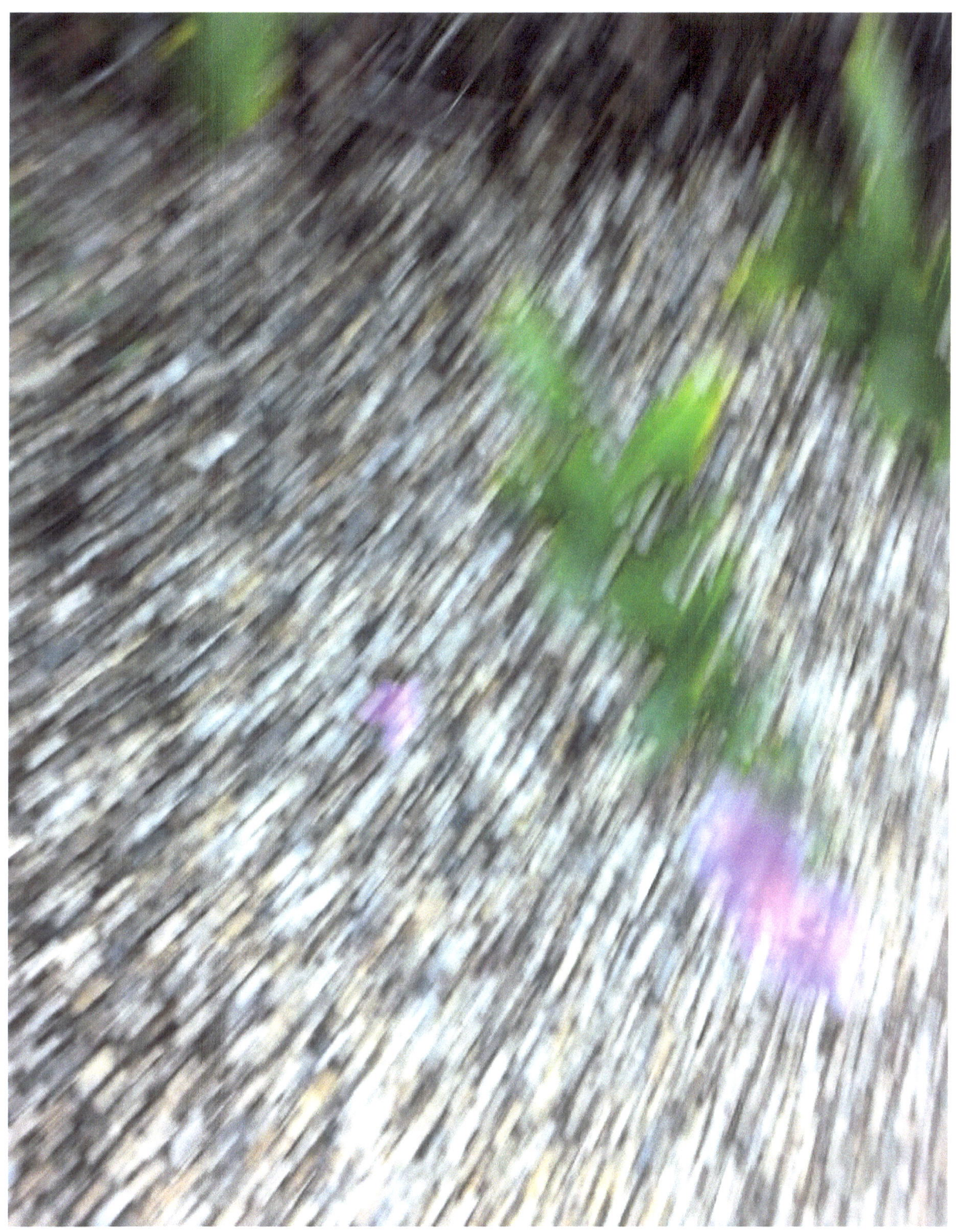

Pebbles and flowers in transit.

Pebbles becomes a flow of lines. This tells us that rotations makes the patterns of things change. Now we know how pressure rotates in nature and transforms one pattern to another. How grains of meat came from little globes of atoms and bubbles of acids.

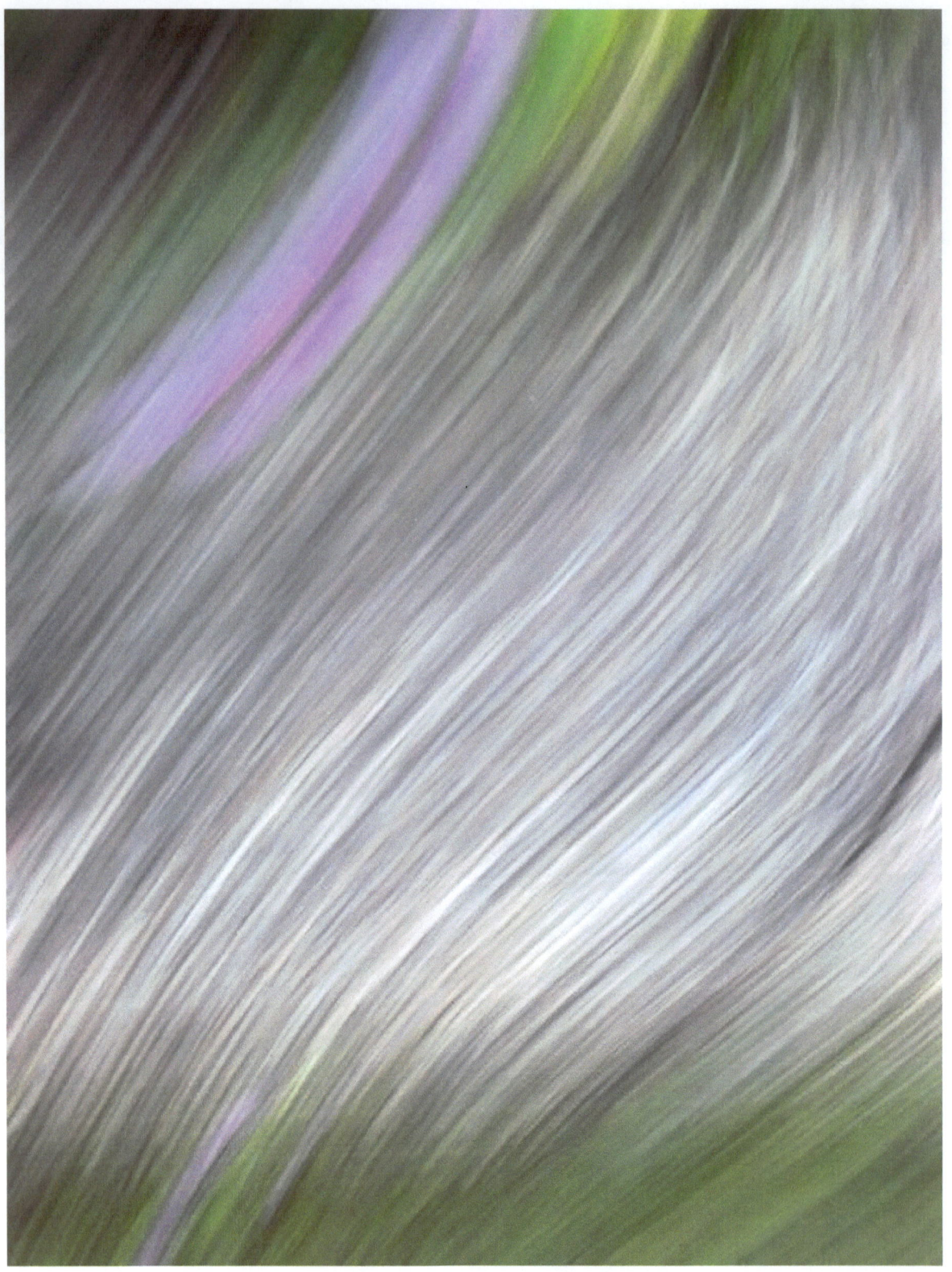

In the previous photo the pebbles become rectangles in this photograph the pebbles become lines. Formation of life structure from acids and minerals transform into streaky meat, skin patterns and so on, because of rotational pressure.

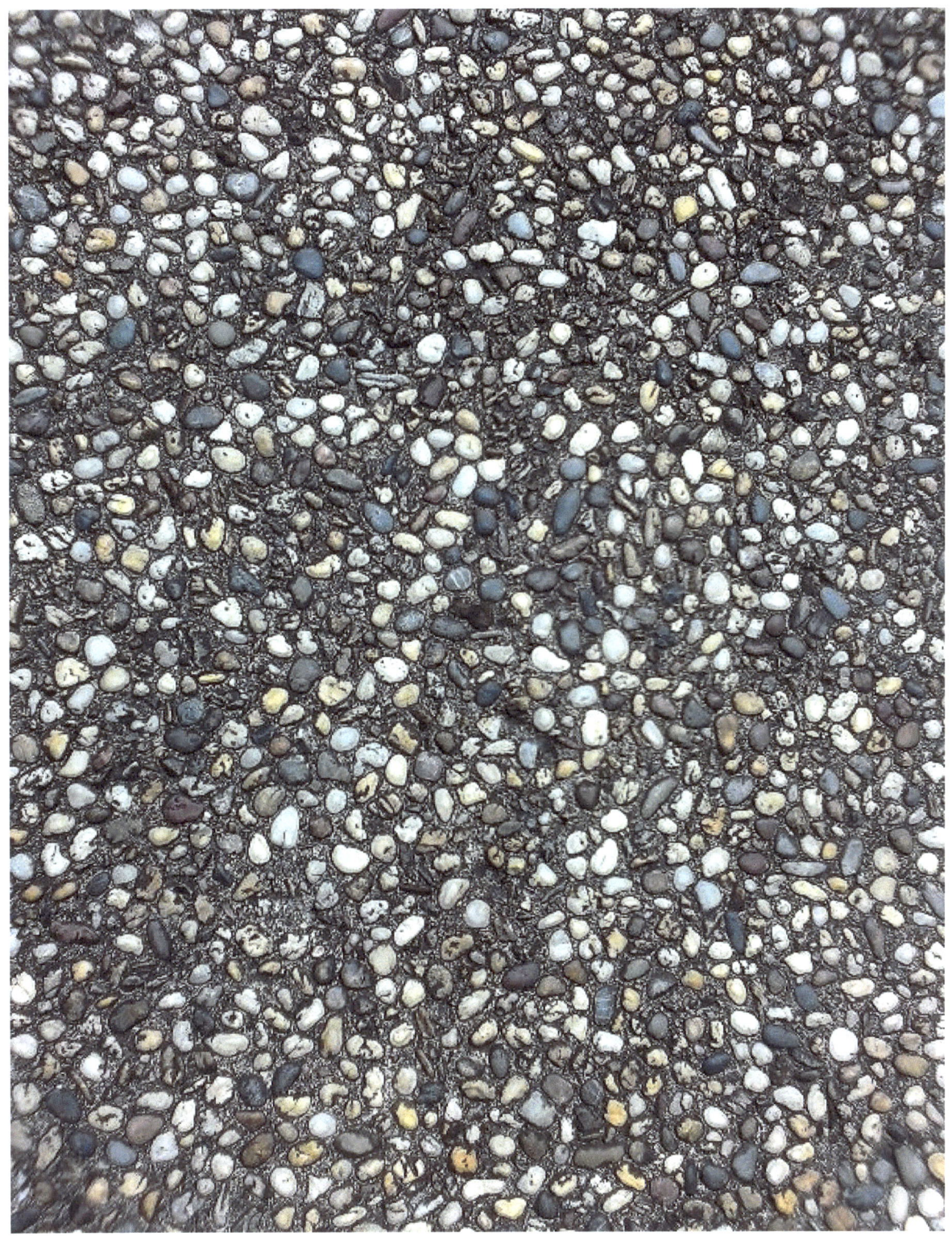

Pebbles on the concrete looks like rotated in the water and become smooth round balls. In rotation these pebbles become rectangles and streaky lines like the photographs in previous pages.

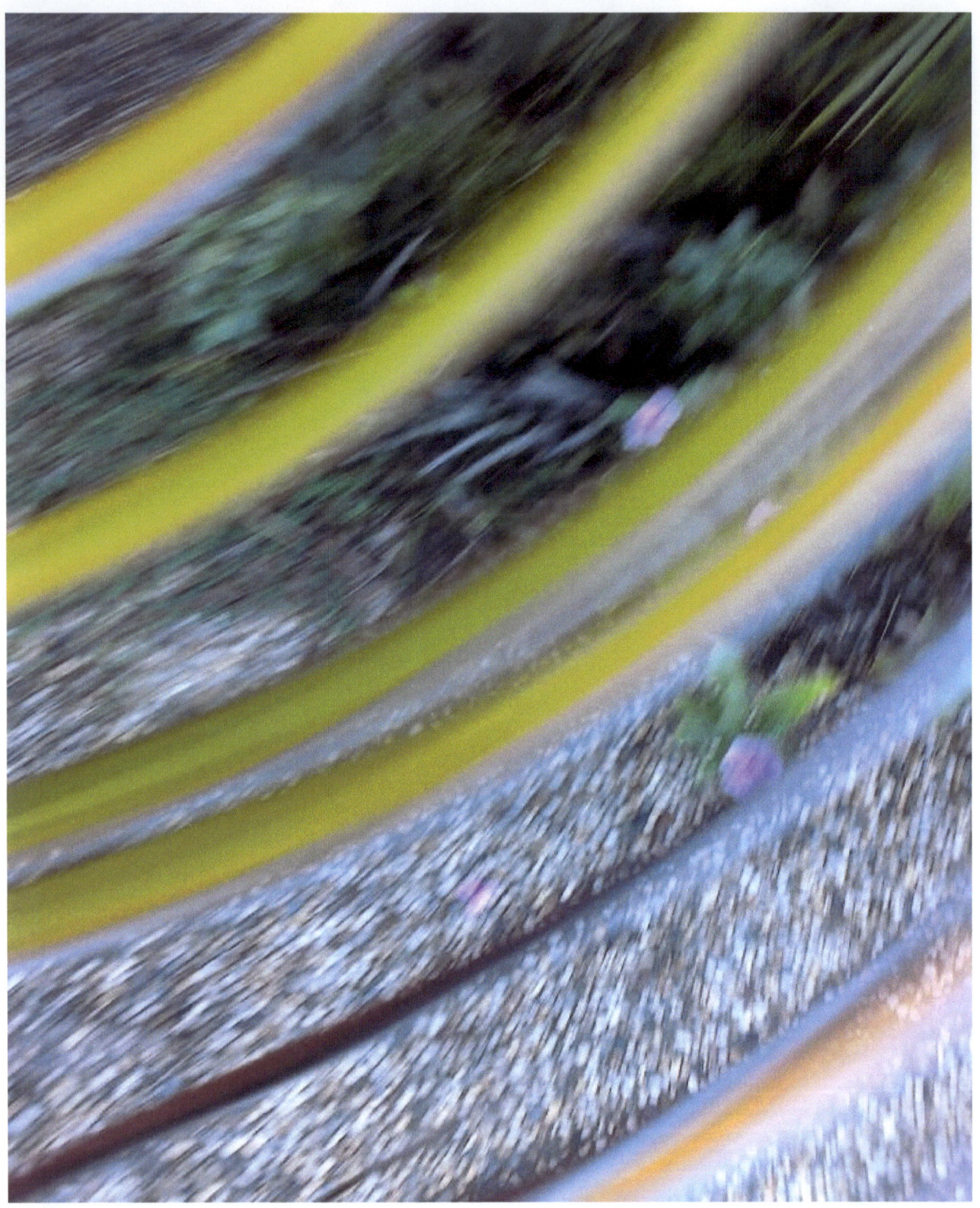

Leaves, pebbles and plants in transit. These round pebbles become squares and rectangle in rotations or movements. How rotational pressure and light created all the shapes including the geometrical shapes. Man did not create these shapes pressure and stellar breakages created these shapes. We as humans only applied mathematics and physics to it but mathematics and physics exist in nature. Humans only named them so they could understand nature.

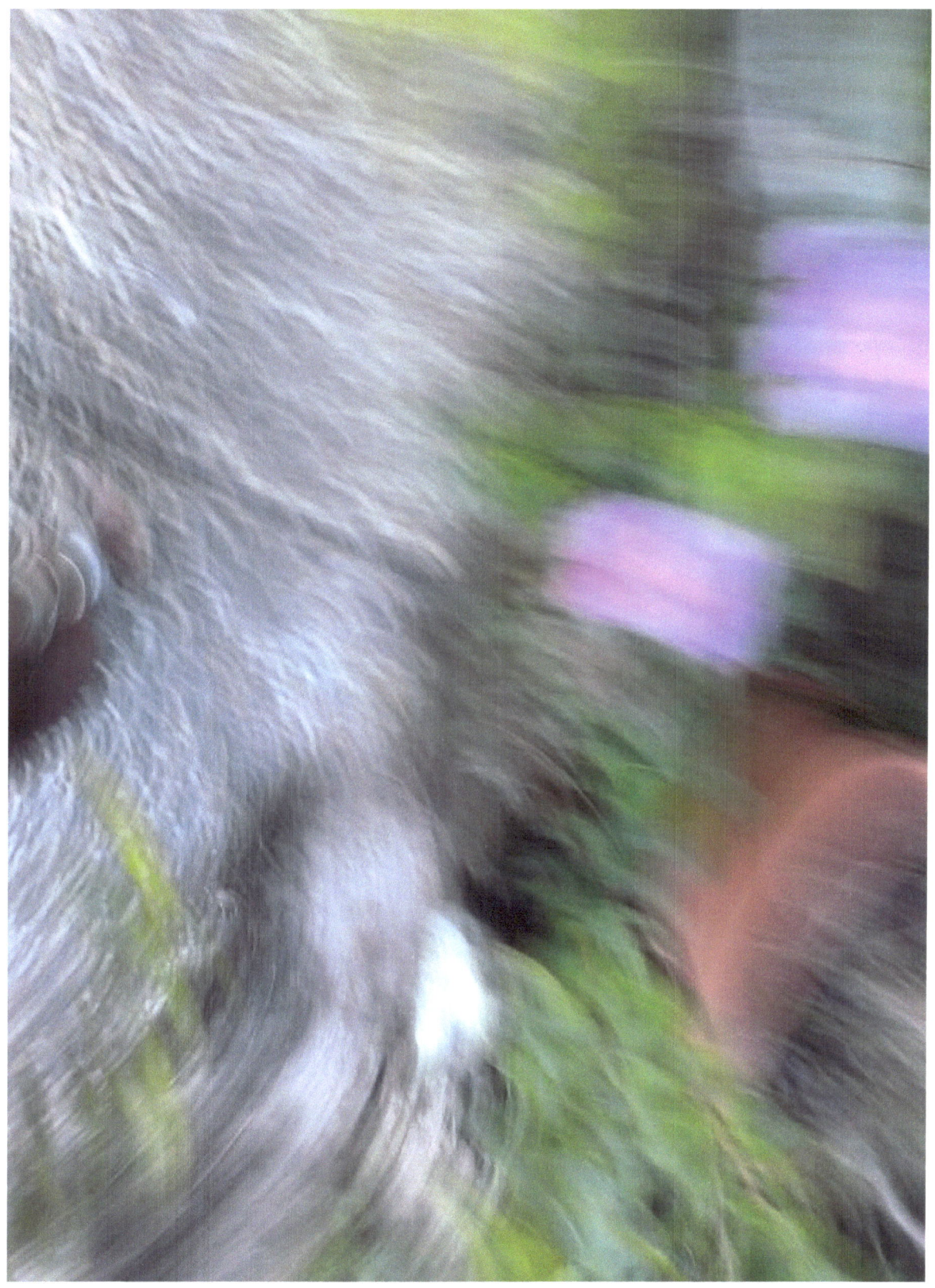

The tree trunk patterns become smaller waves. How rotational pressure and light transforms little globes of atoms, minerals and gases into many life forms.

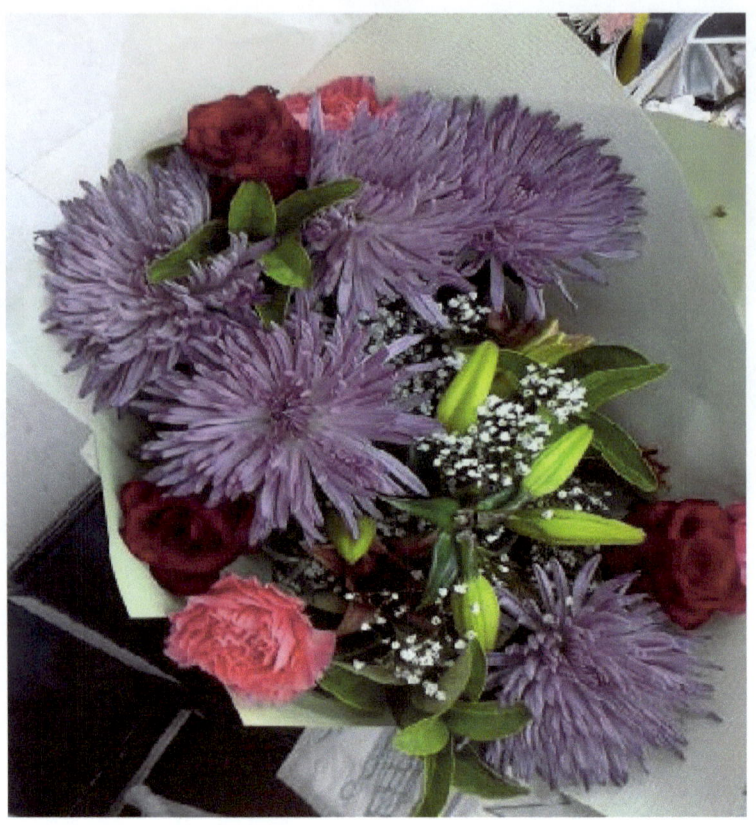

Original flowers of photo above and the photo of the same flowers taken while the camera was in transit below.

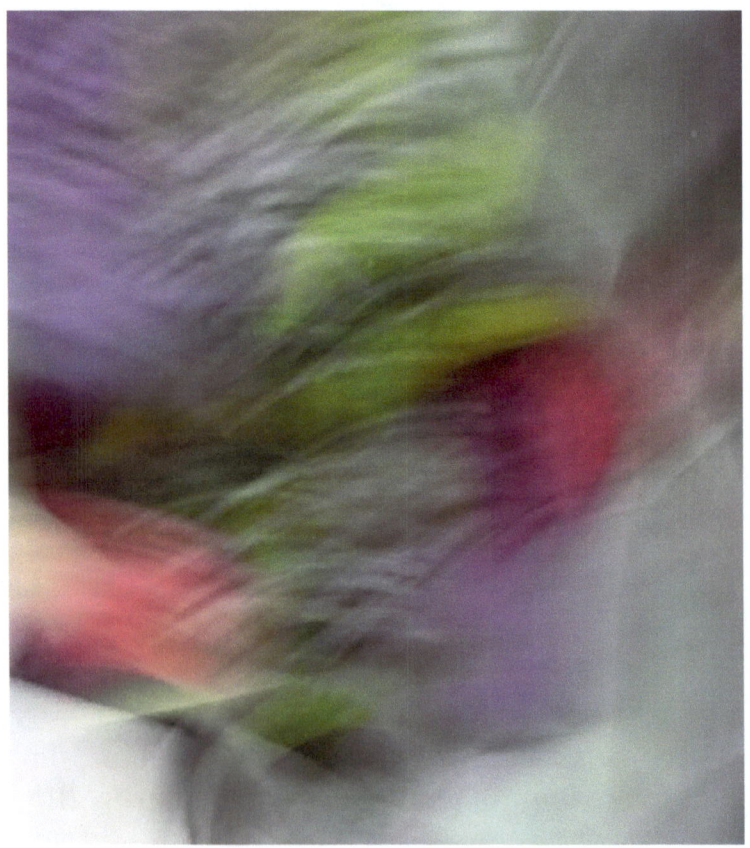

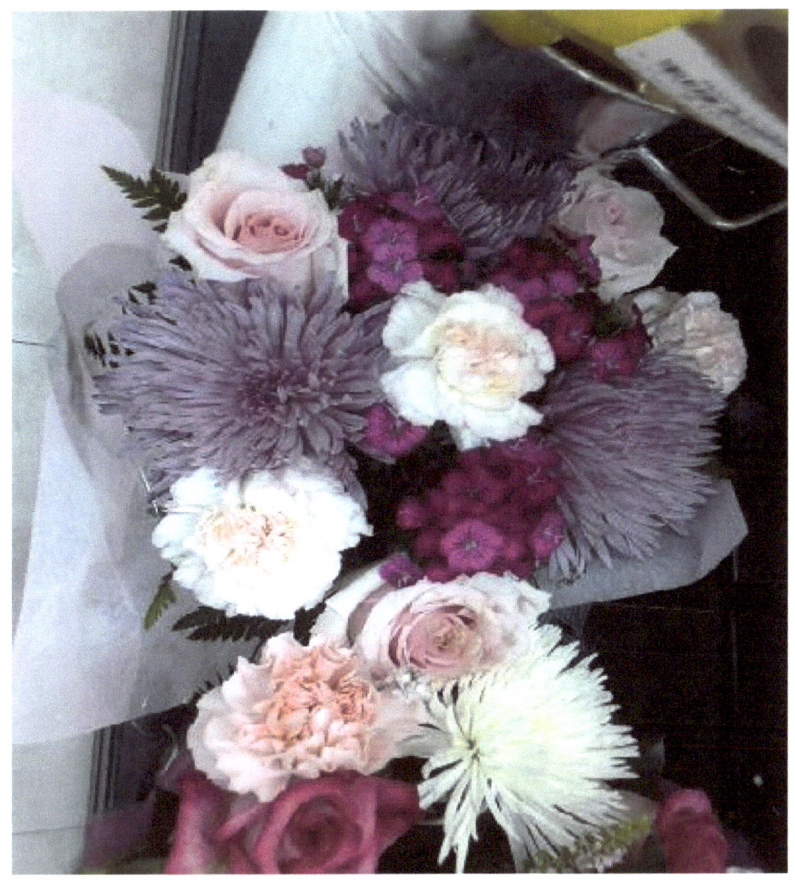

Original flowers of photo above and the same flowers, photo taken in transit below.

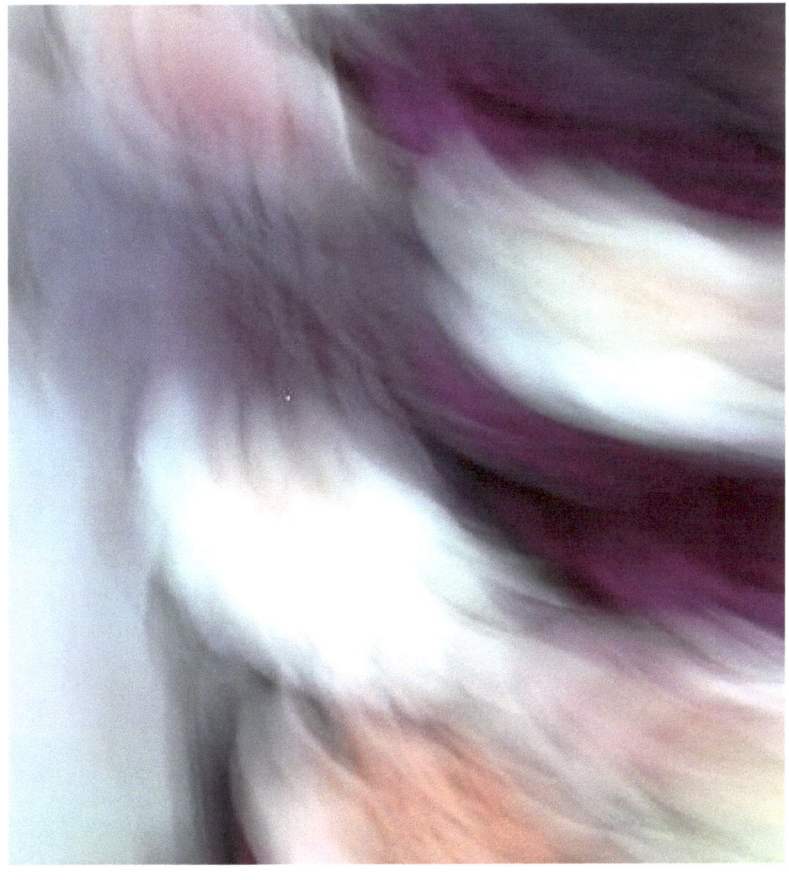

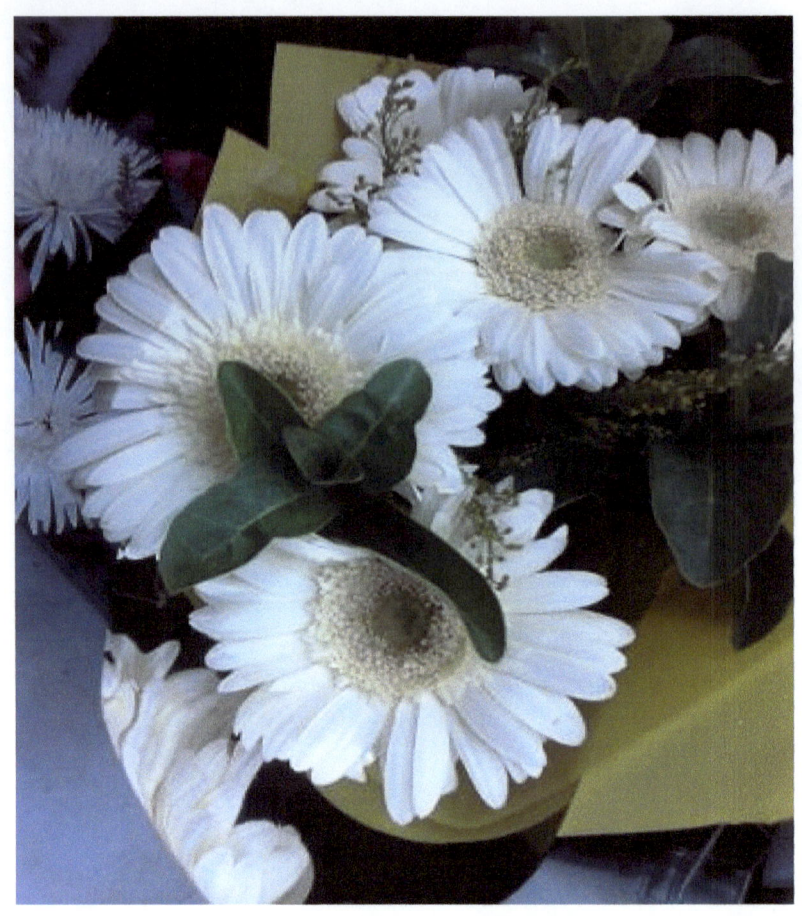

Original flowers of photo above and the same flowers, photo taken in transit below.

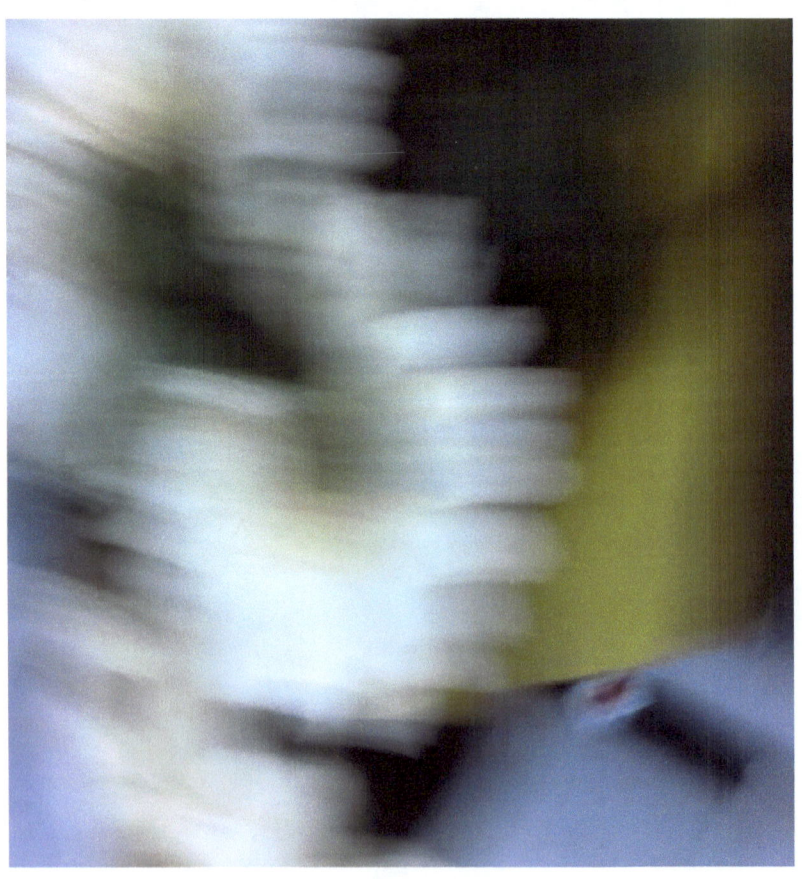

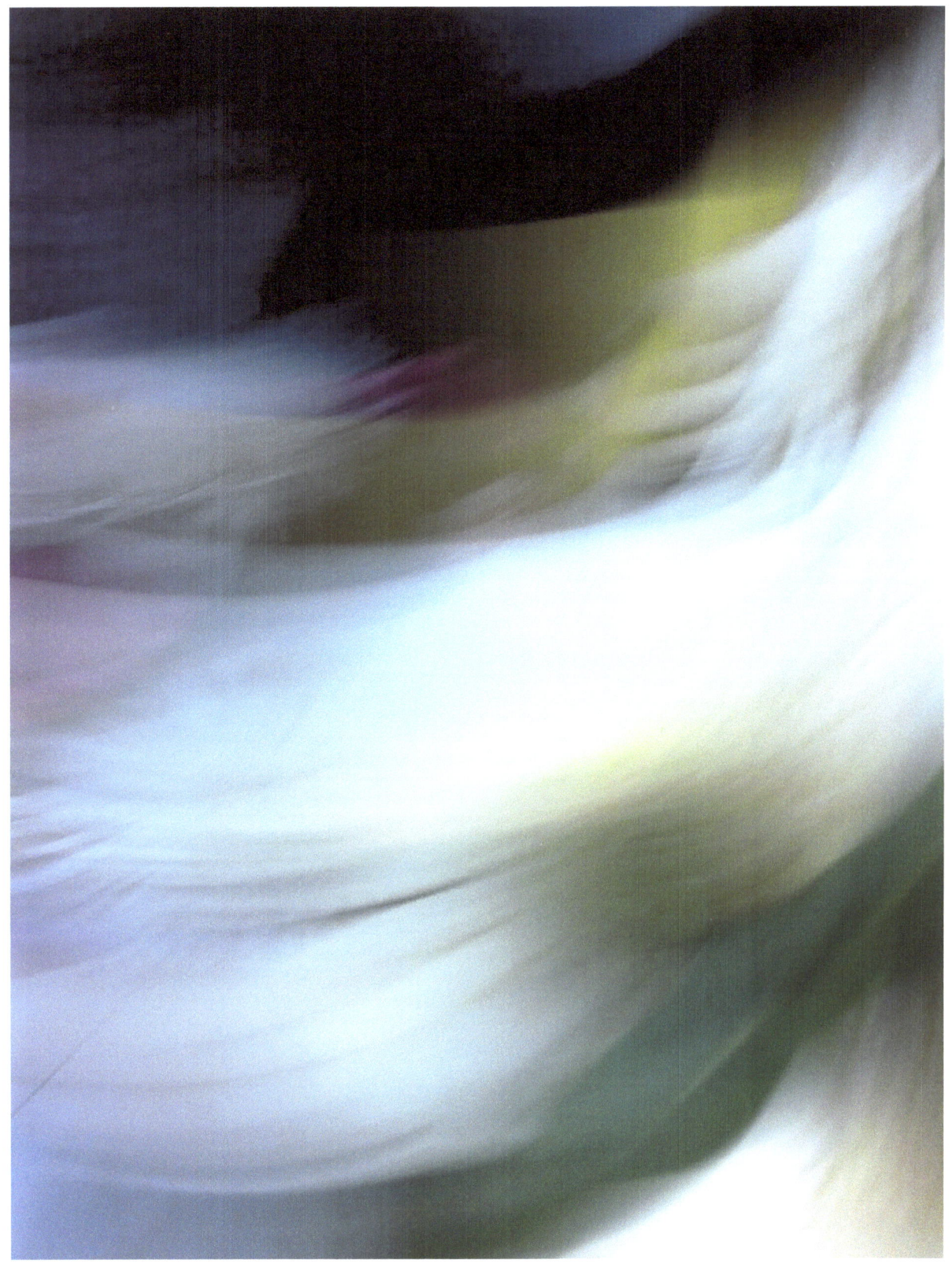

Real flowers produced an abstract photo by taking the photograph while the camera was in transit.

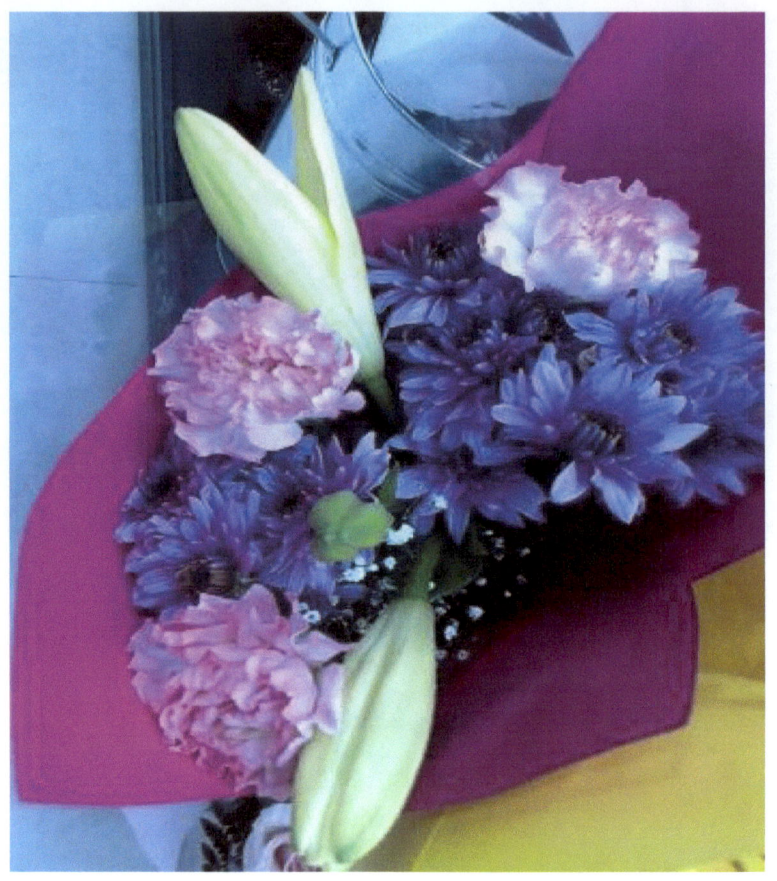

Original flowers of photo above and the same flowers, photo taken in transit below.

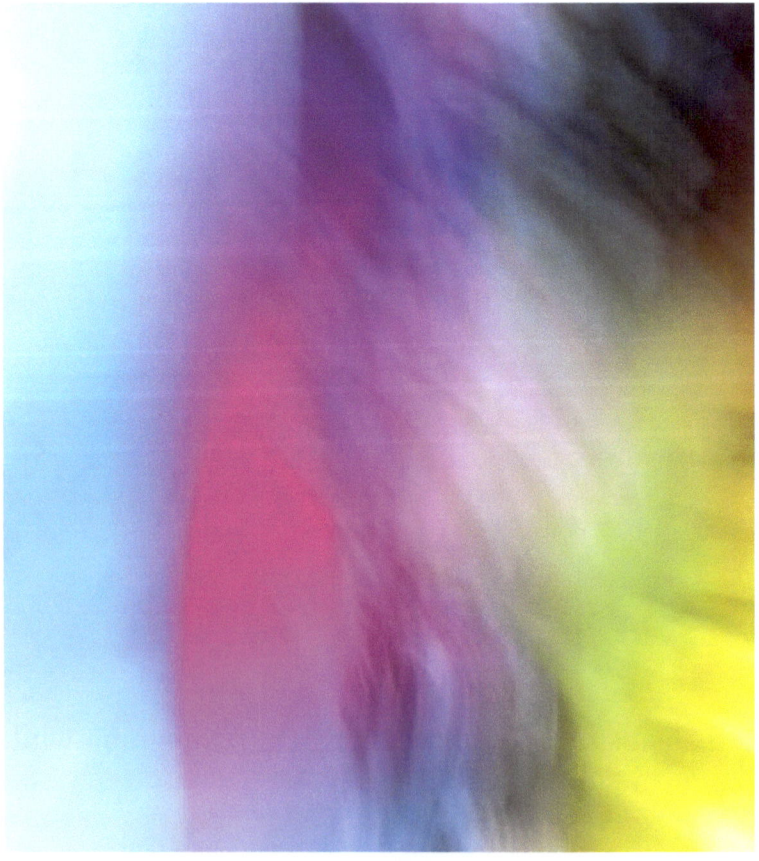

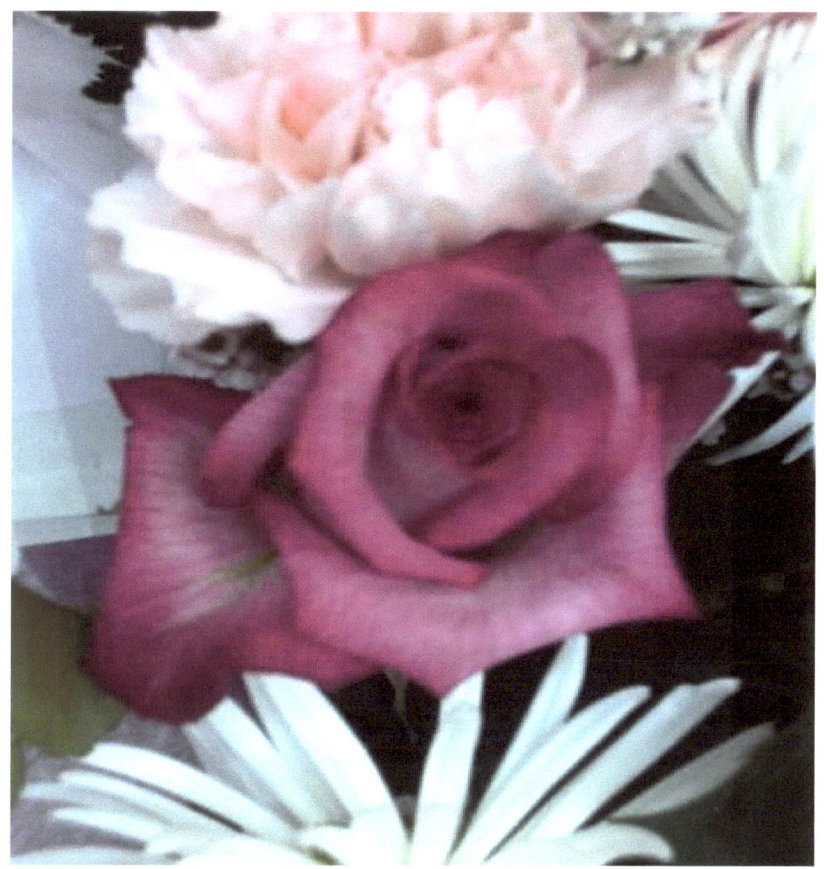

Original flowers of photo above and the same flowers, photo taken in transit below.

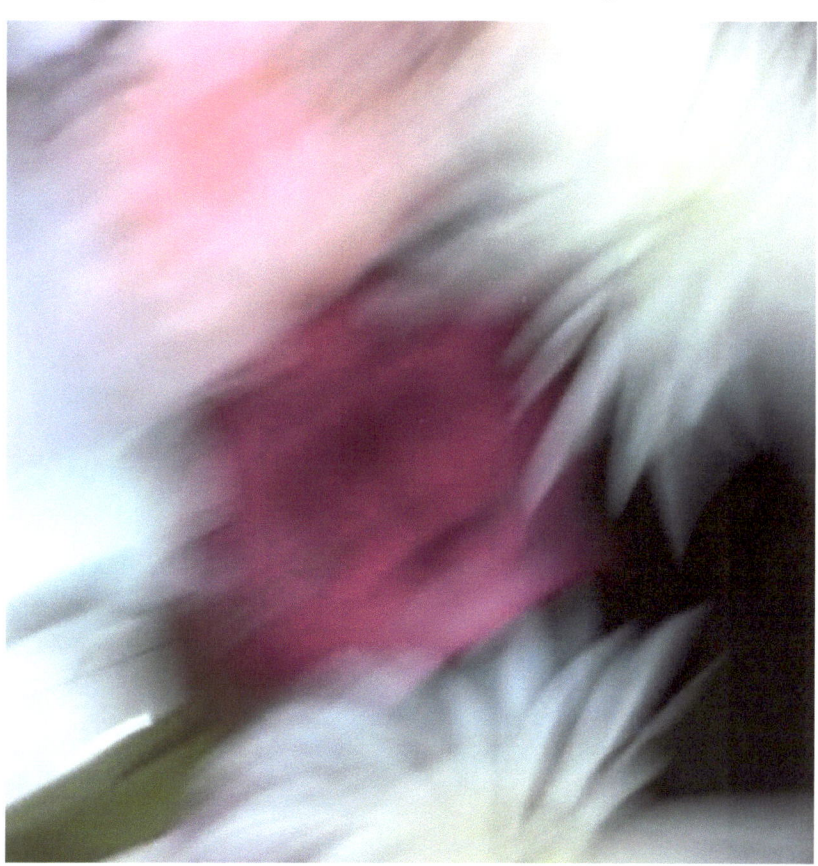

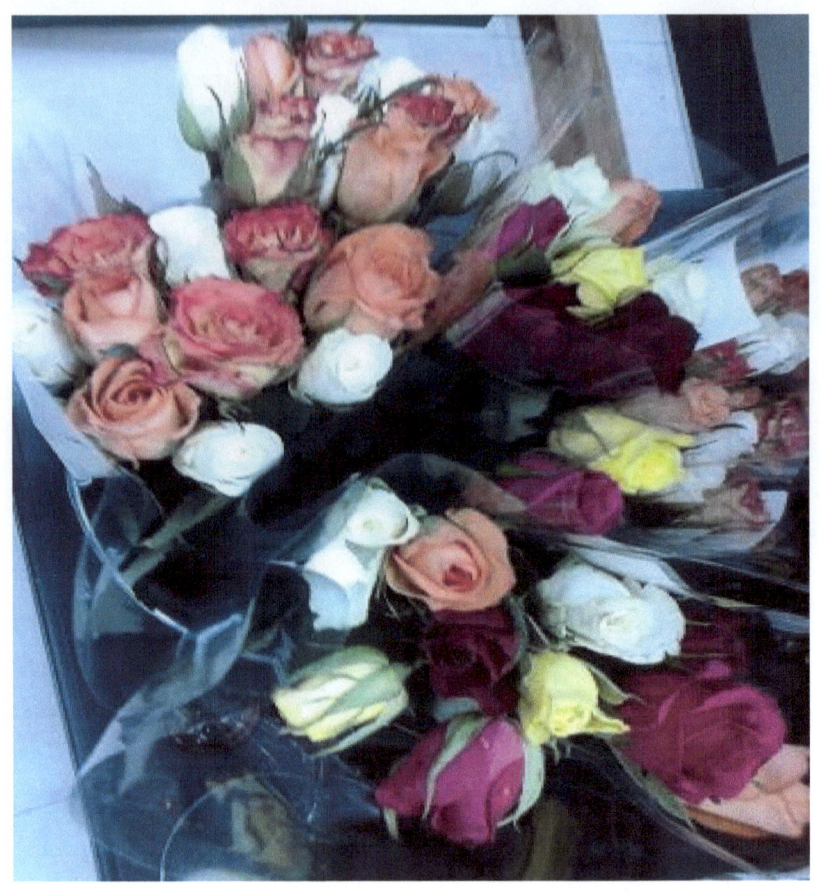

Original flowers of photo above and the same flowers, photo taken in transit below.

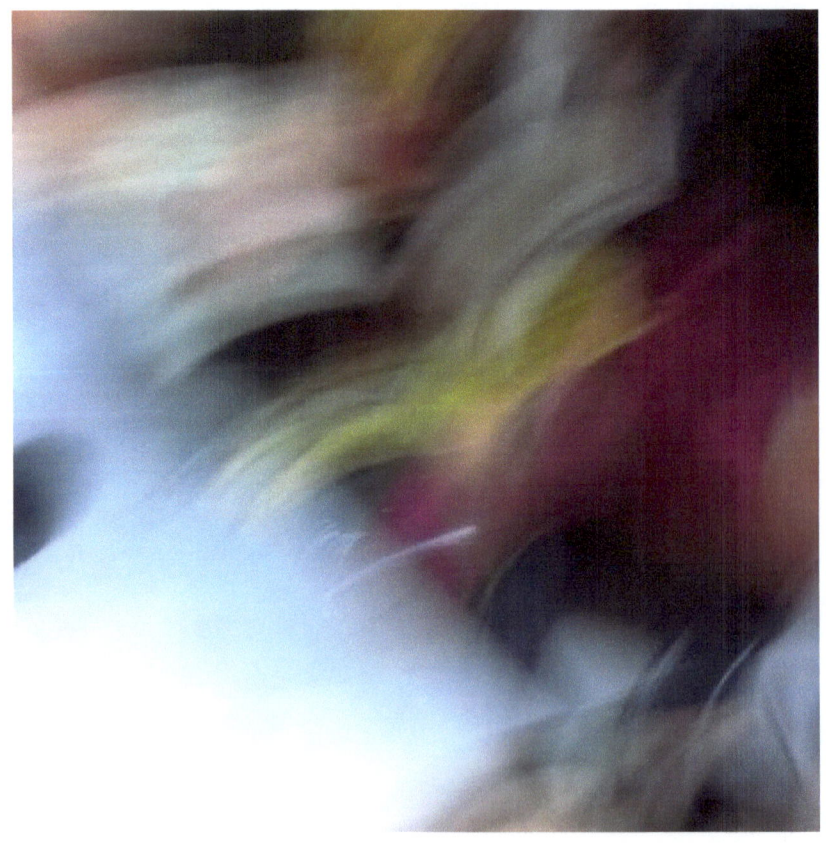

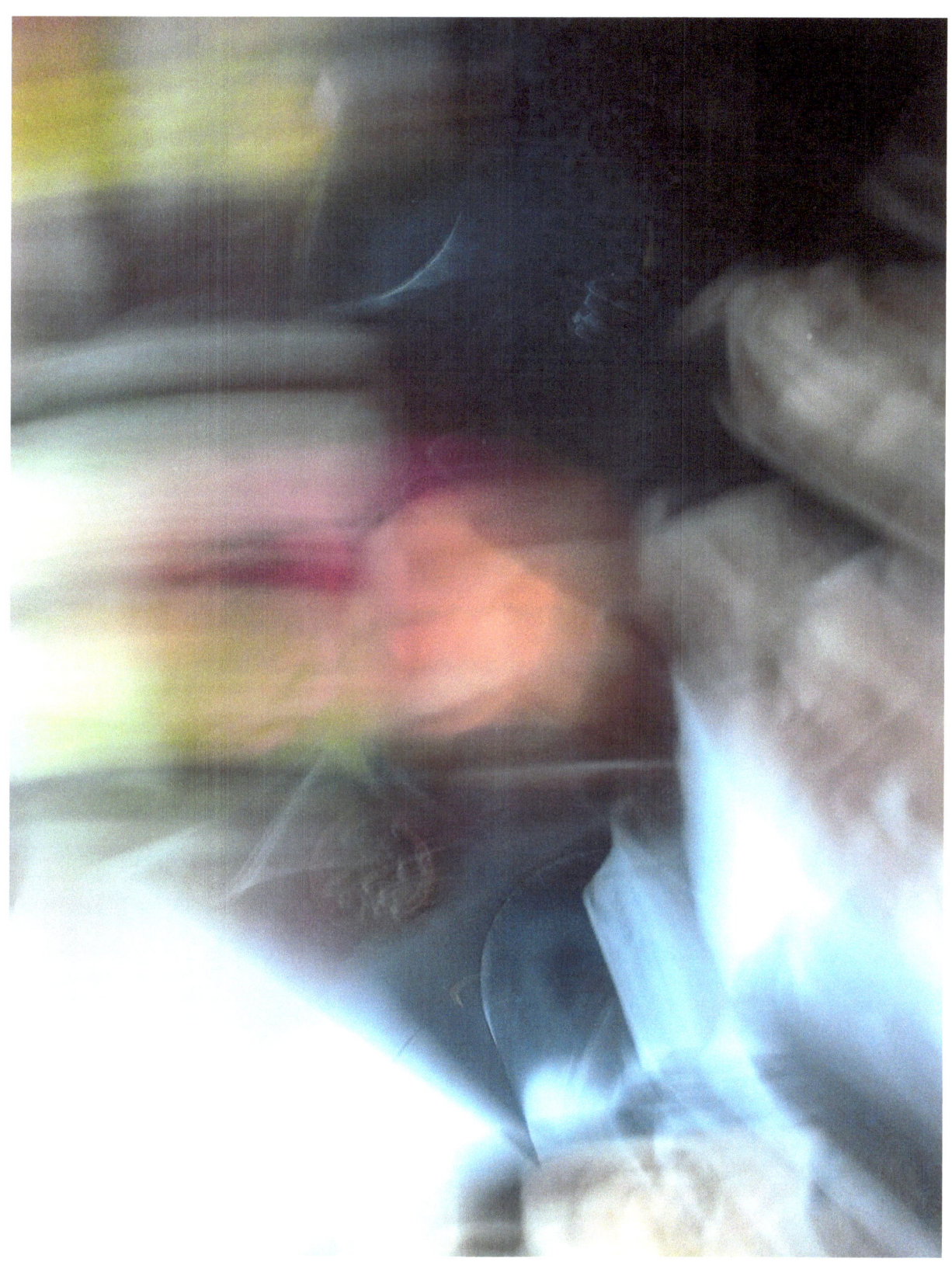

Photographs of flowers taken while the camera was in transit. Looking at the above photograph you would not say it is a photograph of flowers that in the previous page.
When brain is damaged and produces more pressure and rotates faster the images it produces also would look like an abstract art than a real flowers.

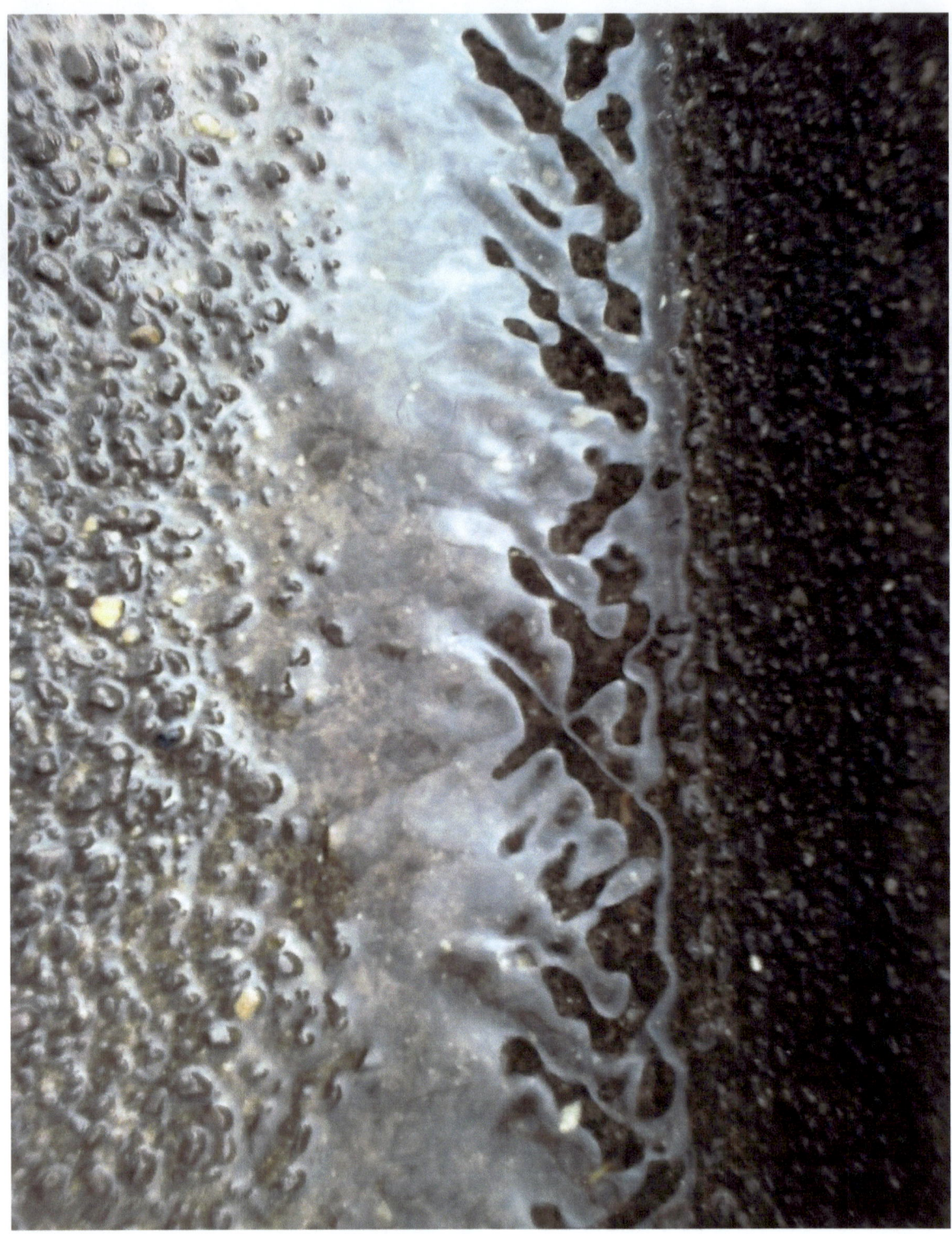

Water moving over pebbles and acids and chemicals moving over flesh, fat makes insects, frogs and lizards' patterns same as the above pattern shown on the photograph. Because body hasn't got an even surface so it produces these sorts of patterns on life forms, because pressure movements are same. Toad on the next page has similar patterns to the water moving over pebbles.

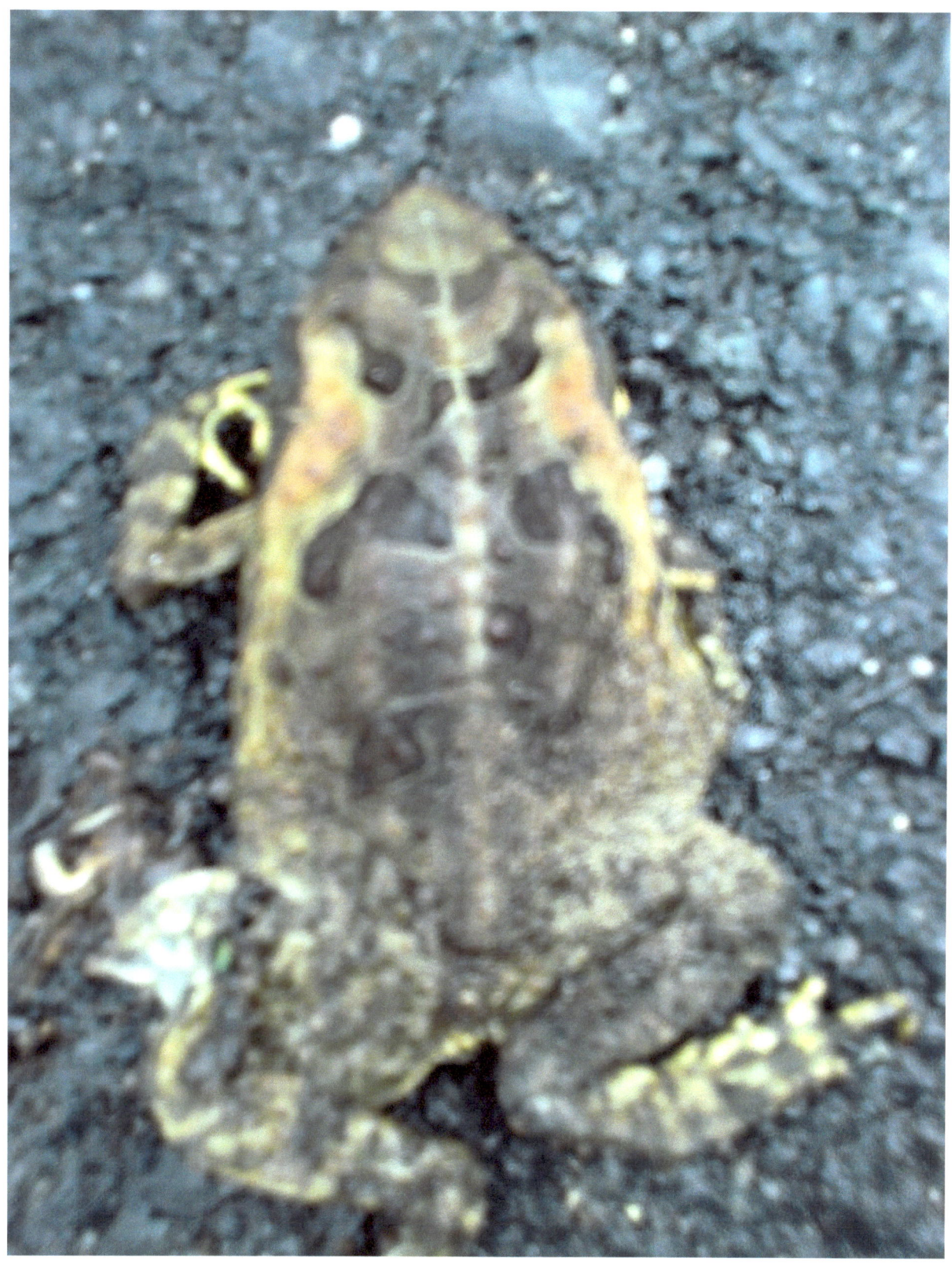

A Toad.

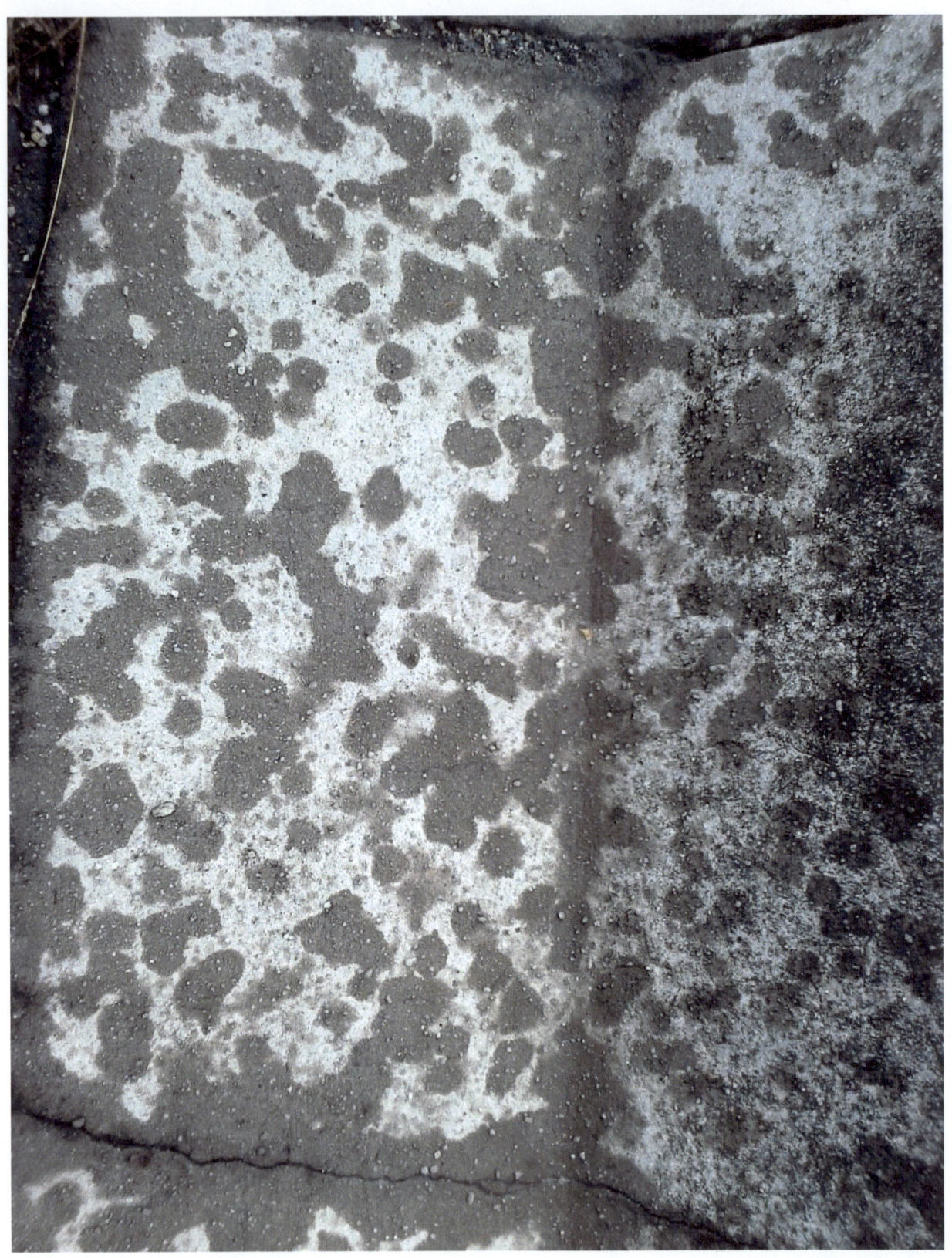

Multiple raindrops created these patterns that you see on many life forms.
How bubbles burst on life forms to make these patterns. A distortion in transit.

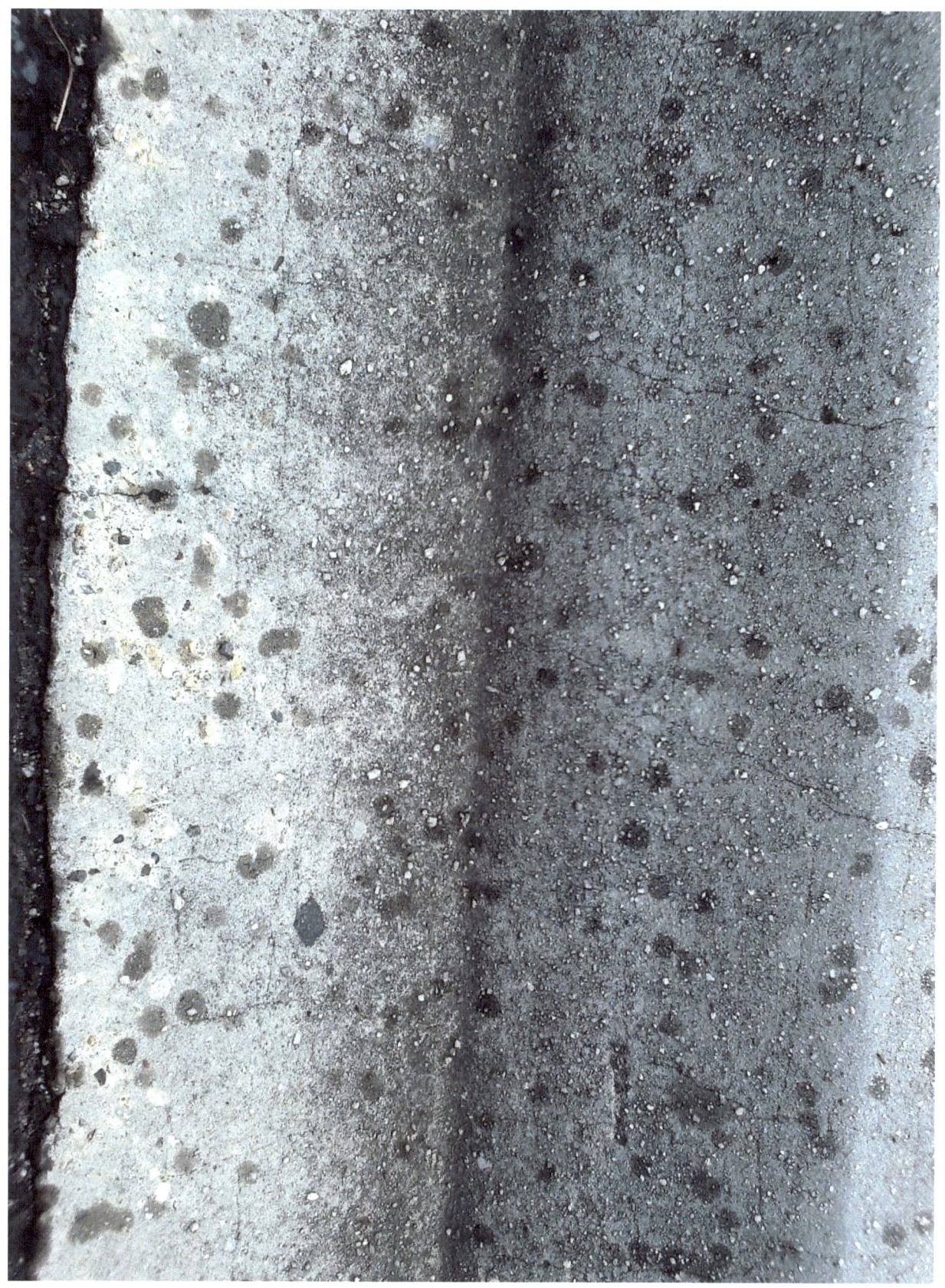

Single rain-drops created this pattern.

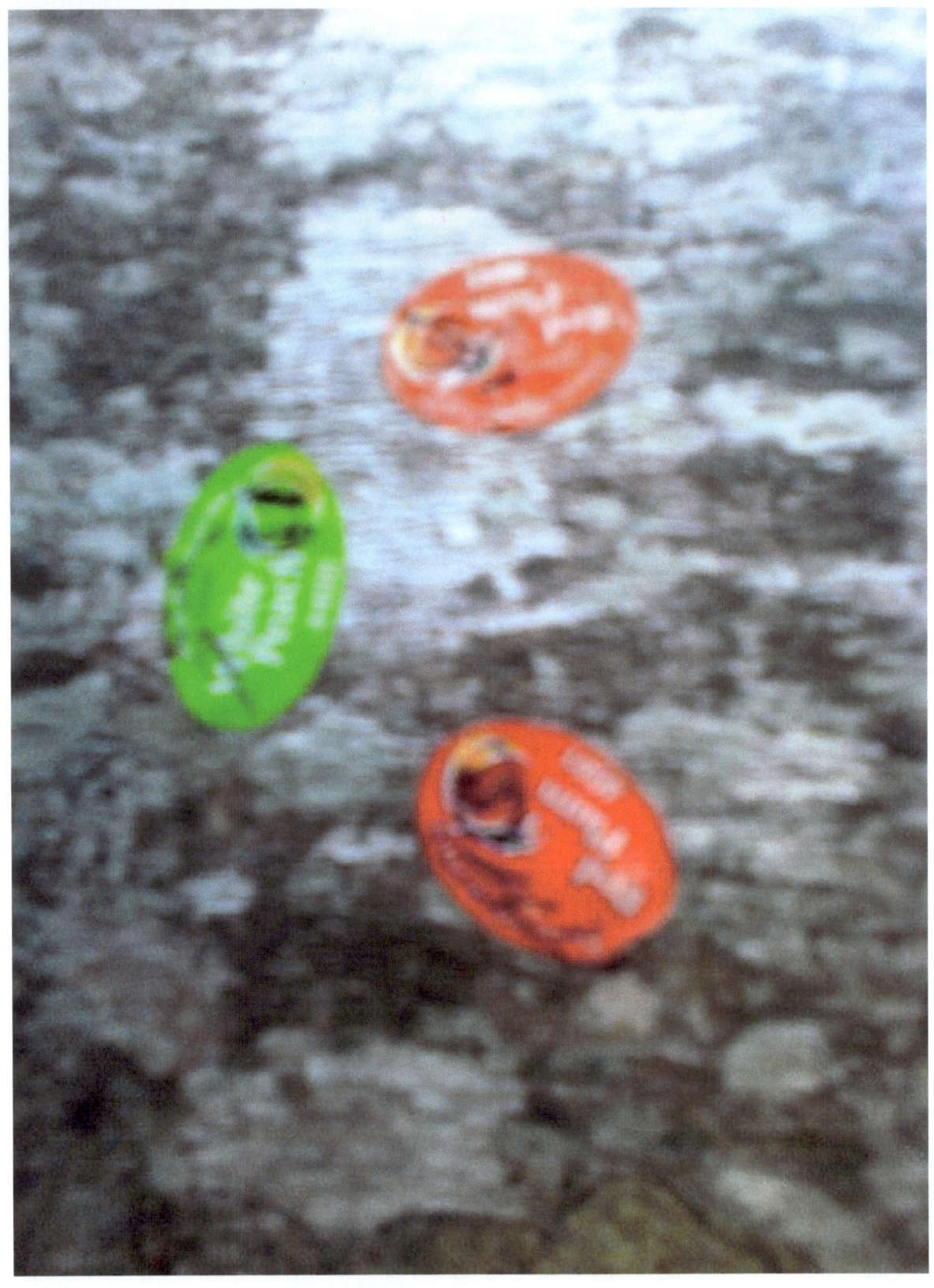

This is a real photo of stickers on a tree trunk and on the next page the same subject photographed in transit.

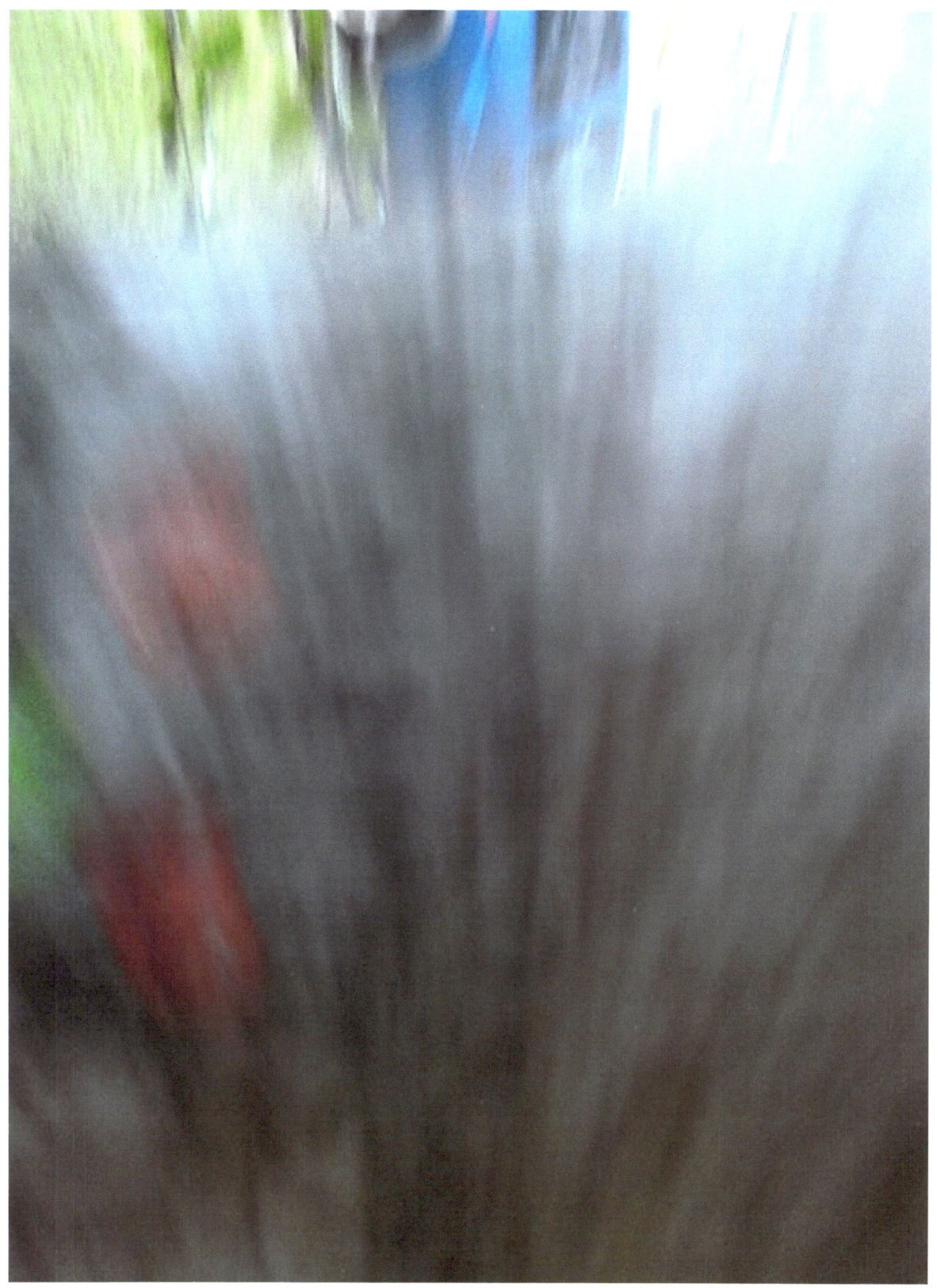

Two reds and a green stickers photographed in transit.

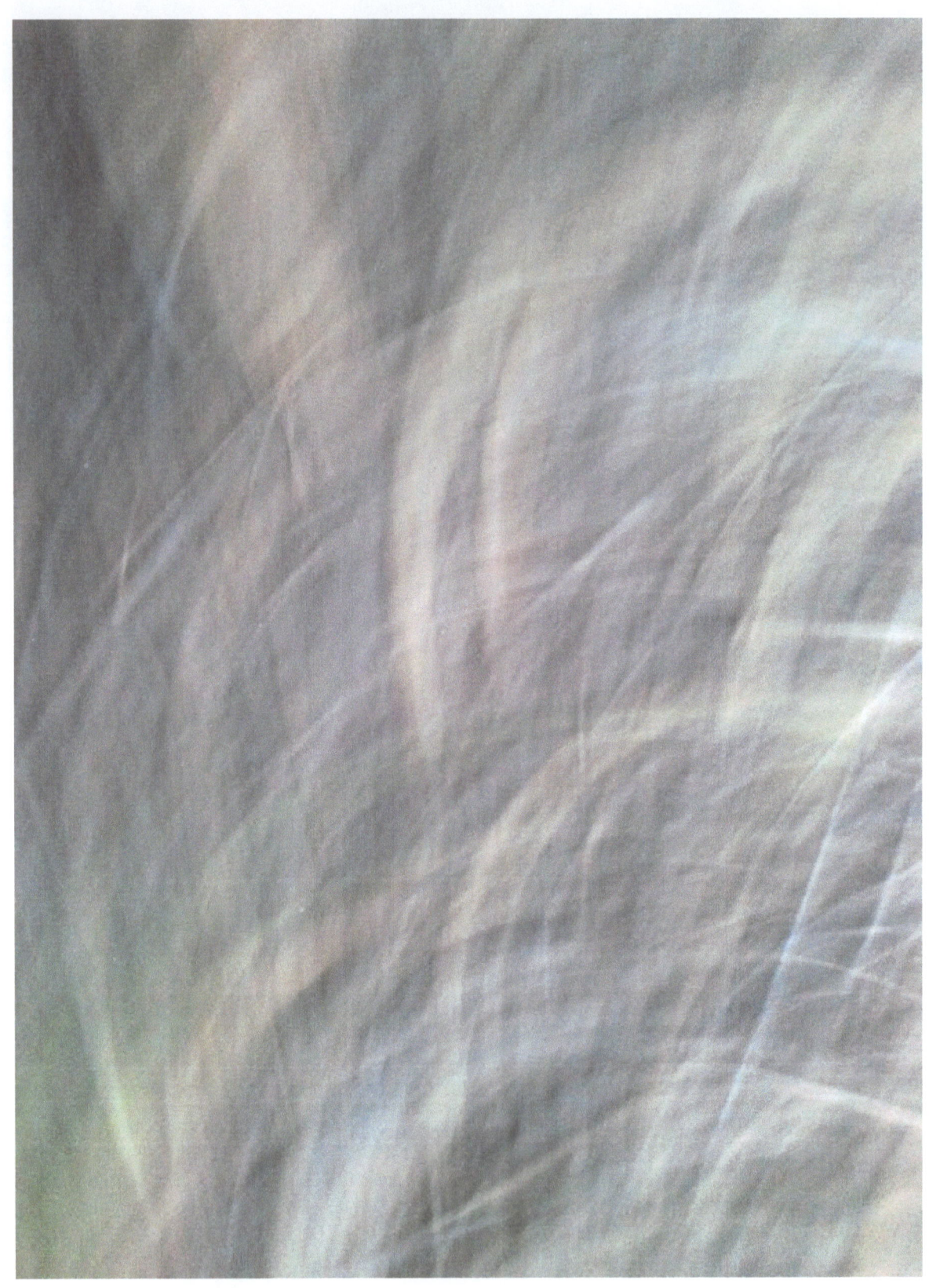

Grass and leaves photographed when camera was in transit.

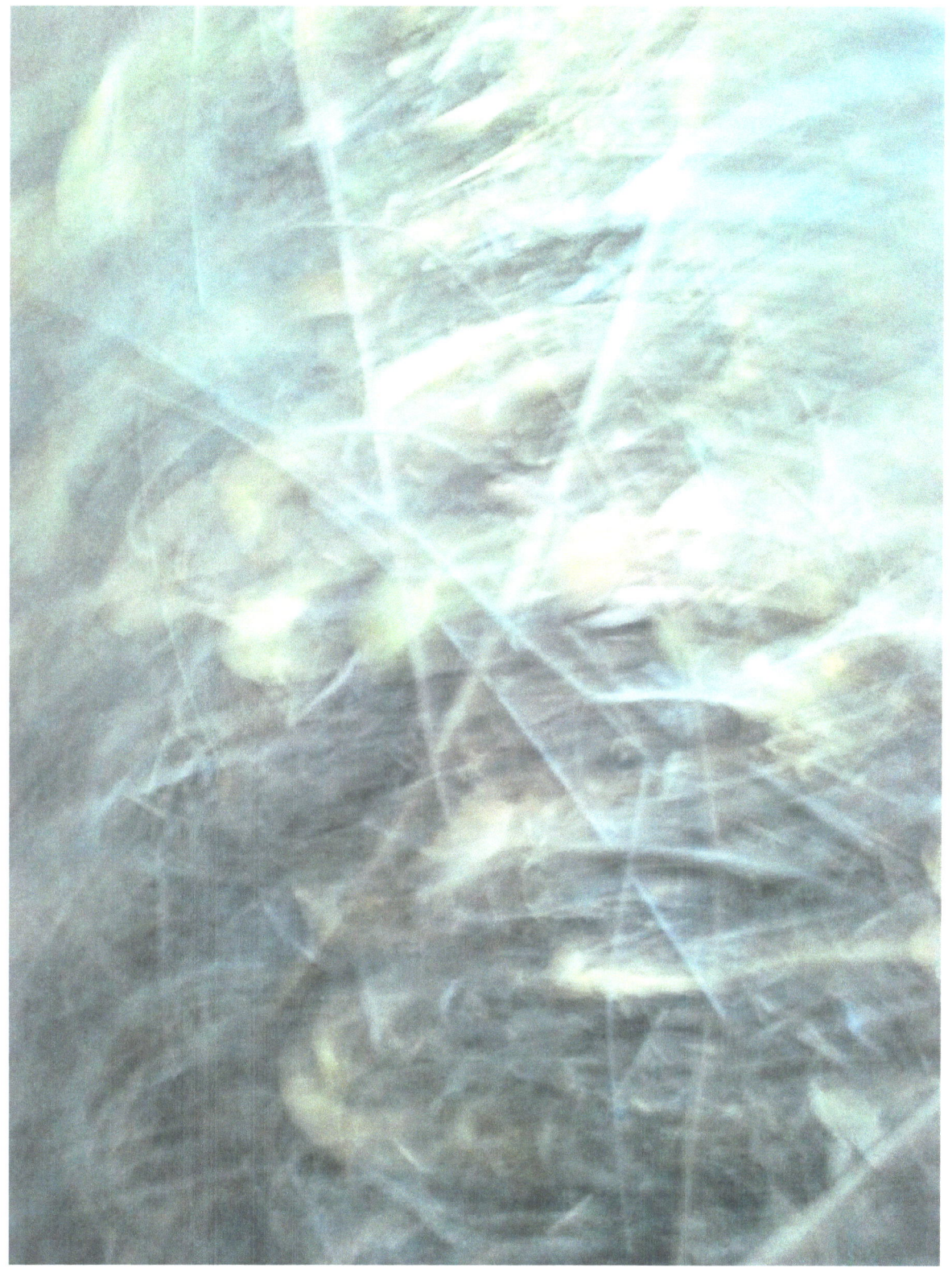

Many rotations formed when photographed with a camera that was in transit.
Multiple objects with a big camera rotations forms many rotations like the solar system.
One big rotation of the camera makes individual plants make their own rotations.

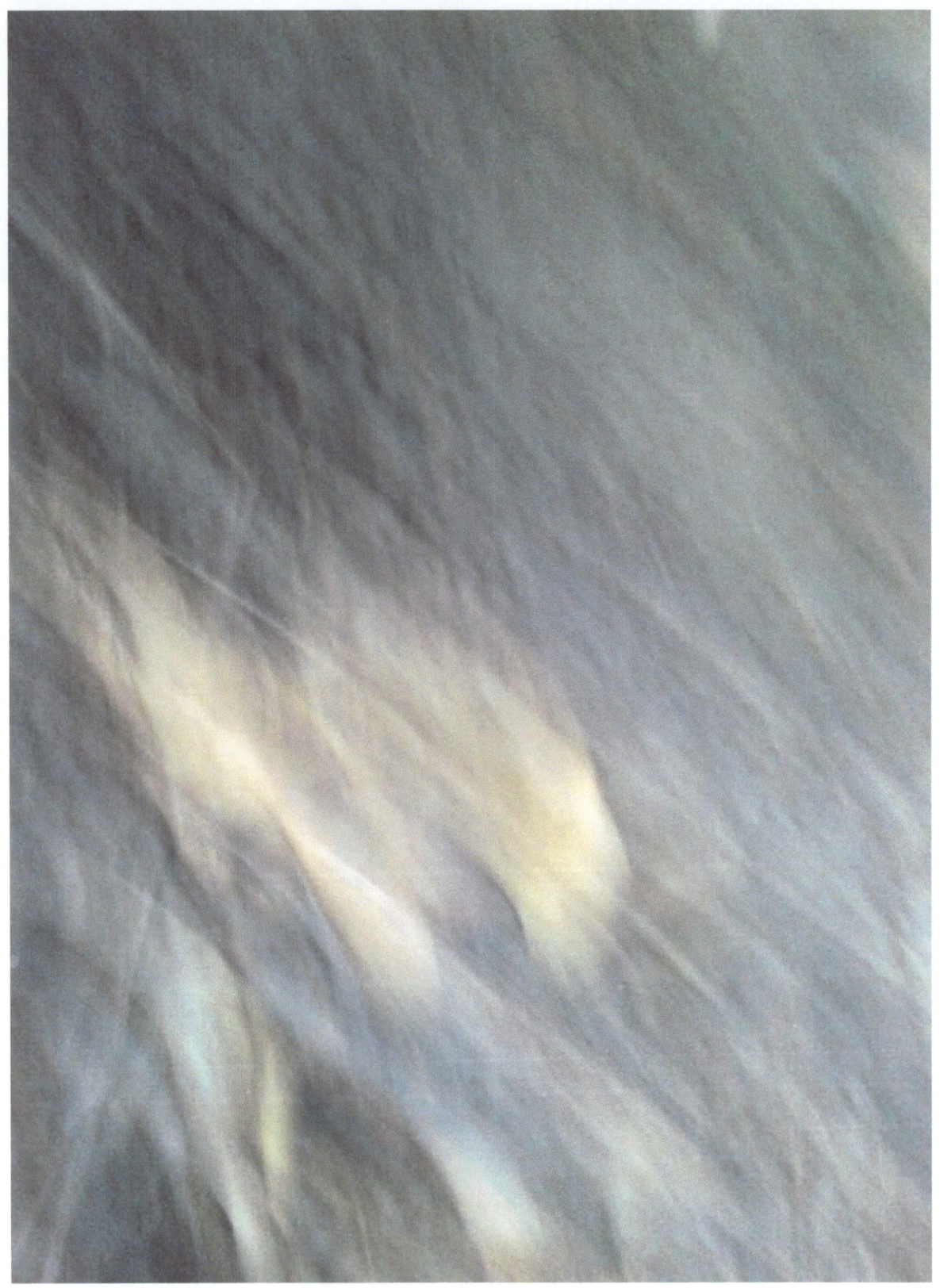

Three dried leaves photographed when the camera was in transit.

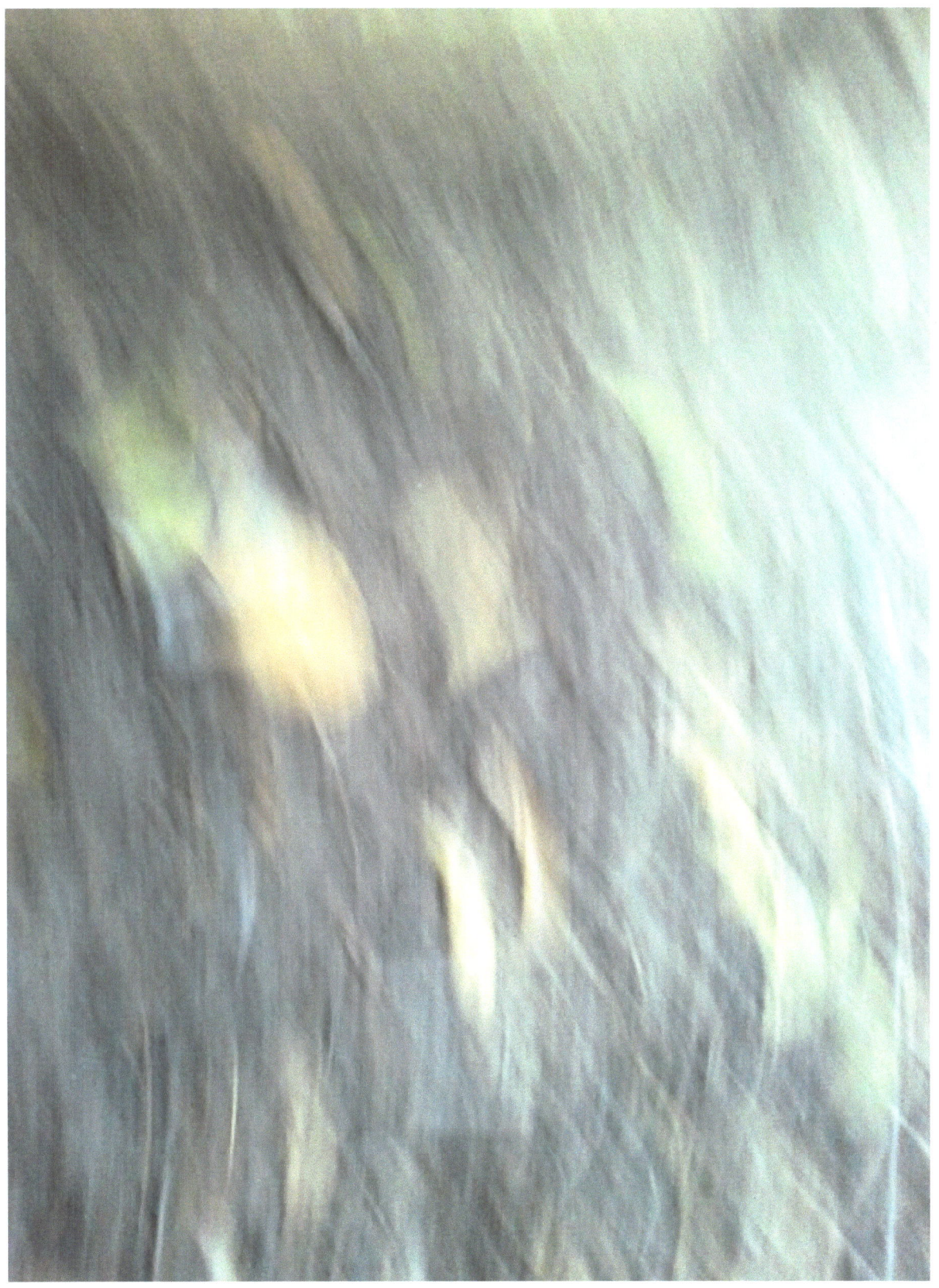

Many green and brown leaves photographed when the camera was in transit.

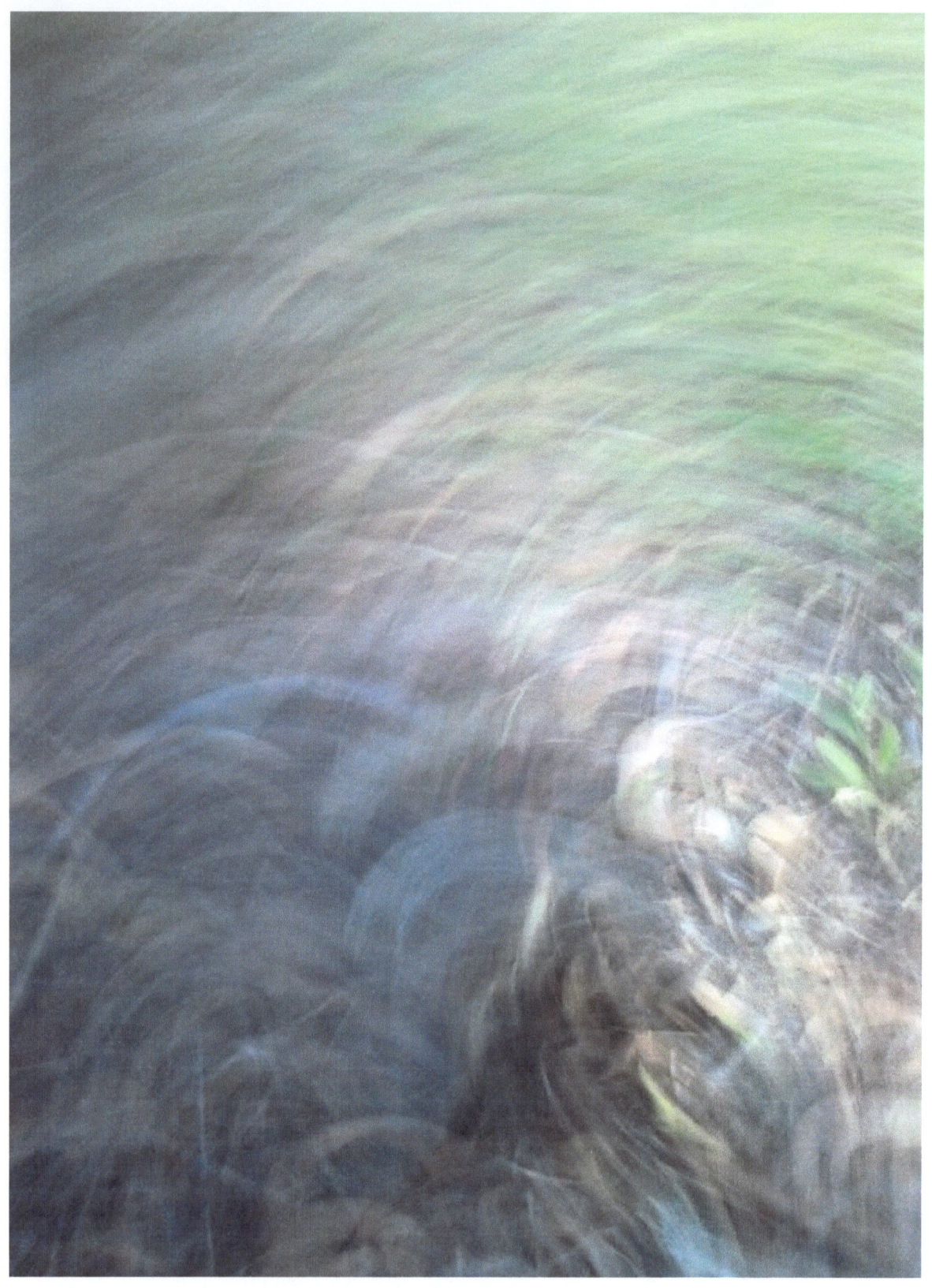

Grass, leaves and mulch photographed when the camera was in transit.

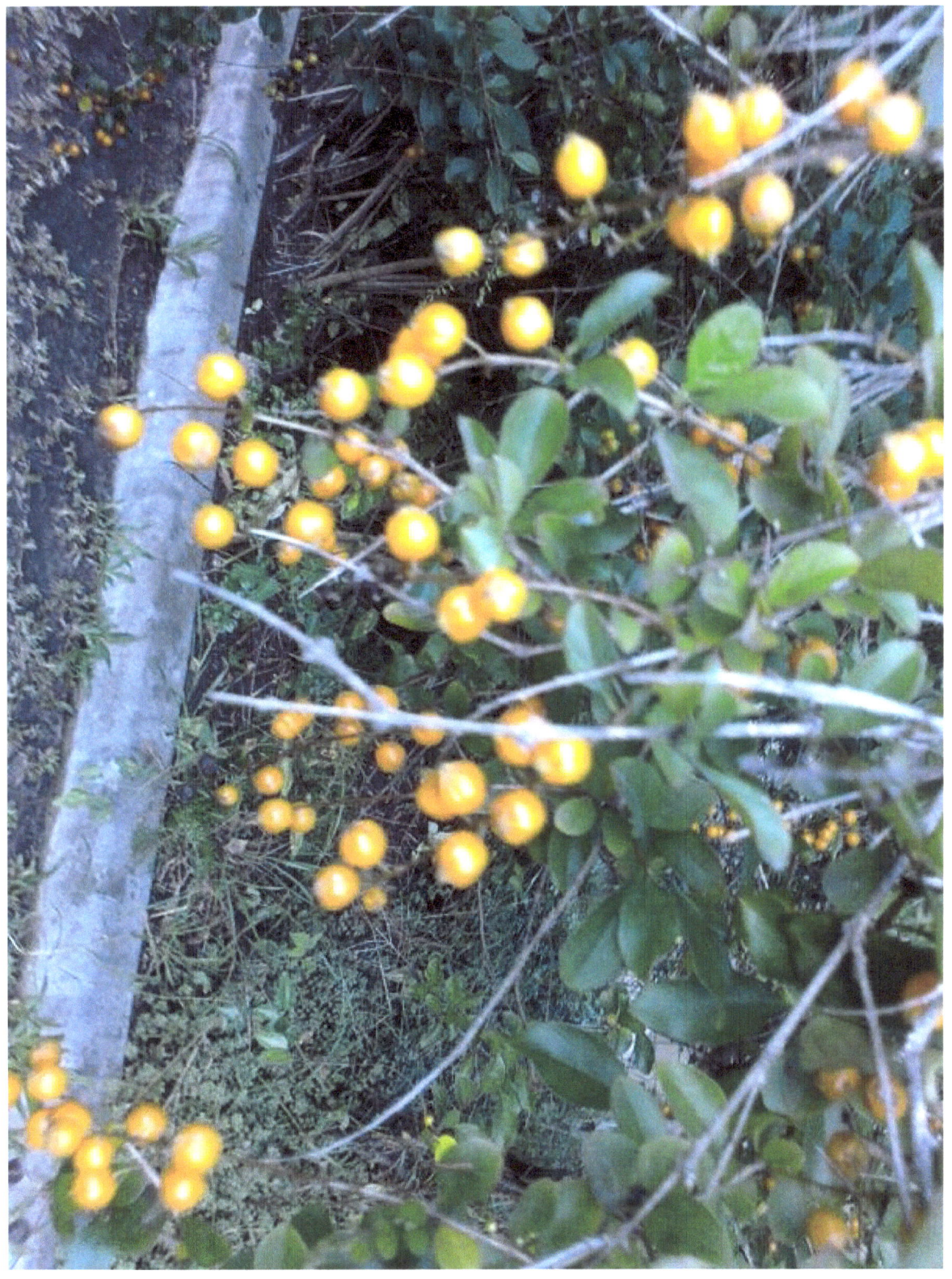

Real photo of a plant and in the next few pages you can see the same photo taken while the camera was in transit.

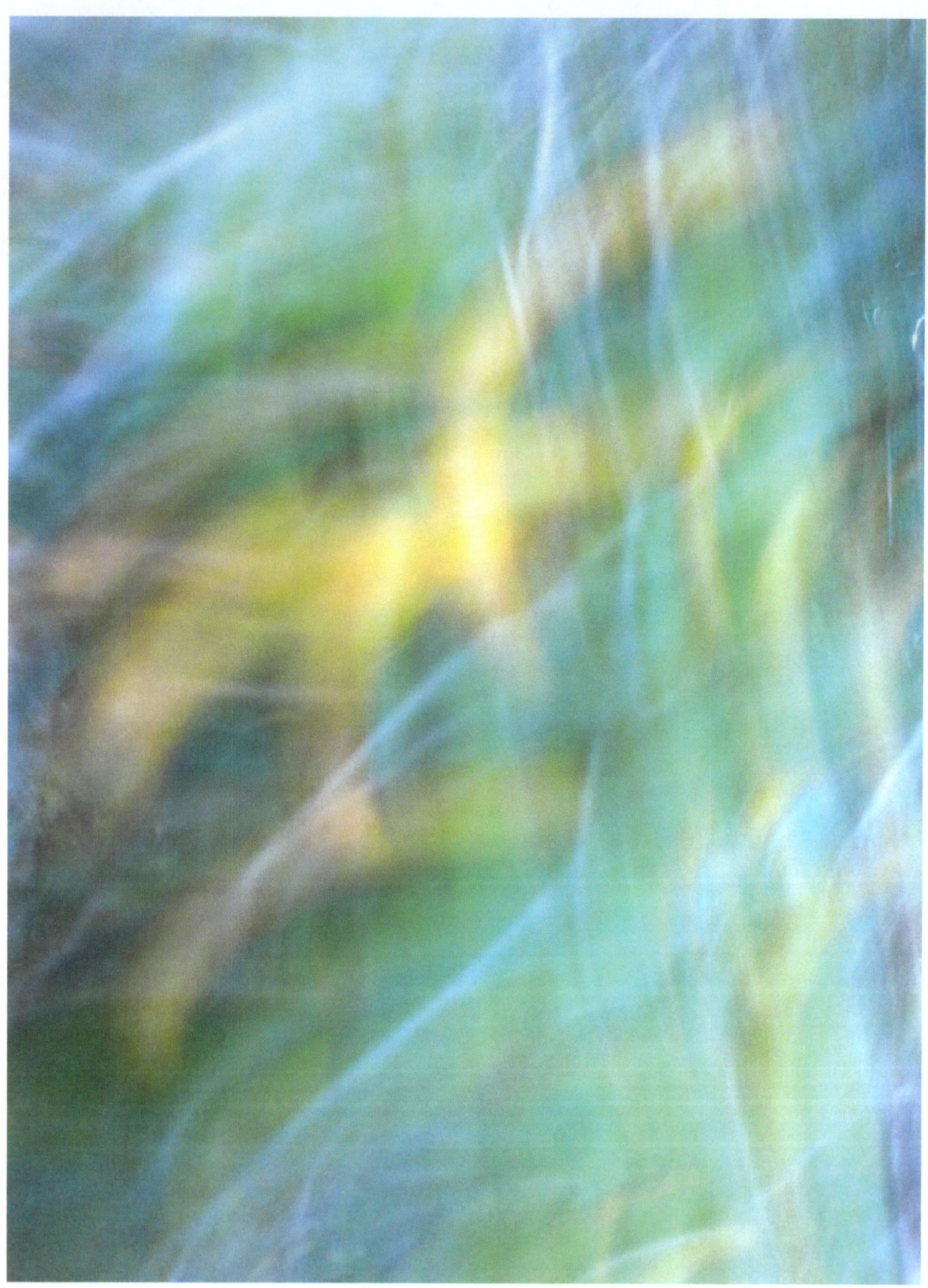

Photo taken in transit.

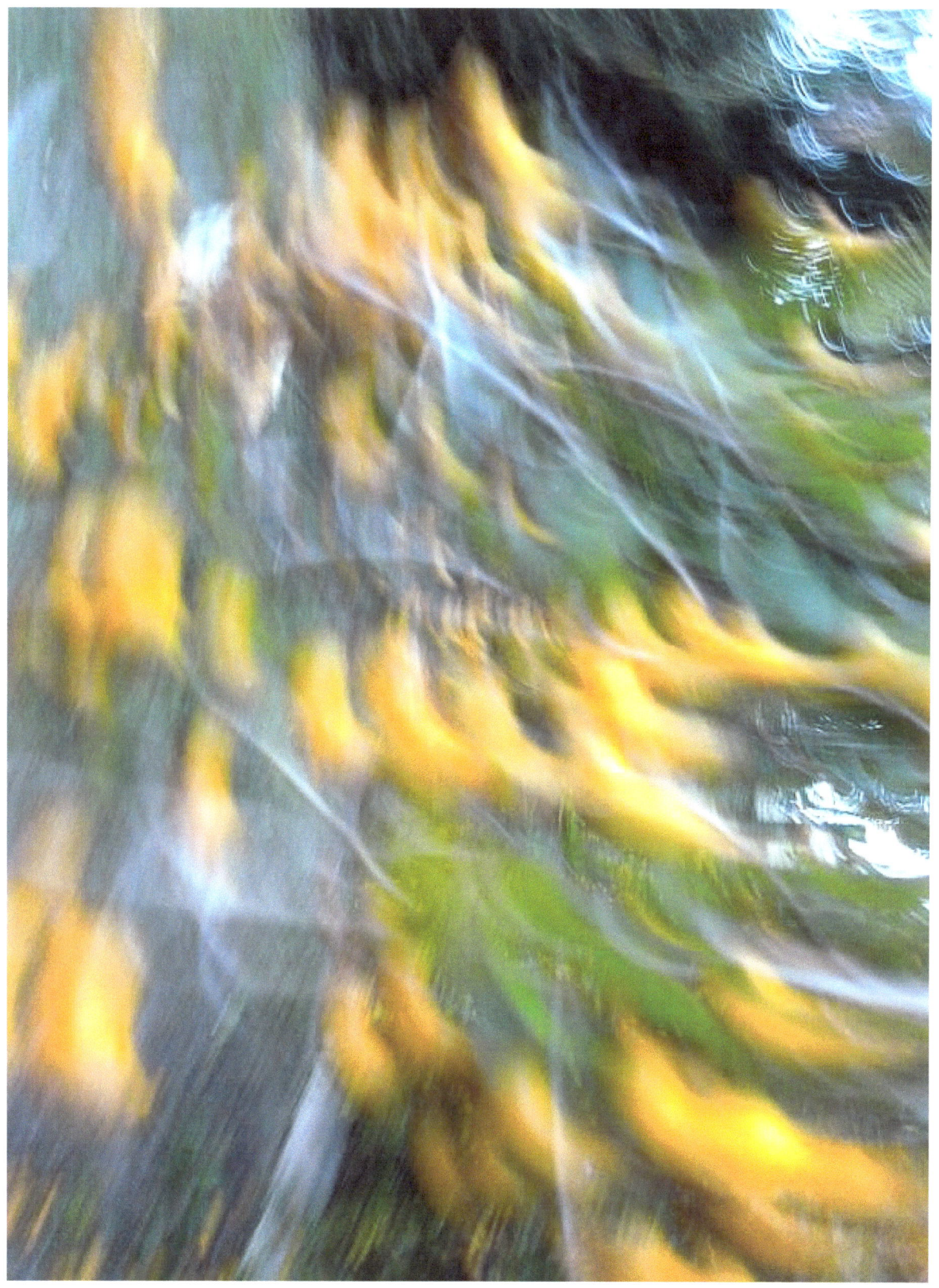

Photo taken in transit shows lines of light also moving.

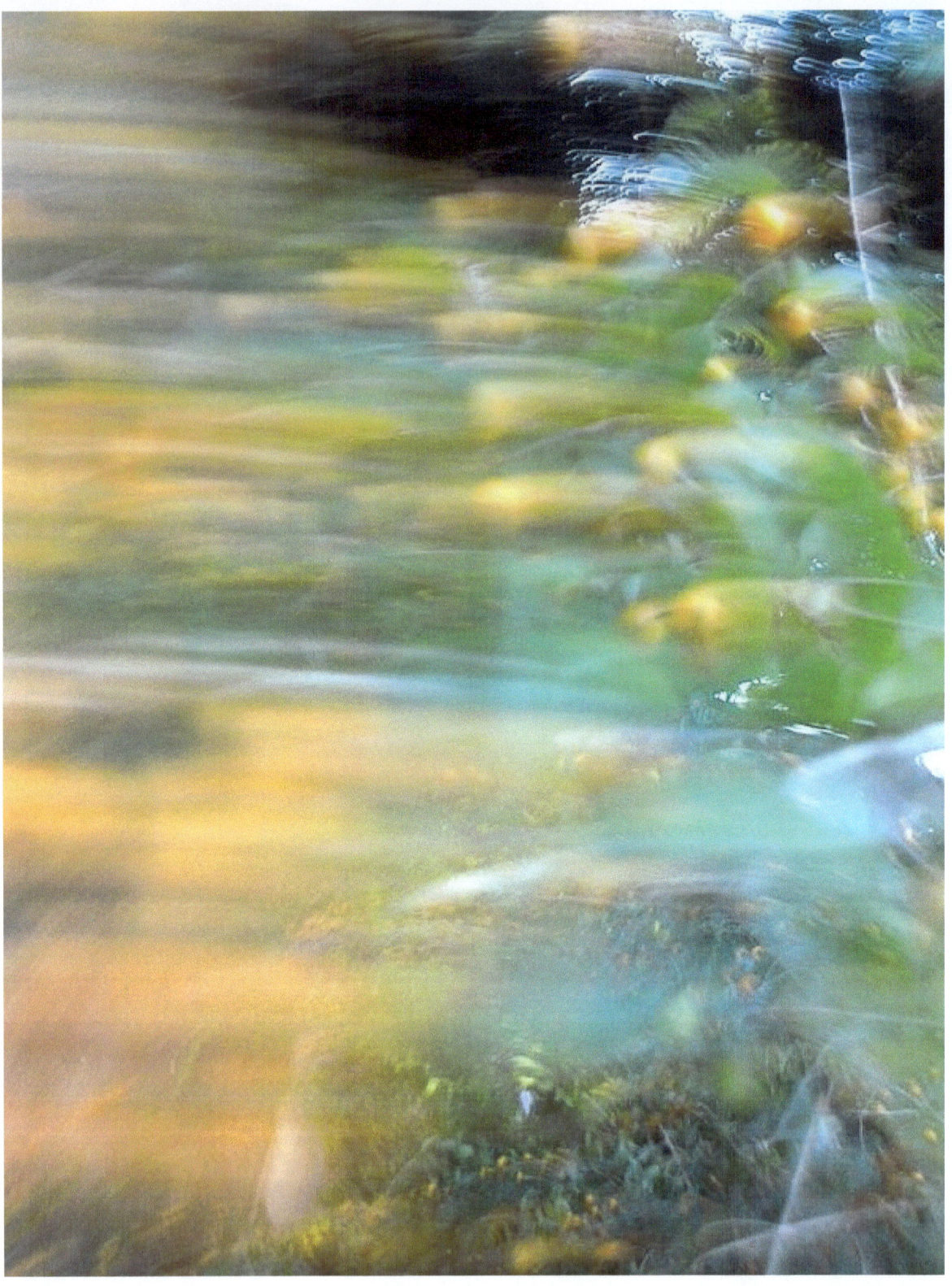

Photo taken in transit show that we can move the light falling off anything. Light has to be powerful and also you can see light moving off small fruits, shows as small bubbles of fruits was moving like light on the photograph.

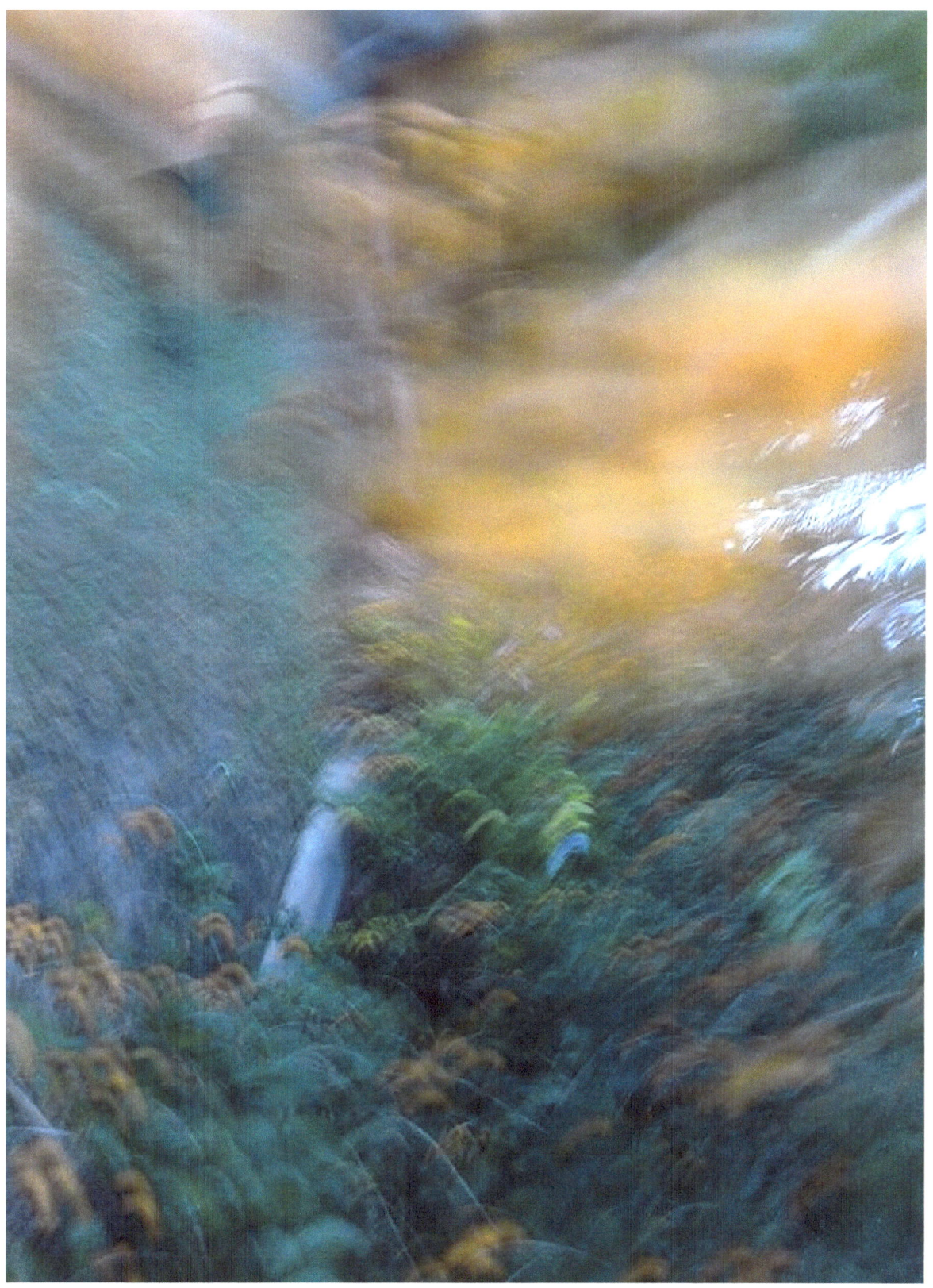

This plant photo taken in transit looks like a landscape.

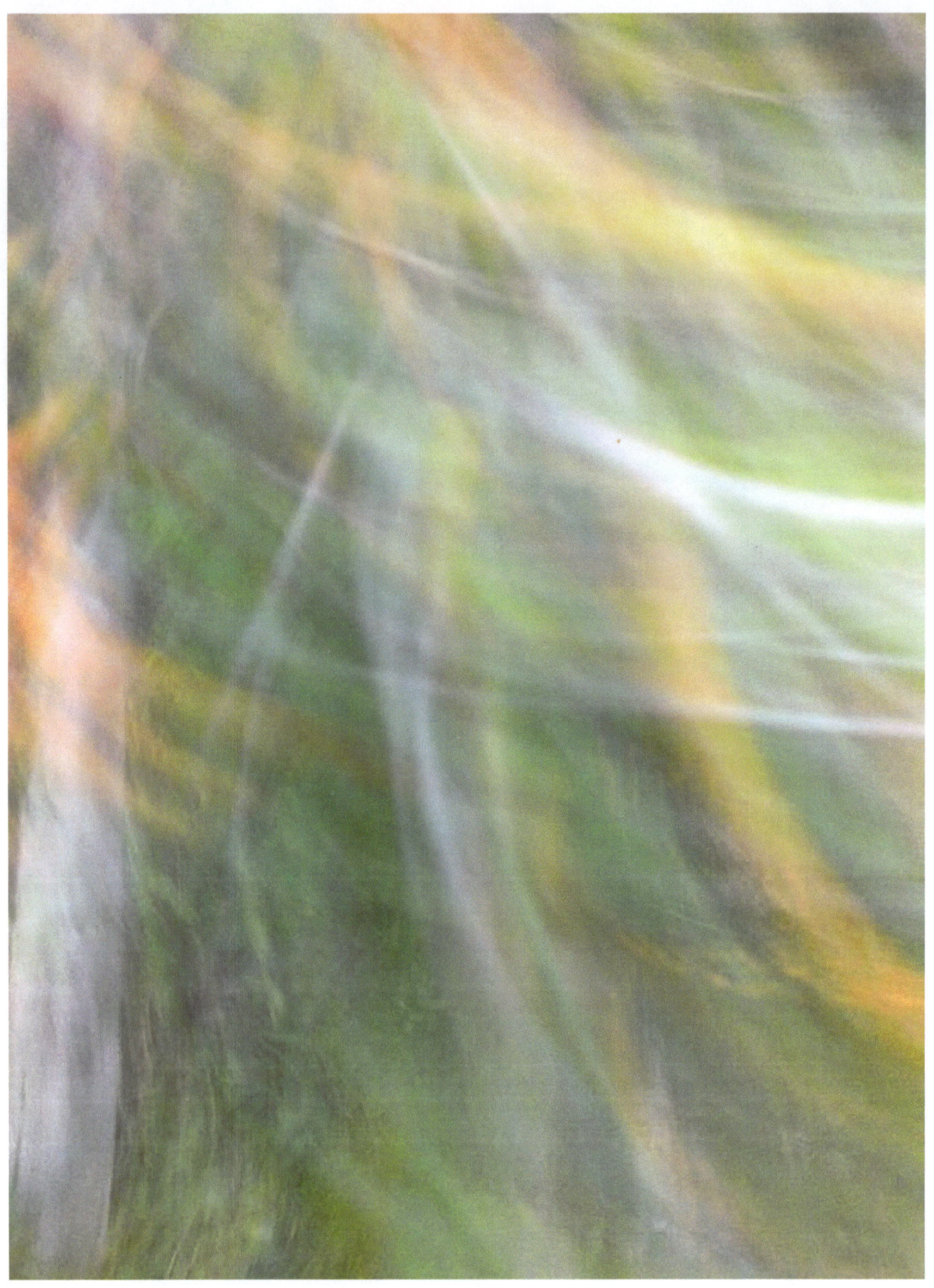

Palm leaves photographed when the camera was in transit.

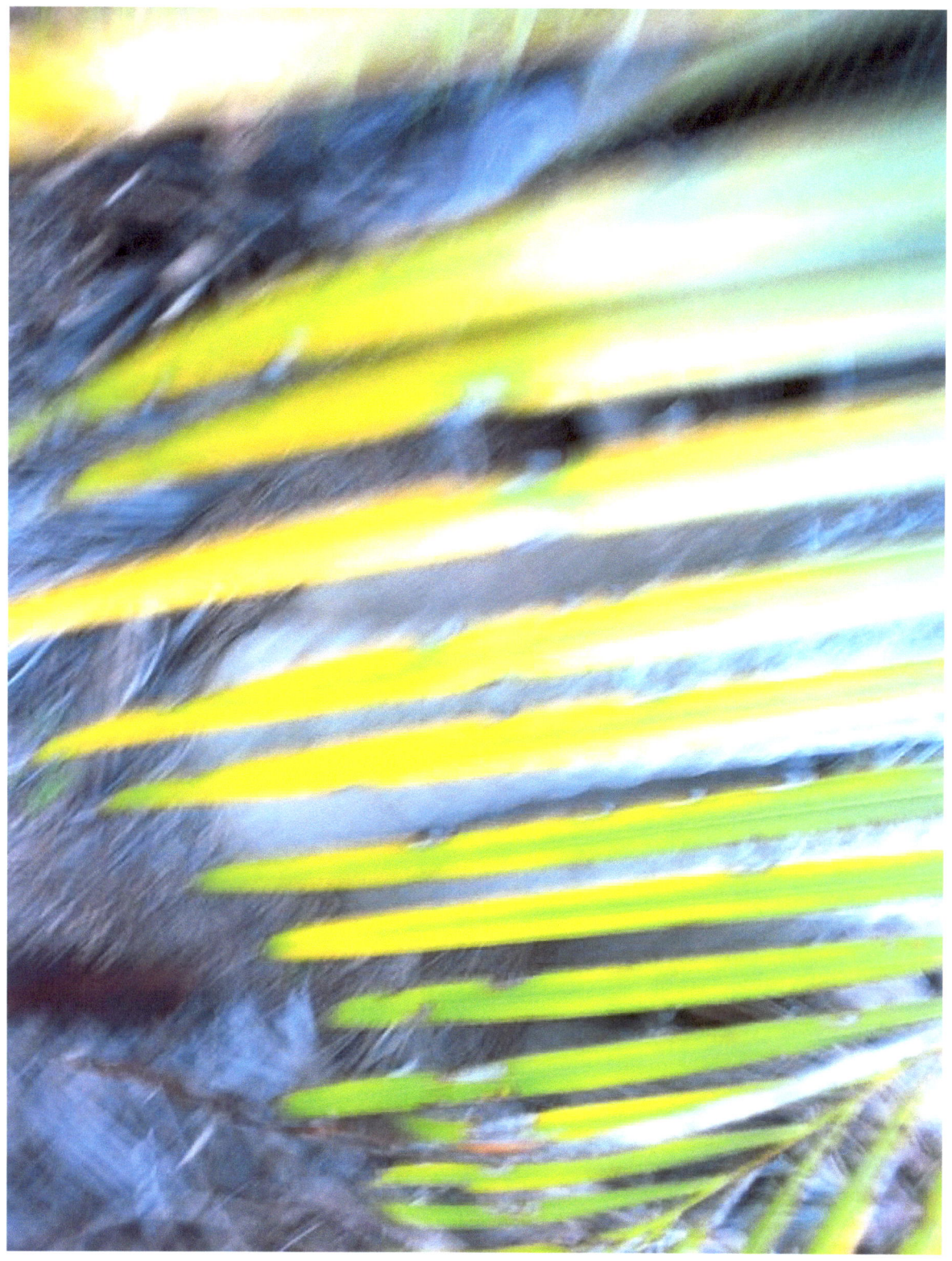

Real photograph of palm leaves and you can see the same subject photographed while the camera was in transit.

Photograph of the plant on the previous page, photographed when the camera was in transit.

Extra movements on the camera made it lighter colours.

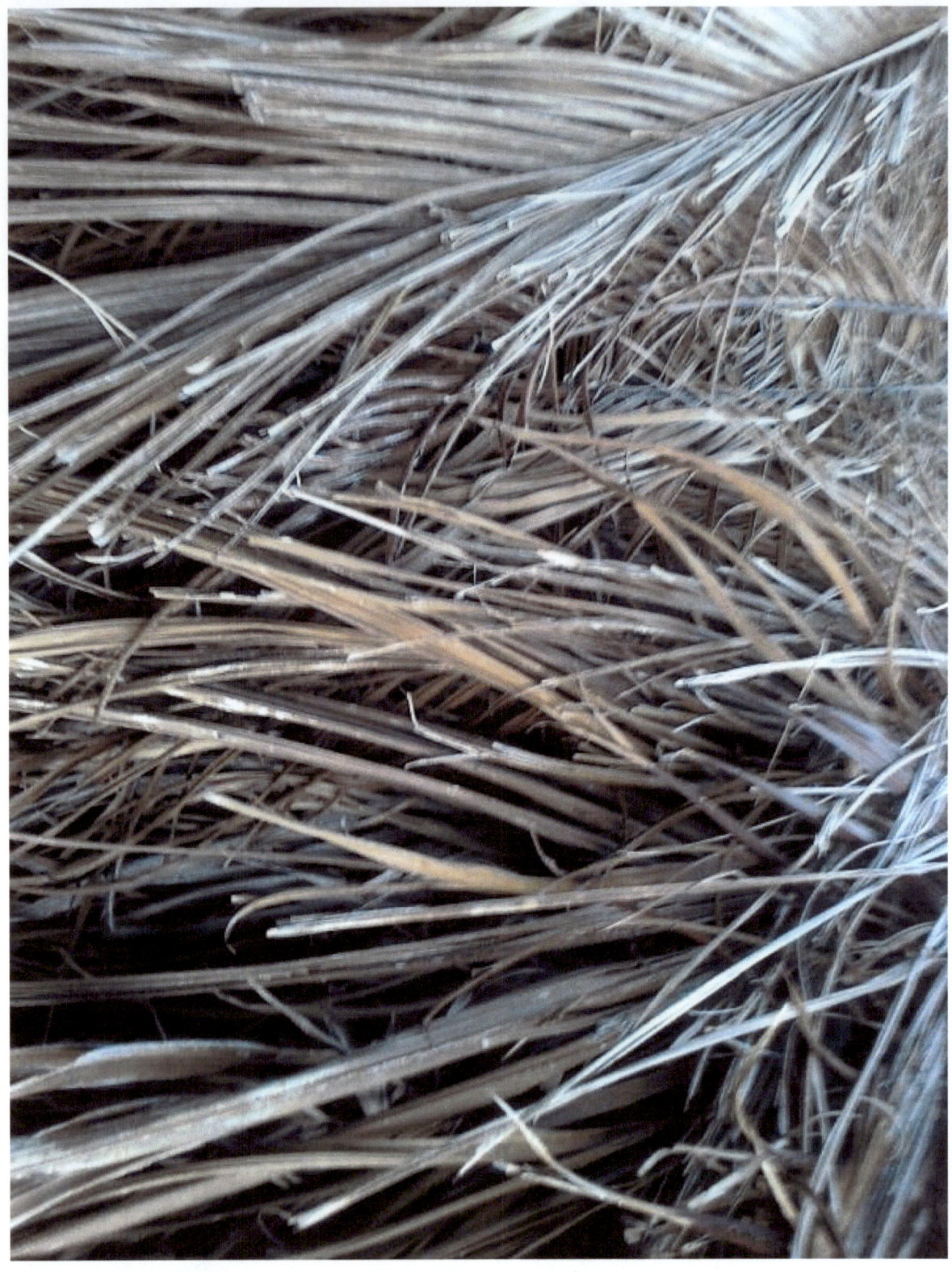

Real photo of palm leaves and you can see the same subject photographed while the camera was in transit on the next few pages.

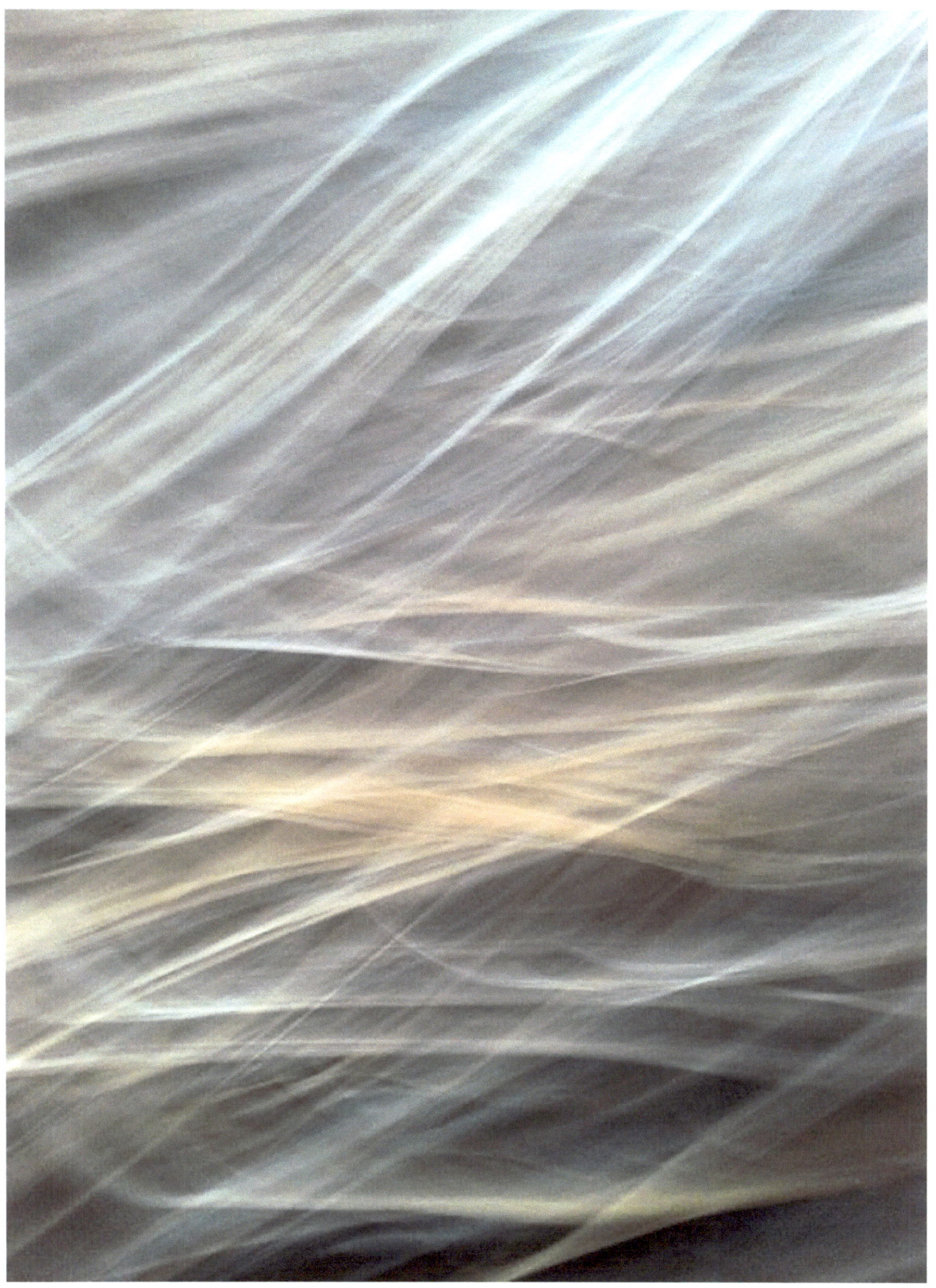

Photograph of dry palm leaves when the camera was in transit.

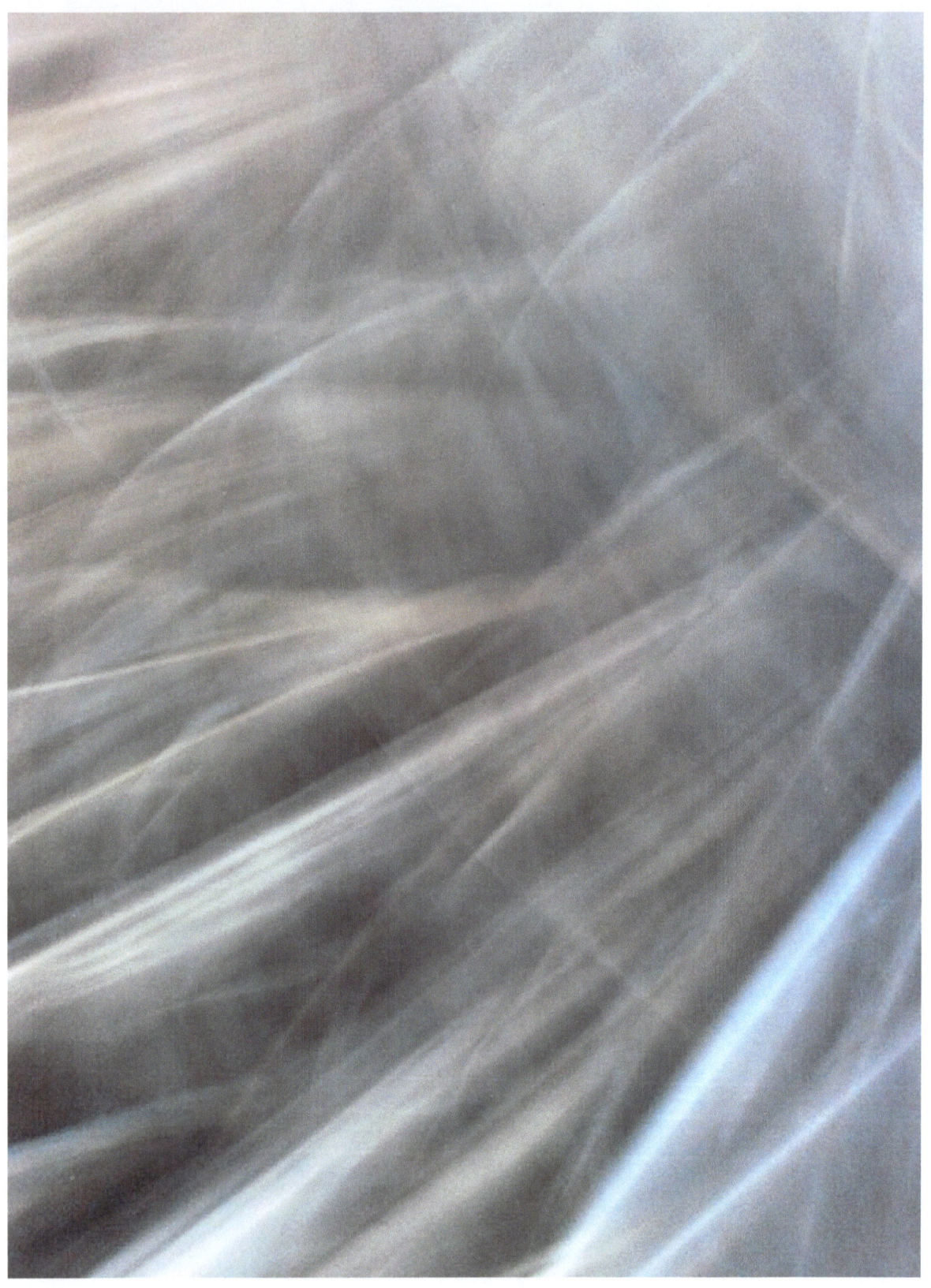

Extra rotation of the camera made photograph lighter.

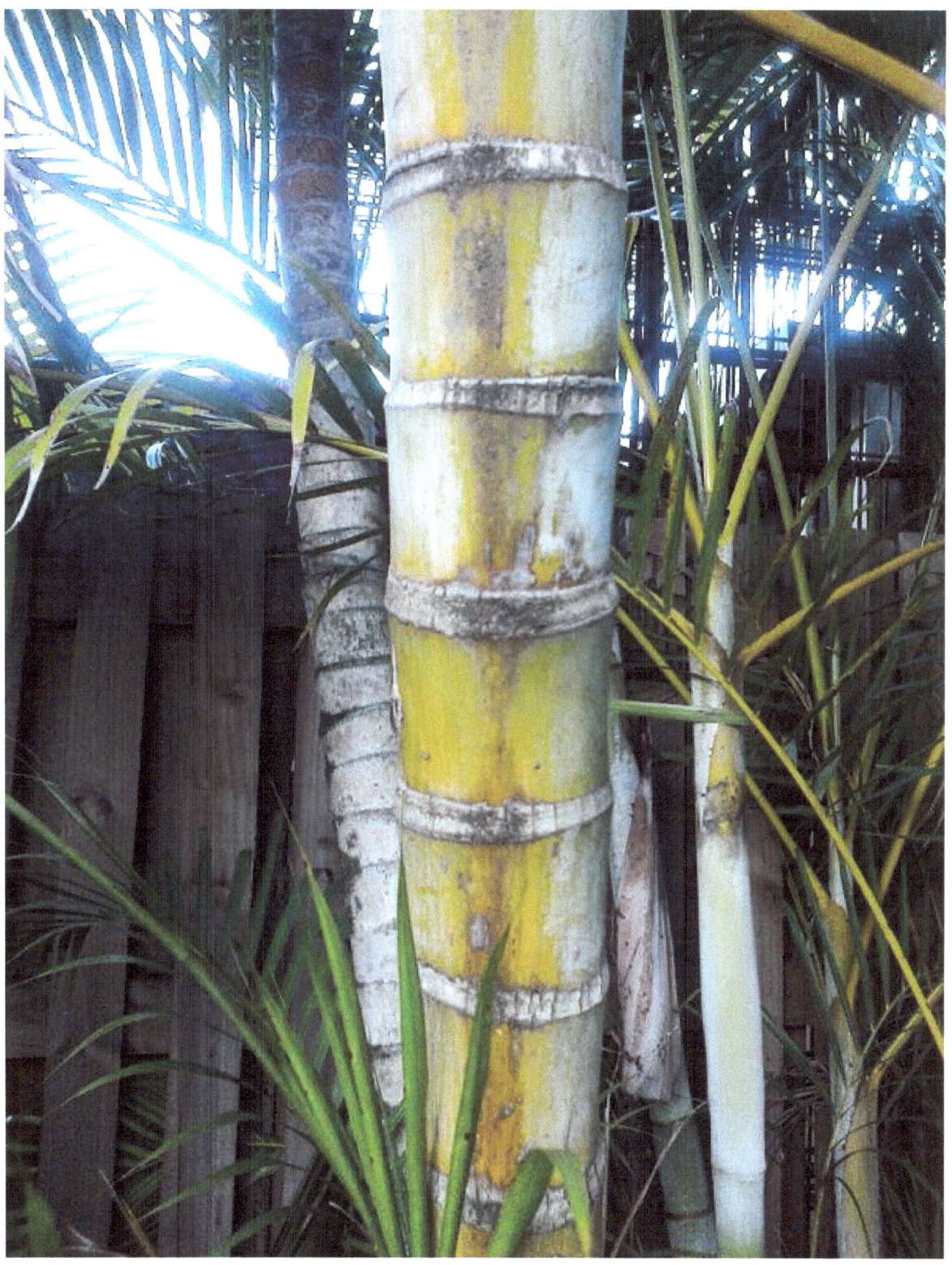

This is the real photograph of palm trees and you can see light between the leaves. On the next page you can see how light can be pulled while photographing with a camera that was in transit.

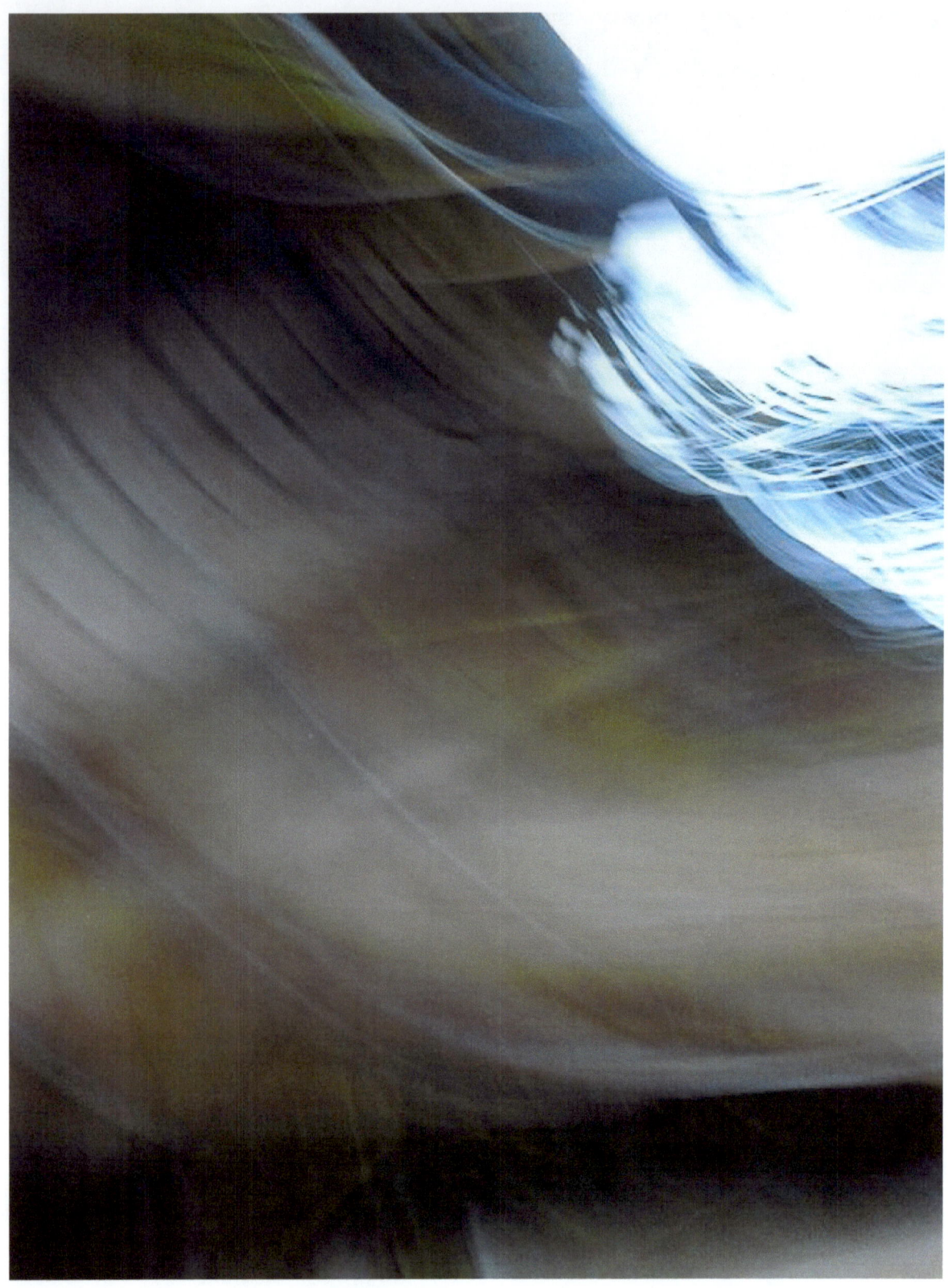

You can see the light pulled to create a feature on the photograph.

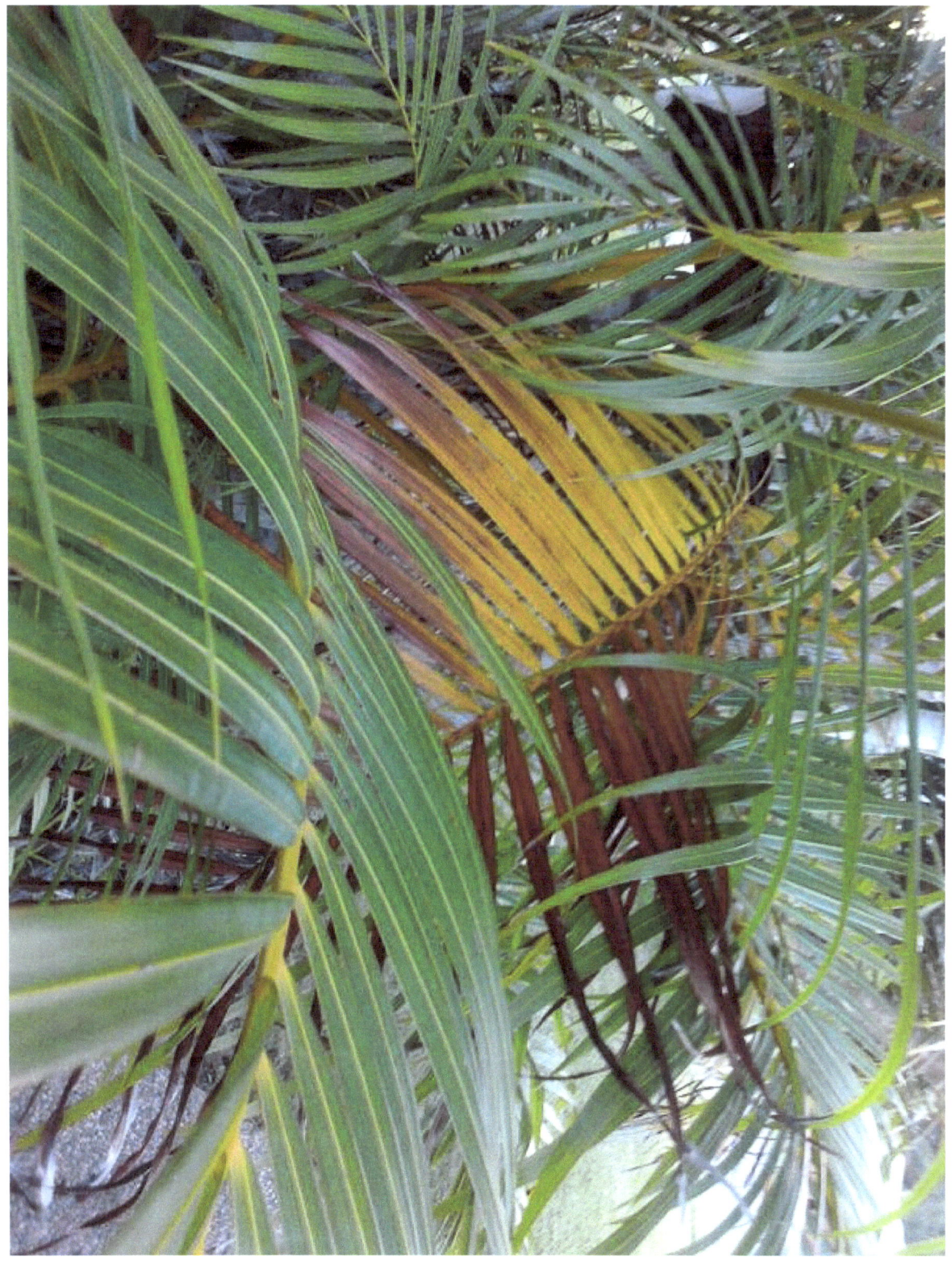

Real photograph of palm leaves and you can see the same subject photographed in transit on the next few pages.

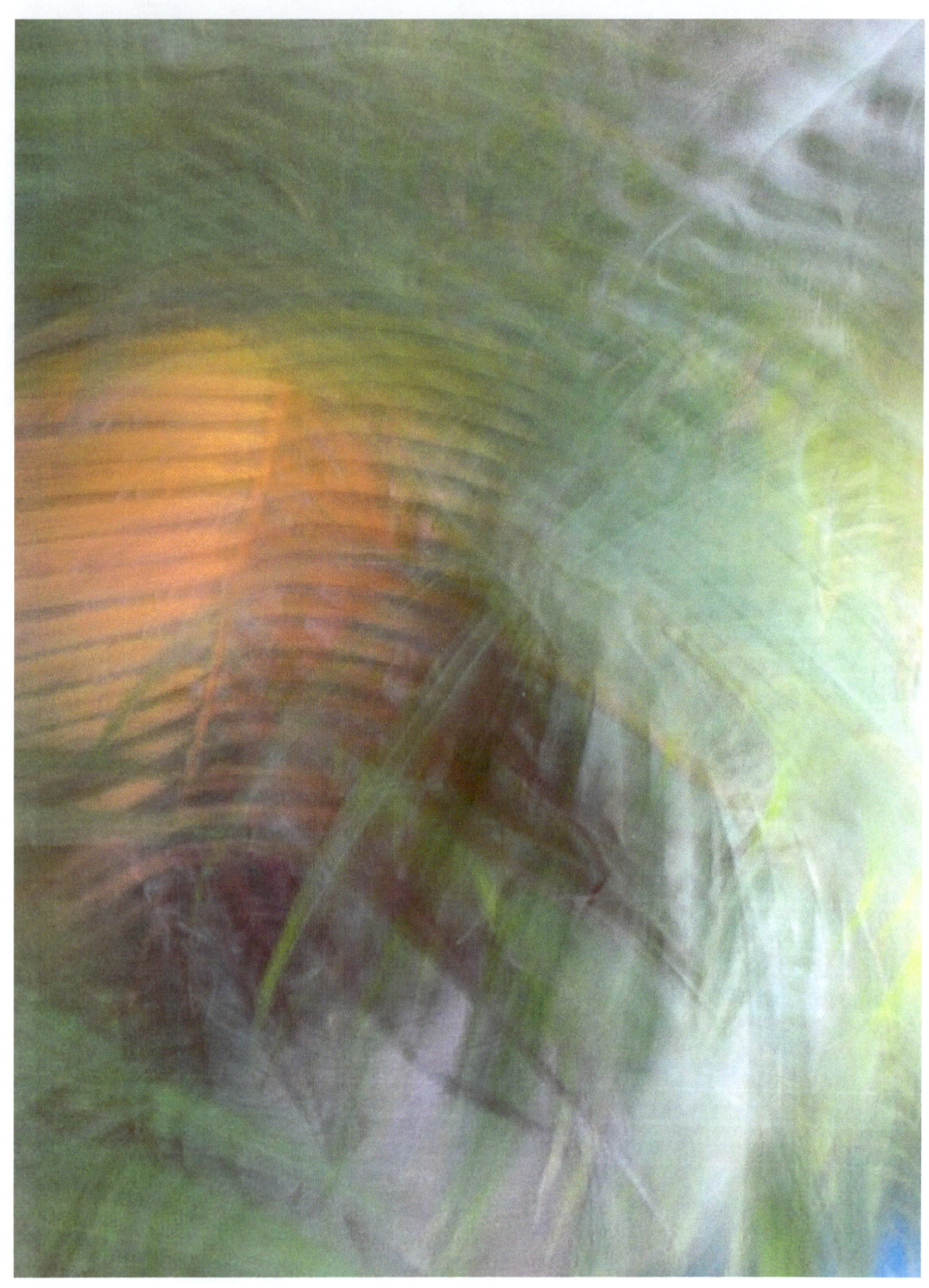

Photographed in transit.

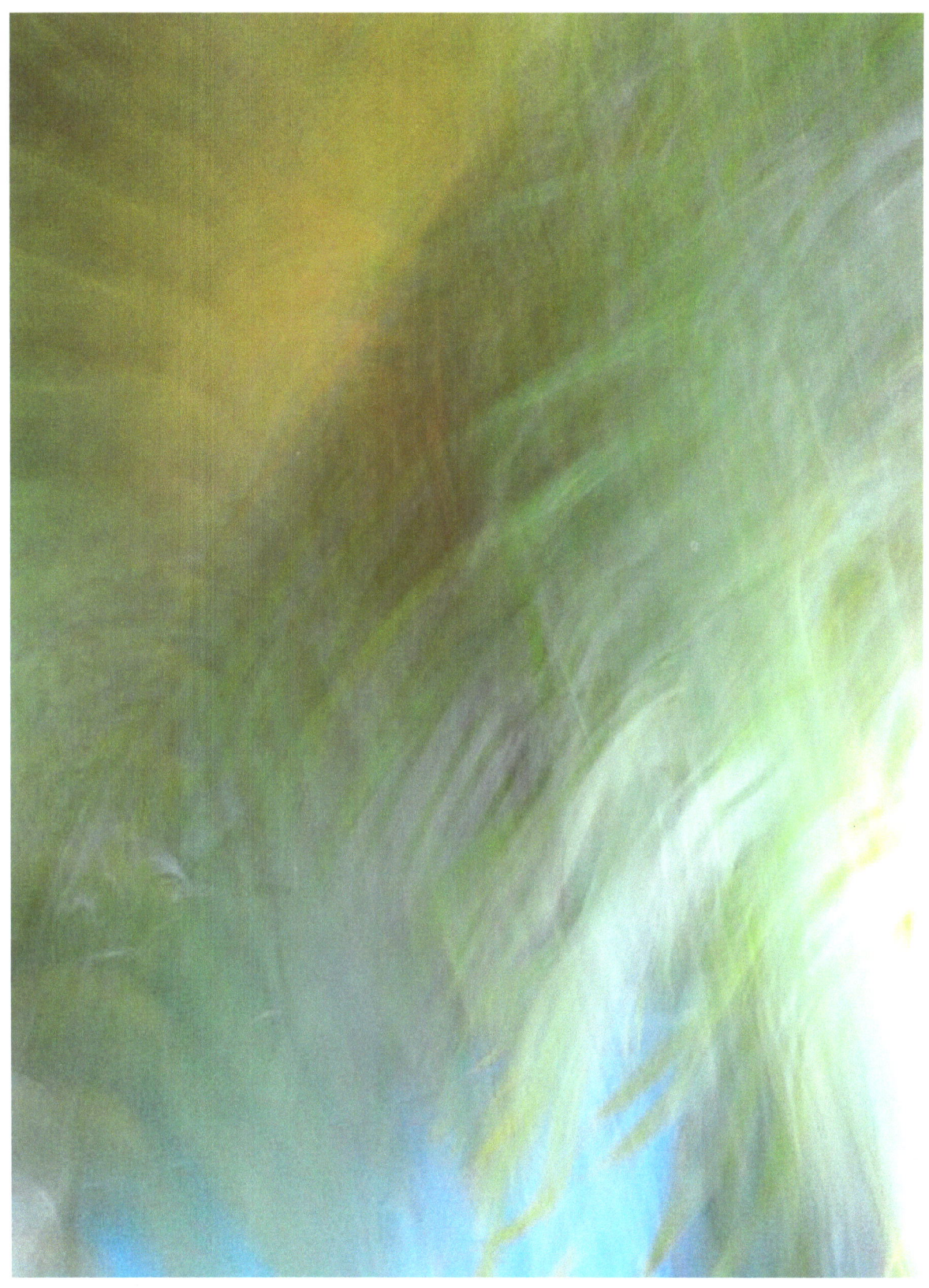

Photographed in transit.

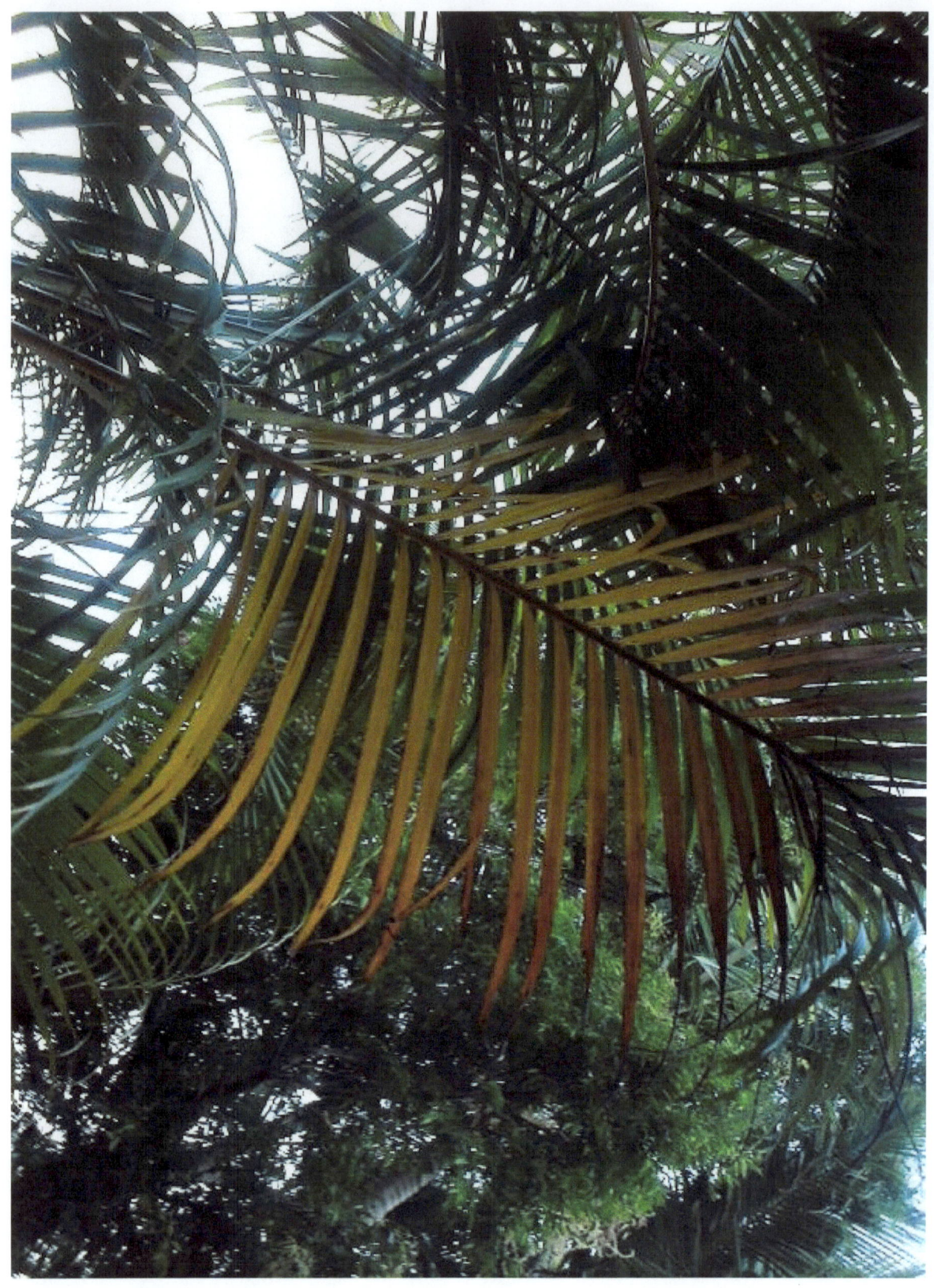

Real photograph of leaves and you can see the light between the leaves. On the next photo you can see how light is pulling out when photographed in transit.

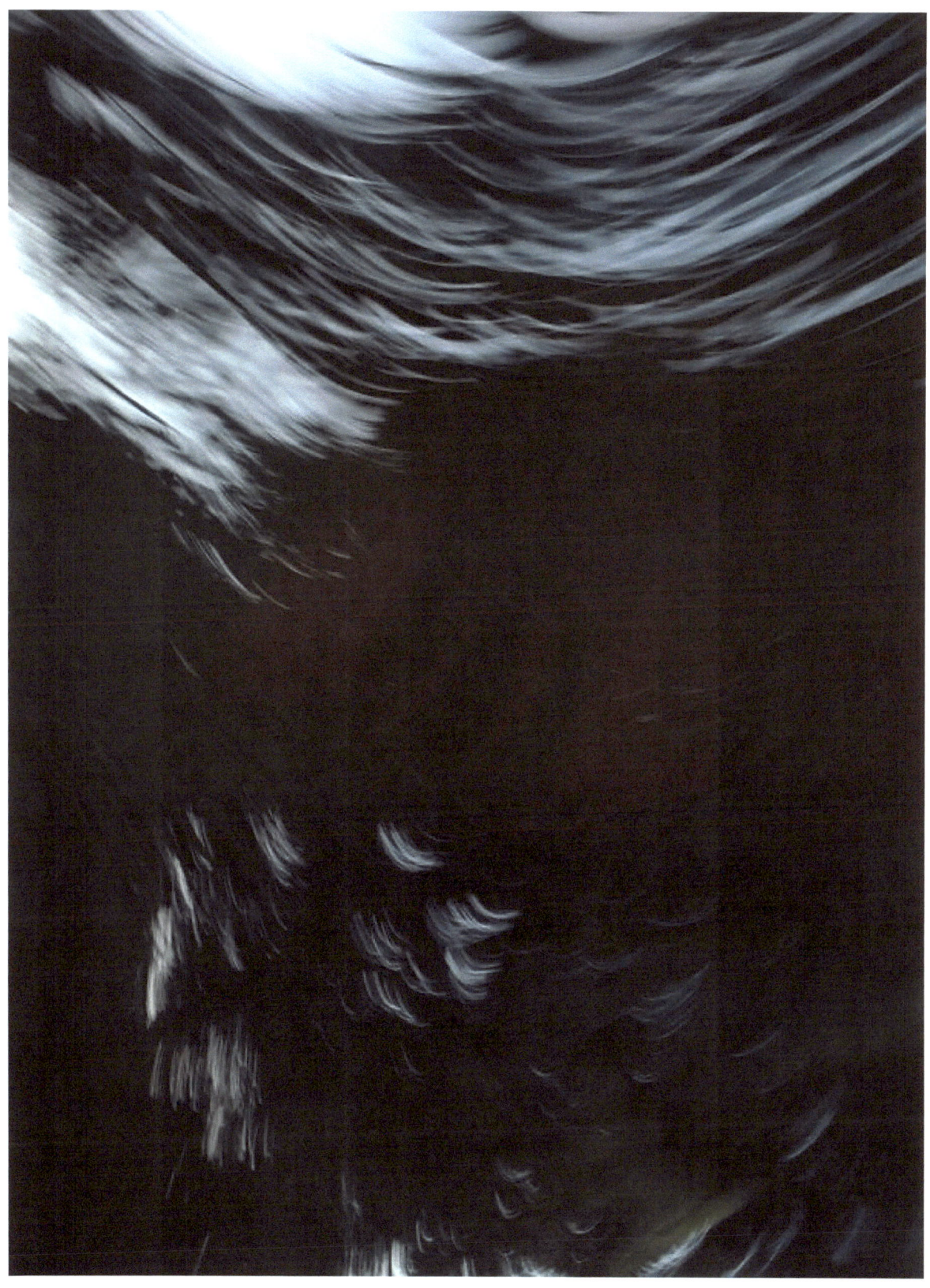

You can make the light move when you take photographs in transit. Light has to be highly **luminous** make it move.

Light moving in a streaky ways in rotation of the camera.

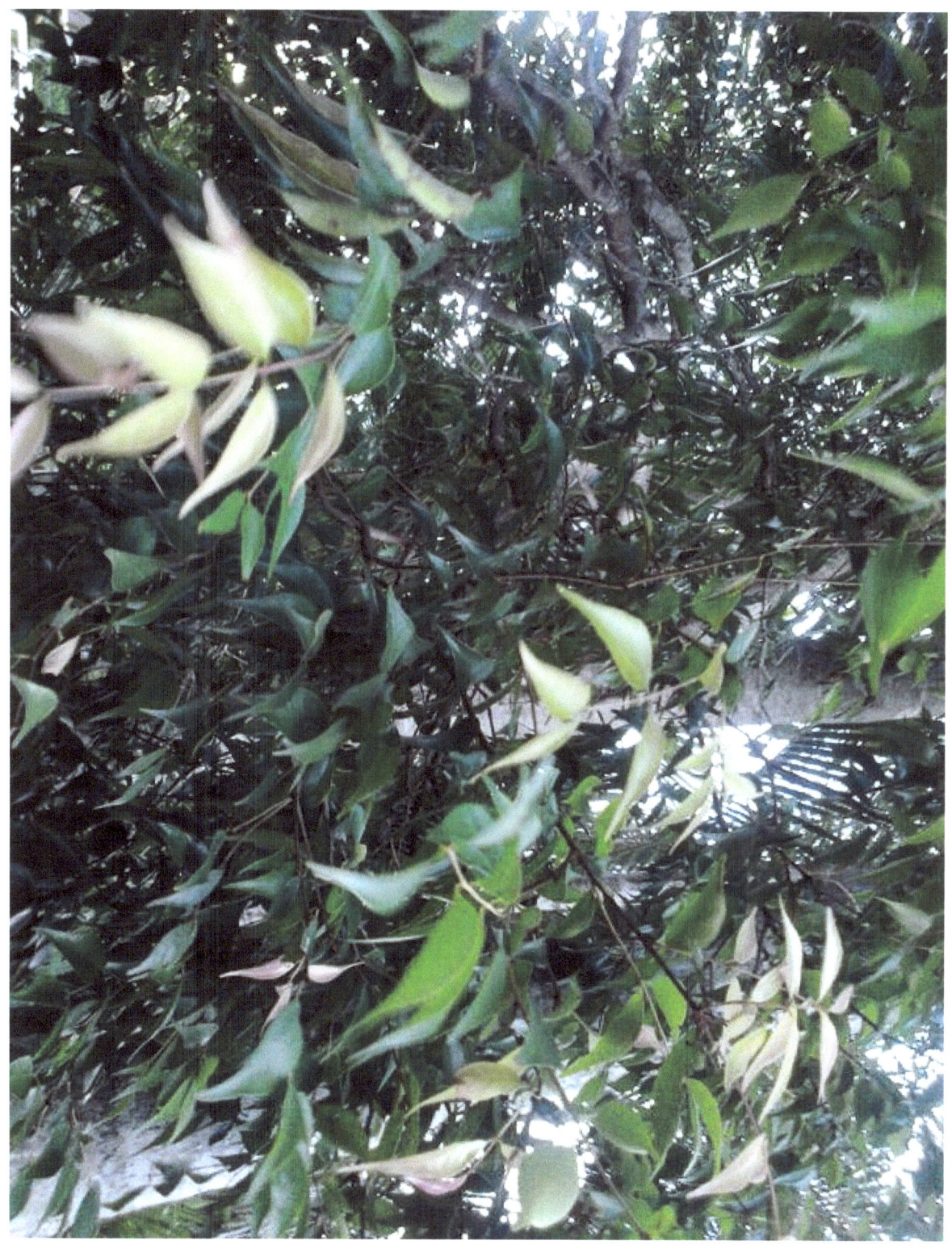

Real photograph of leaves and you can see on the next page how light you see in between leaves is pulled out when photographed in transit.

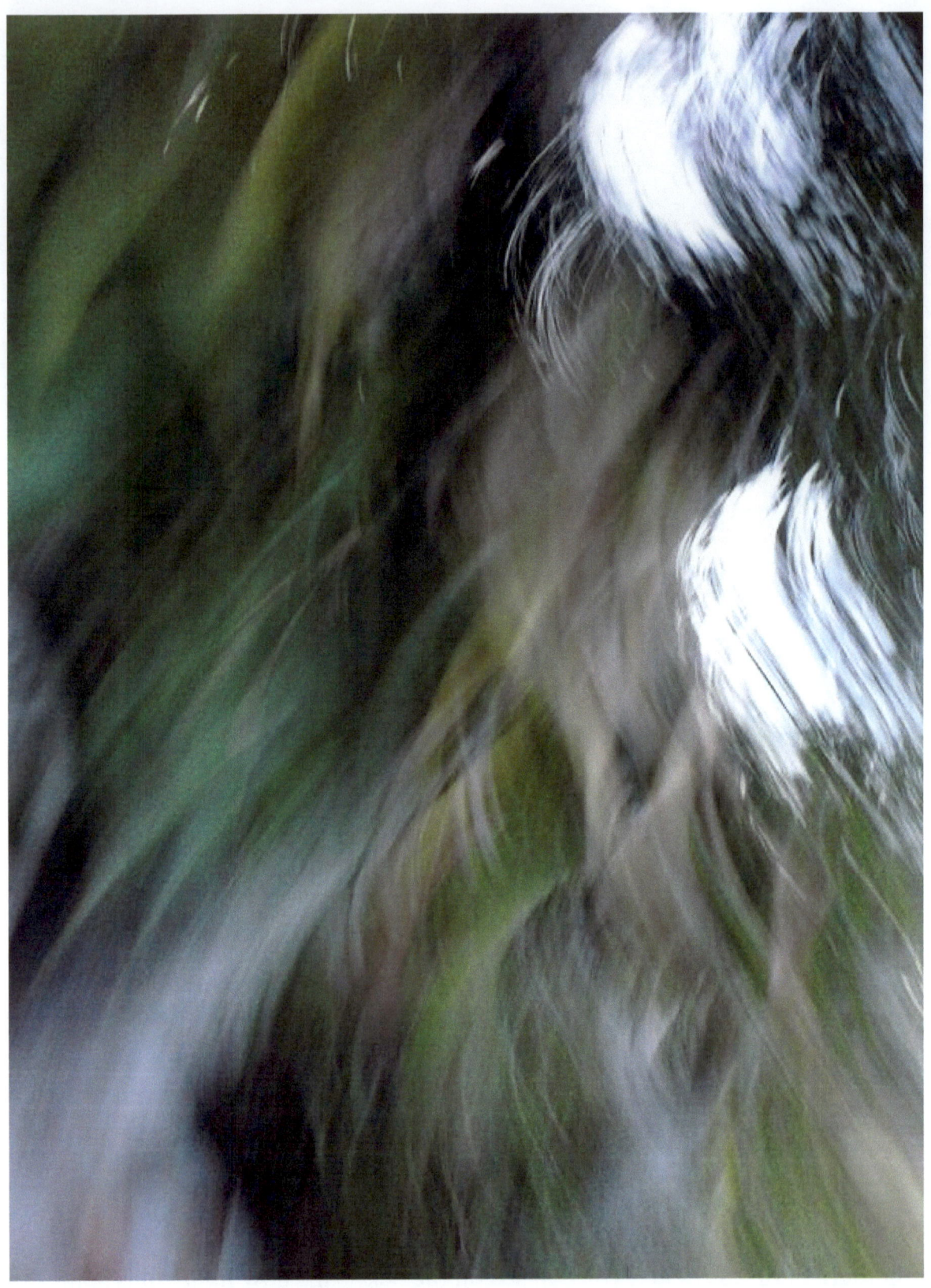

When photographed in transit you can see light moved as well.

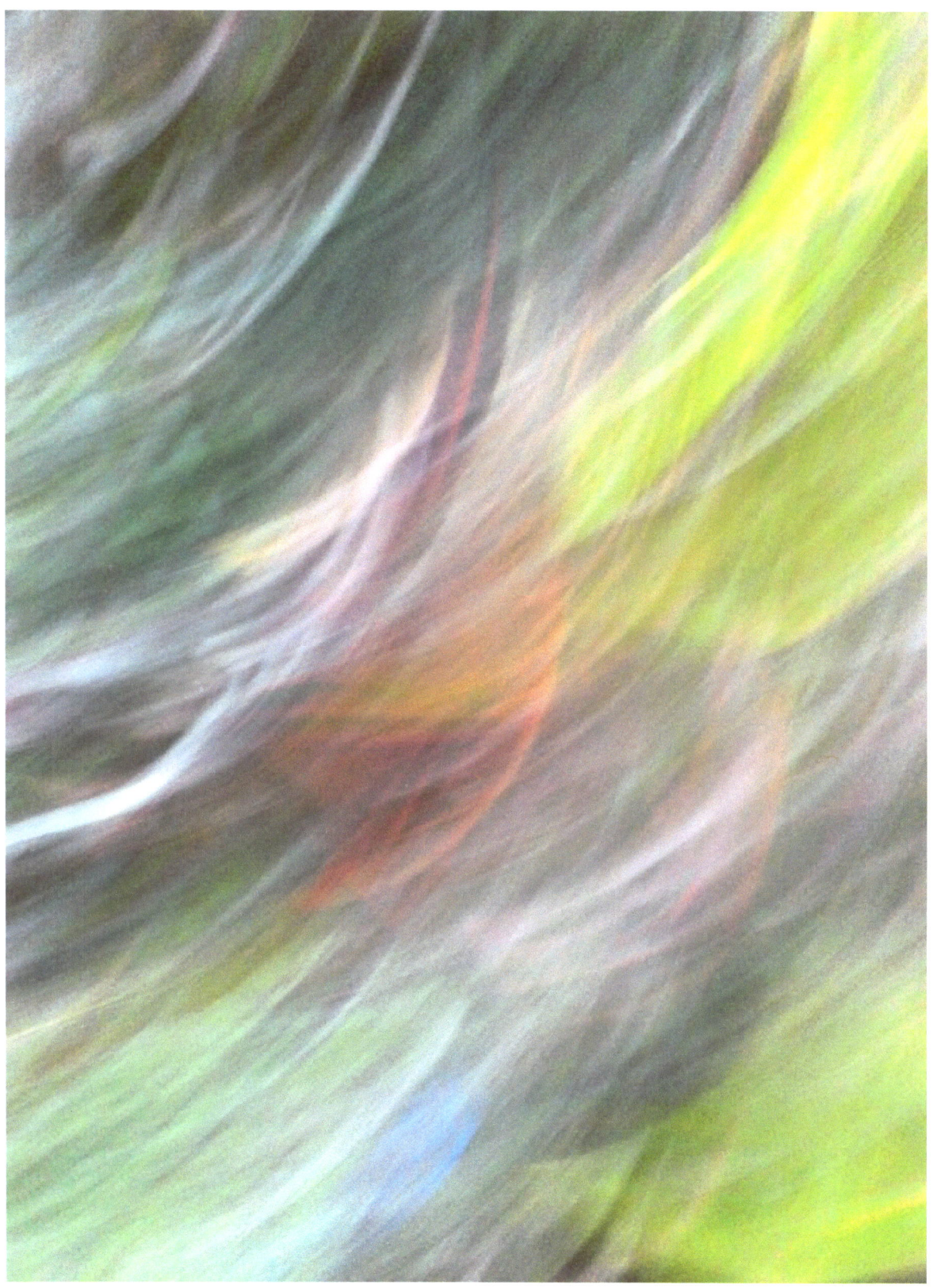
Photographs of colourful leaves when the camera was in transit.

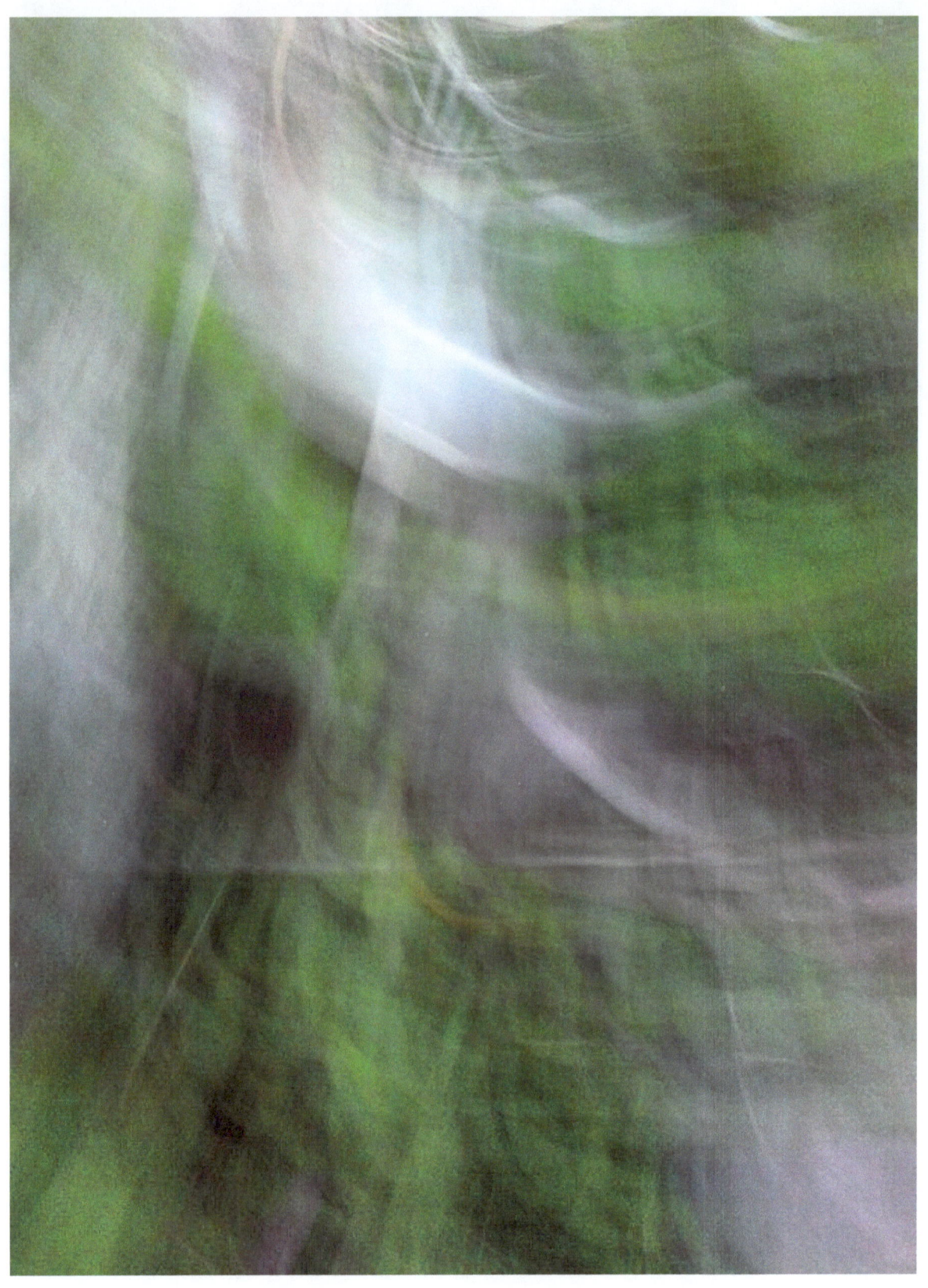

Waves of leaves when photographed with a camera in transit.

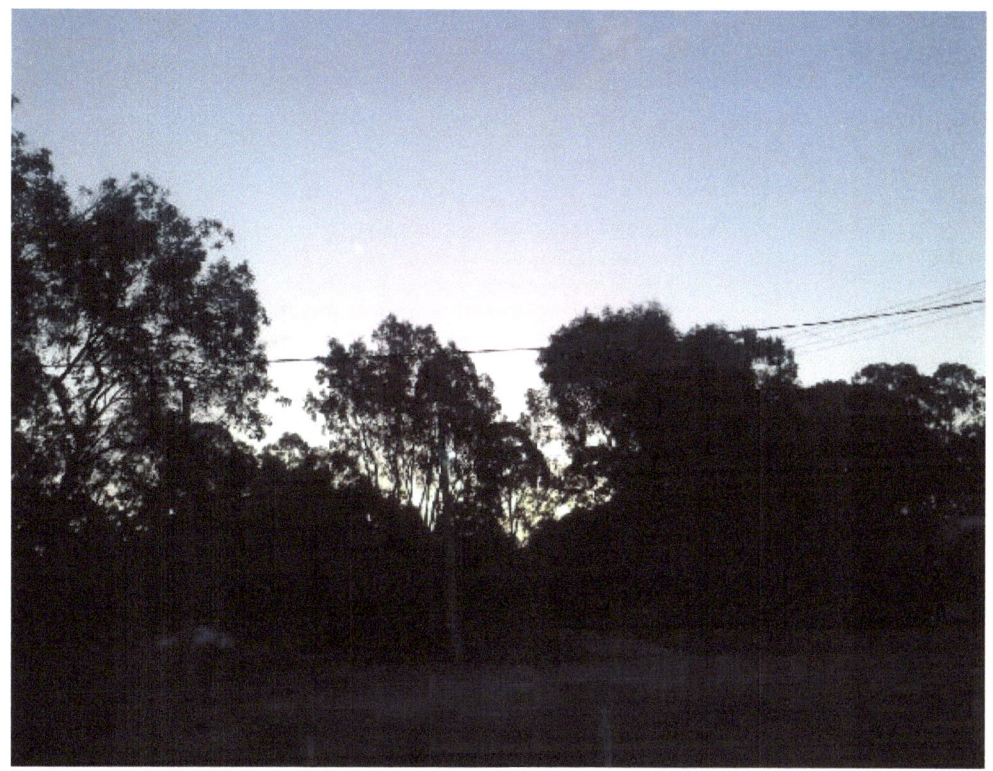

Real sunset photograph taken in the evening and you can see when the same subject photographed in transit pulls the light shows on the photograph below.

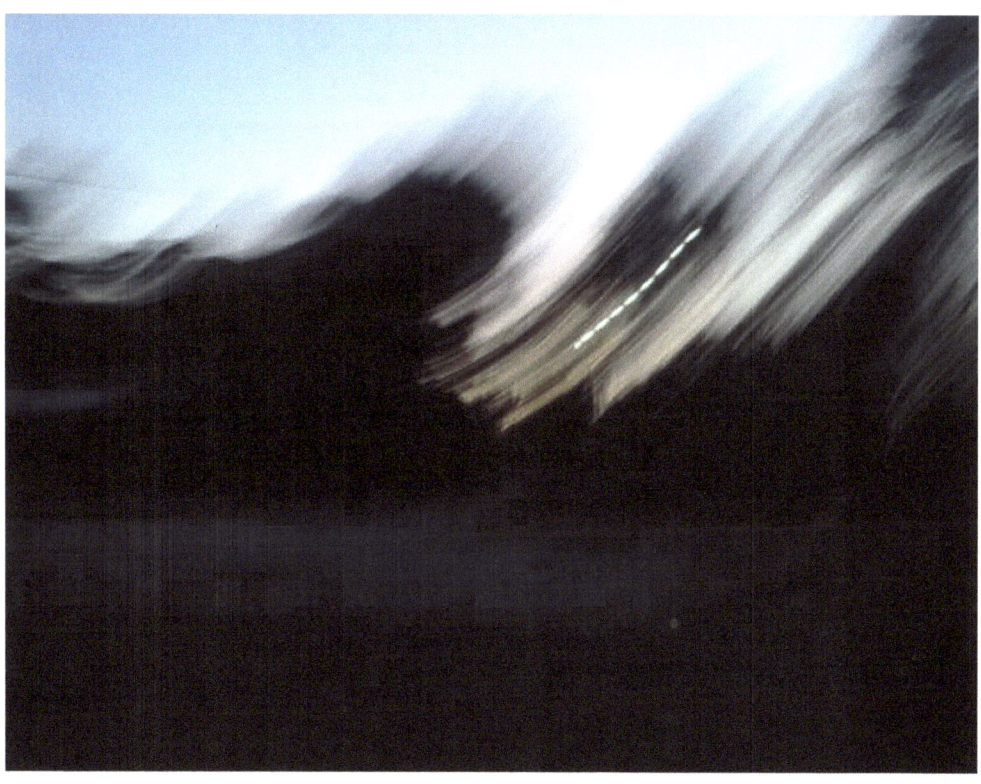

You can also see light moving in segments. Pressure moves in segments as well it would not have a continuous long flow.

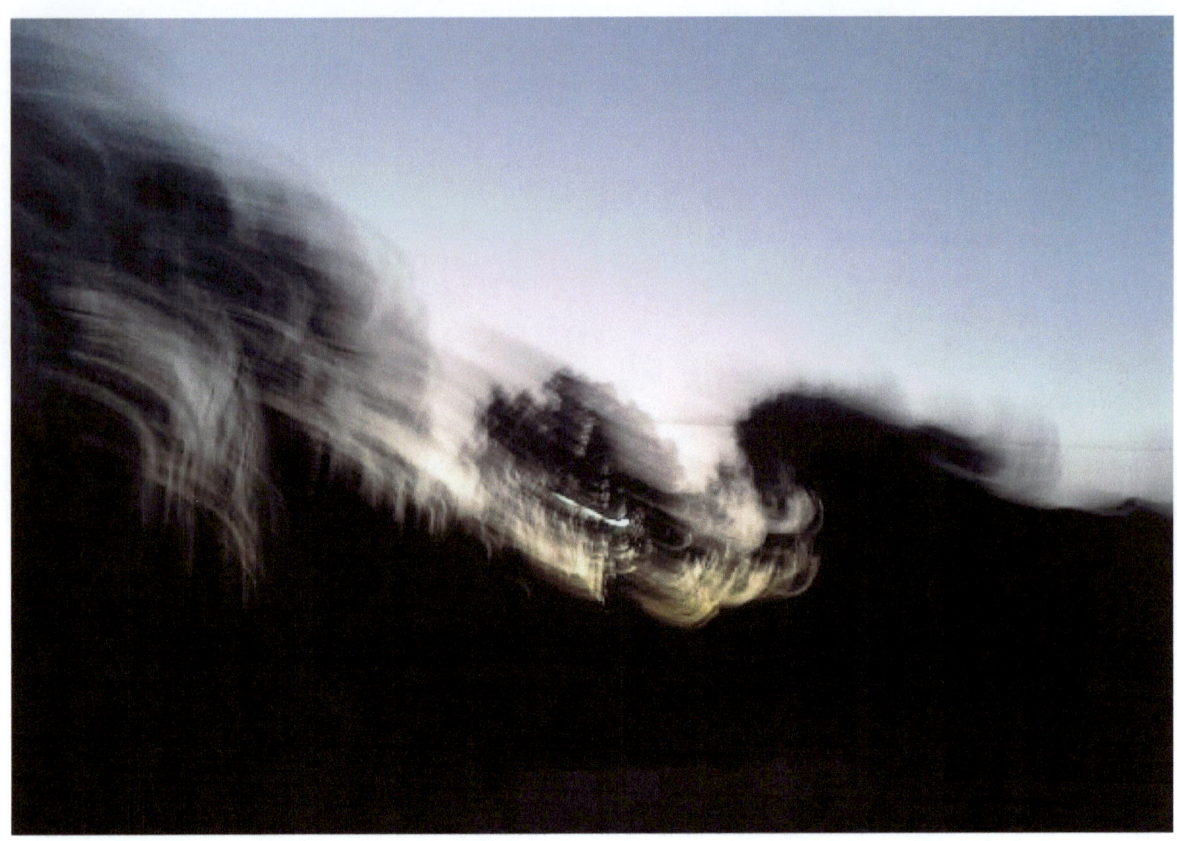

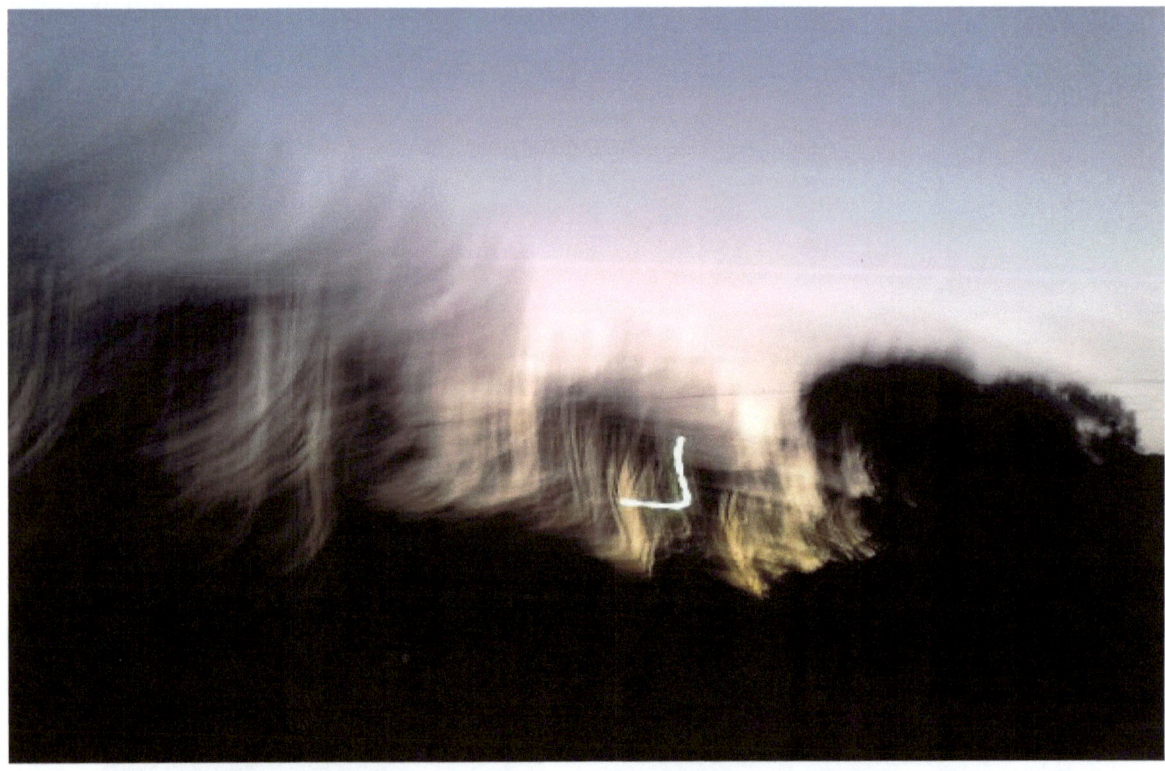

You can see in rotation of light breaking in segments like our back bones. Rotation can transform from stellar breakages to segments.

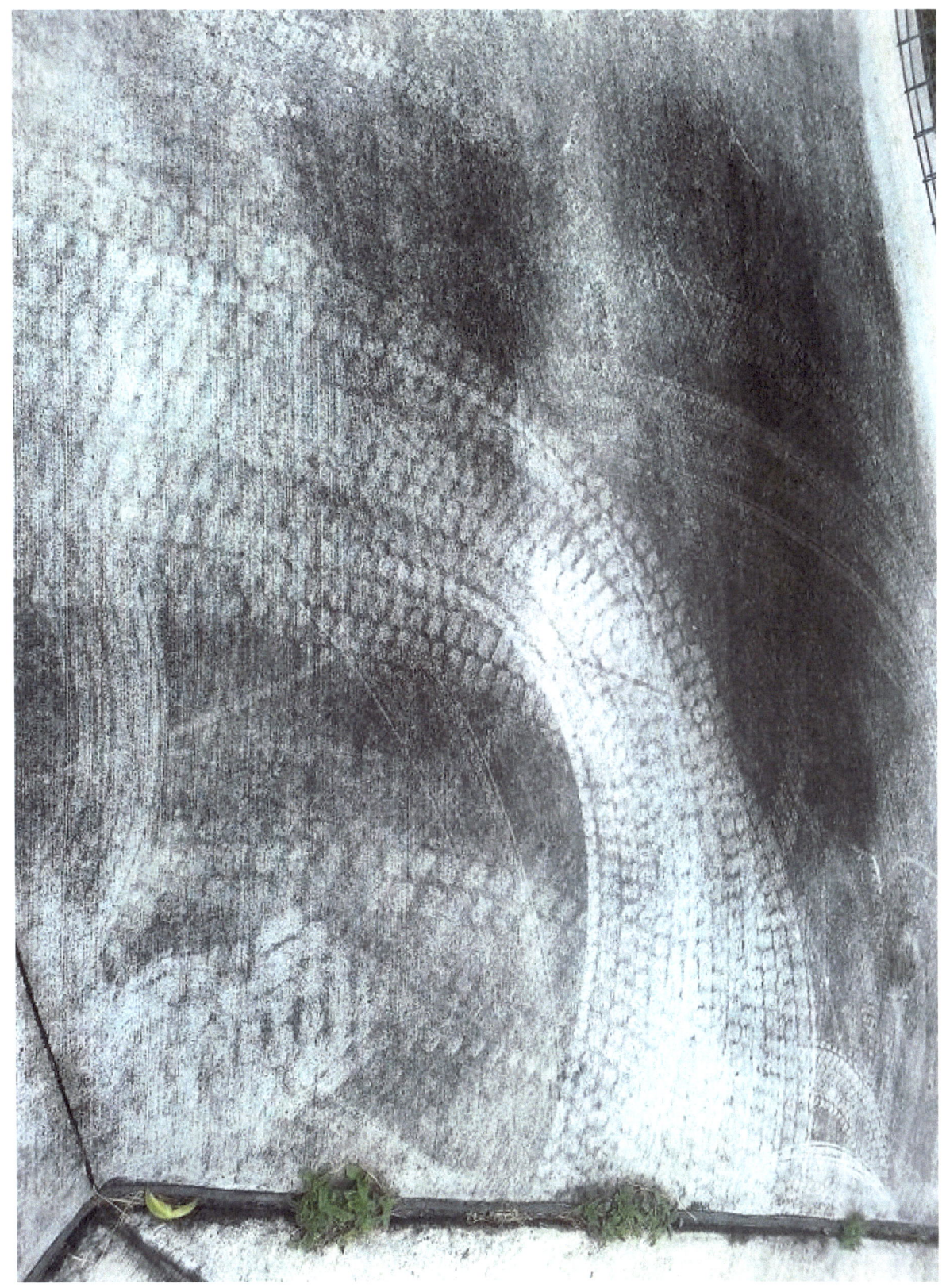

Movements of tyre thread changing from its original size to smaller because of rotation.

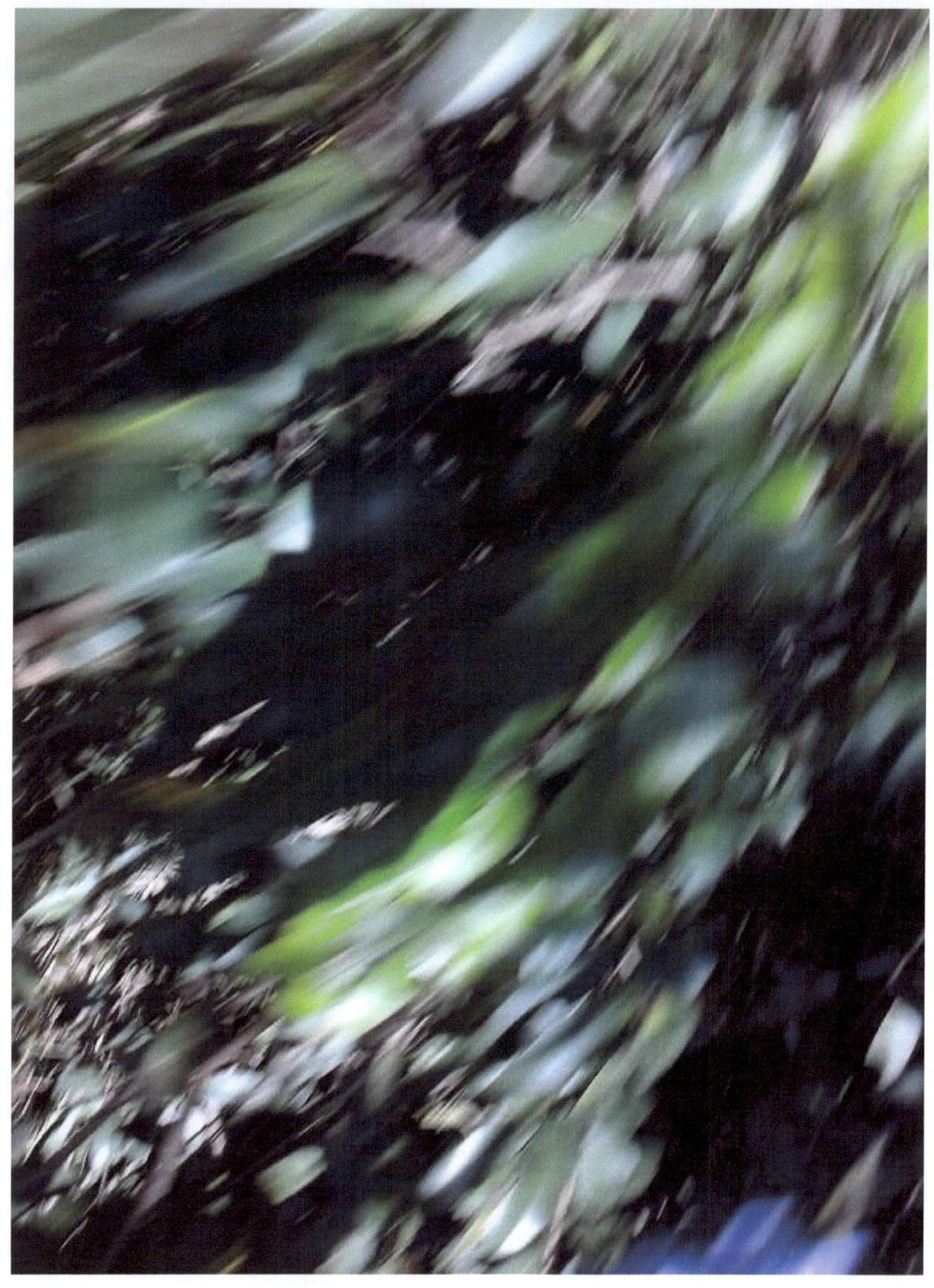

Movements of leaves in rotation.

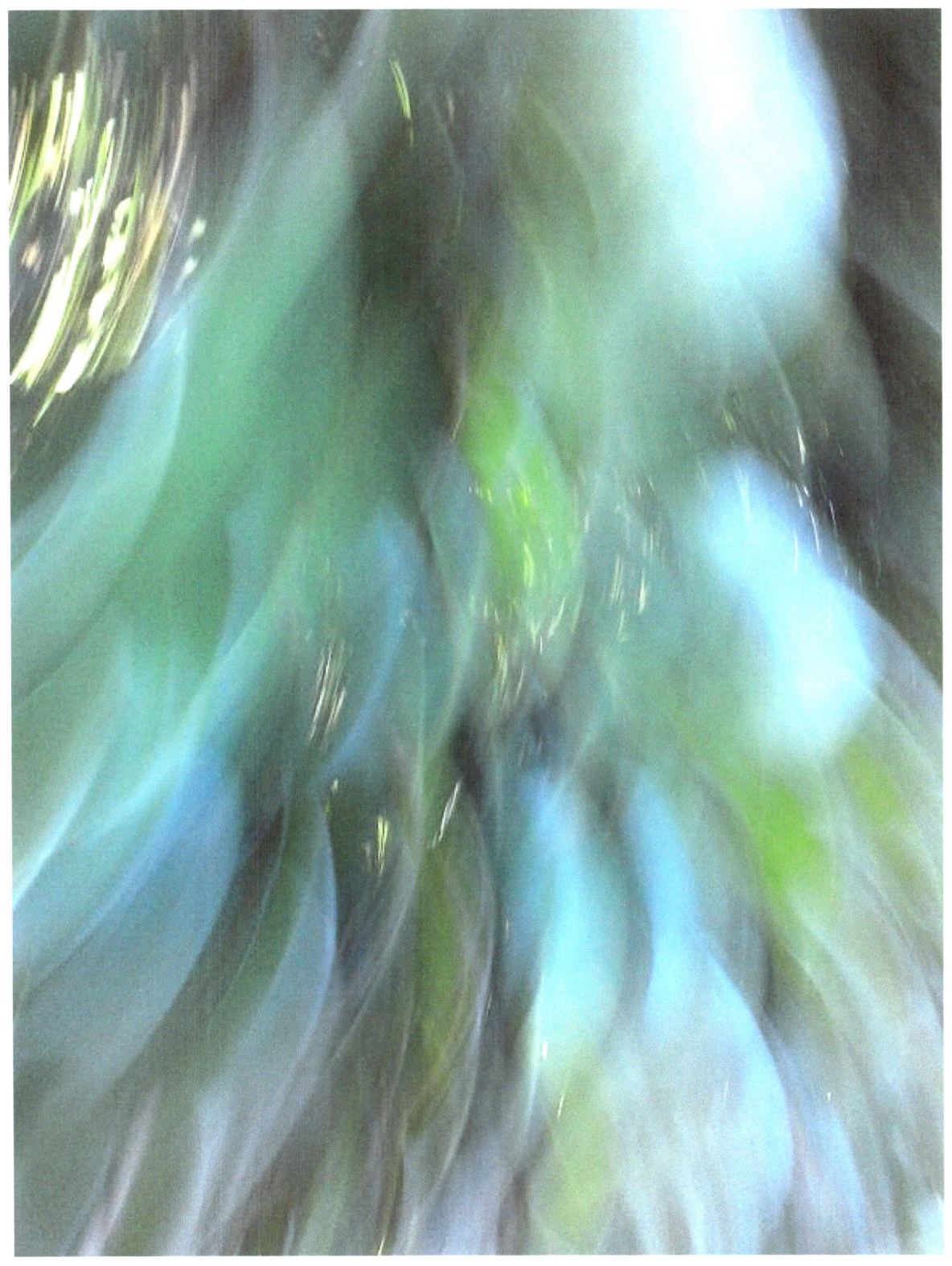

Leaves become waves in rotation like the water. These are some of the patterns you see on skin of humans and animals.

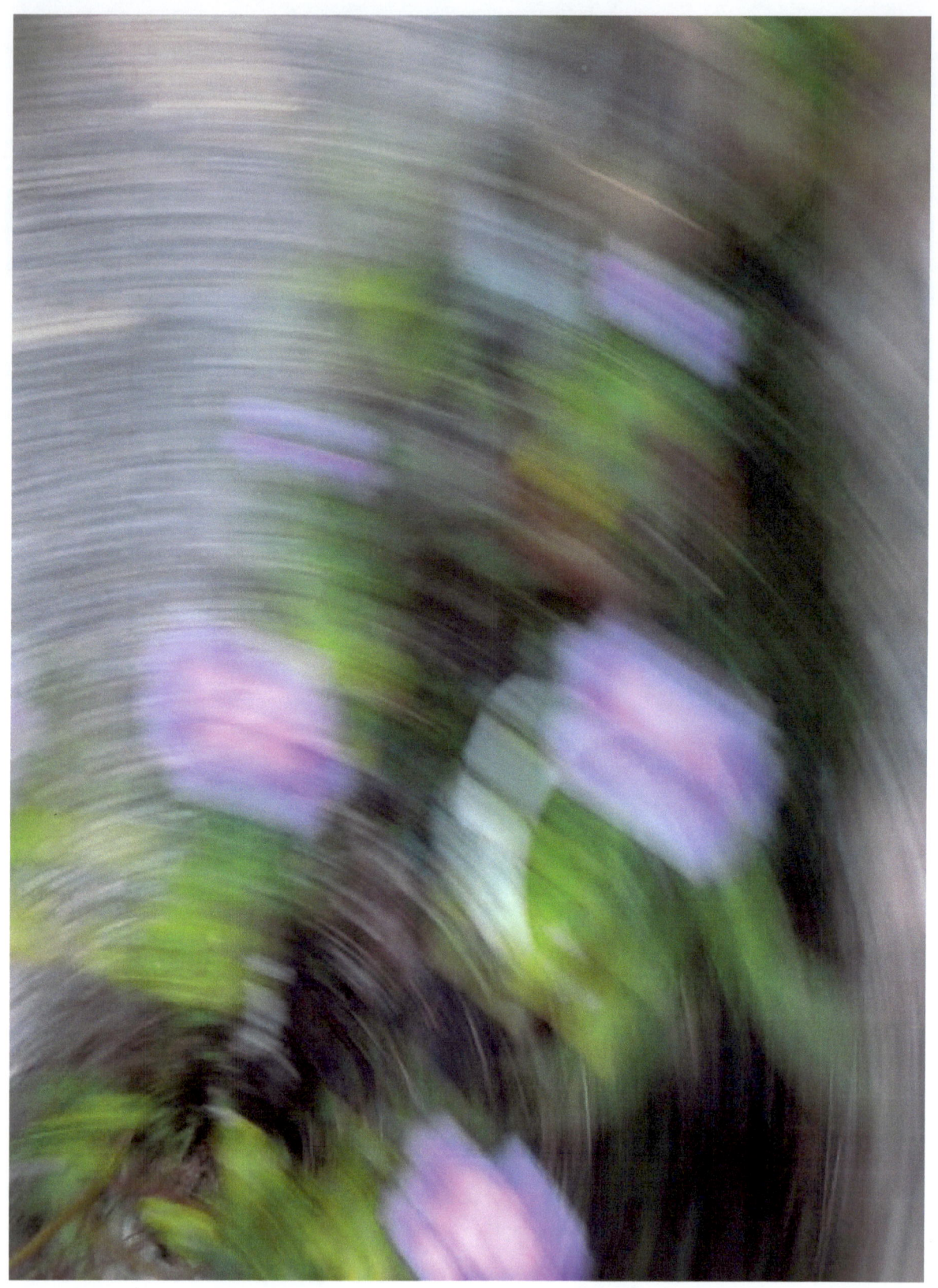

Movement of the camera distorted the flowers and leaves.

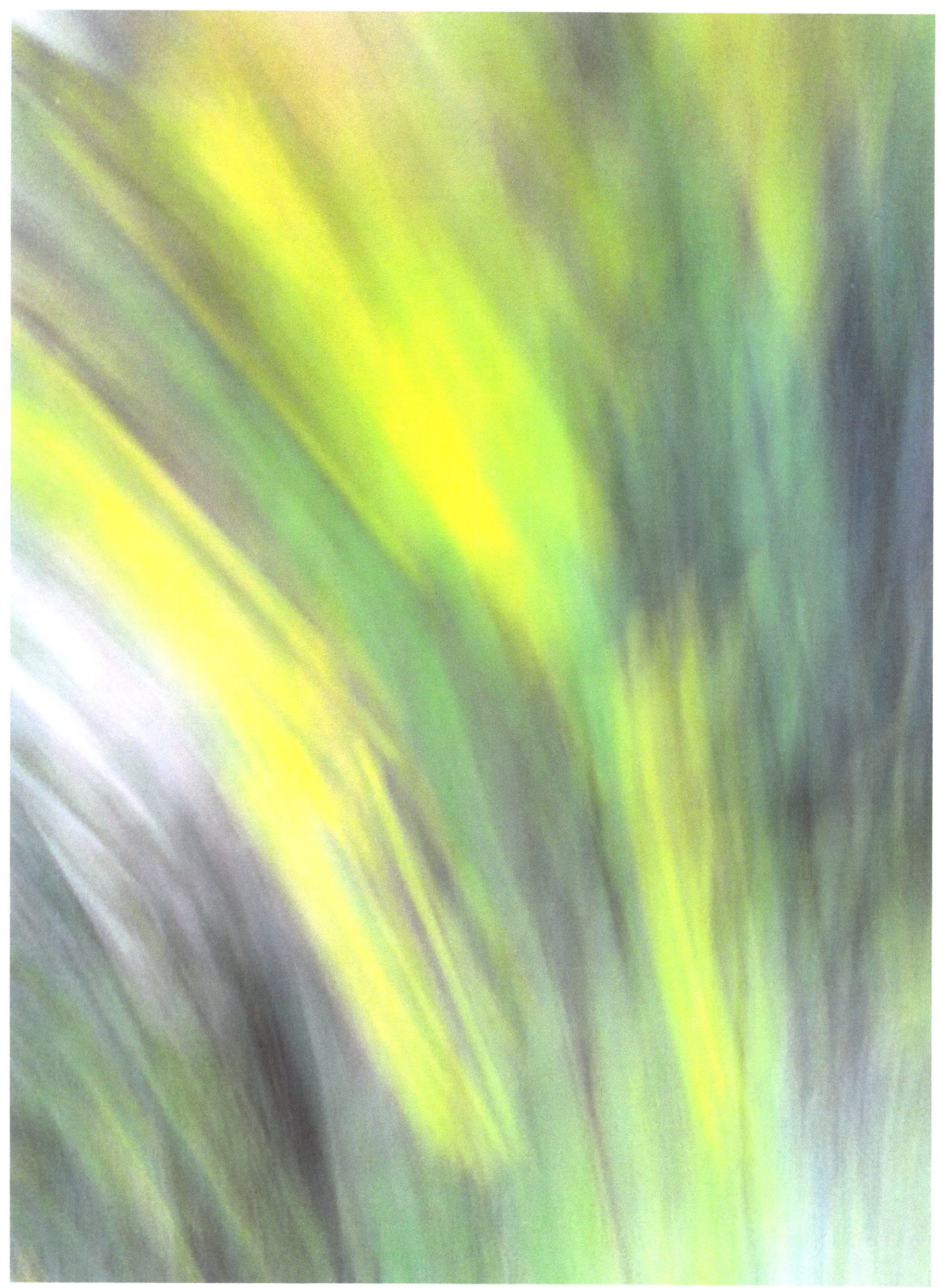

Colour mixing in rotation.

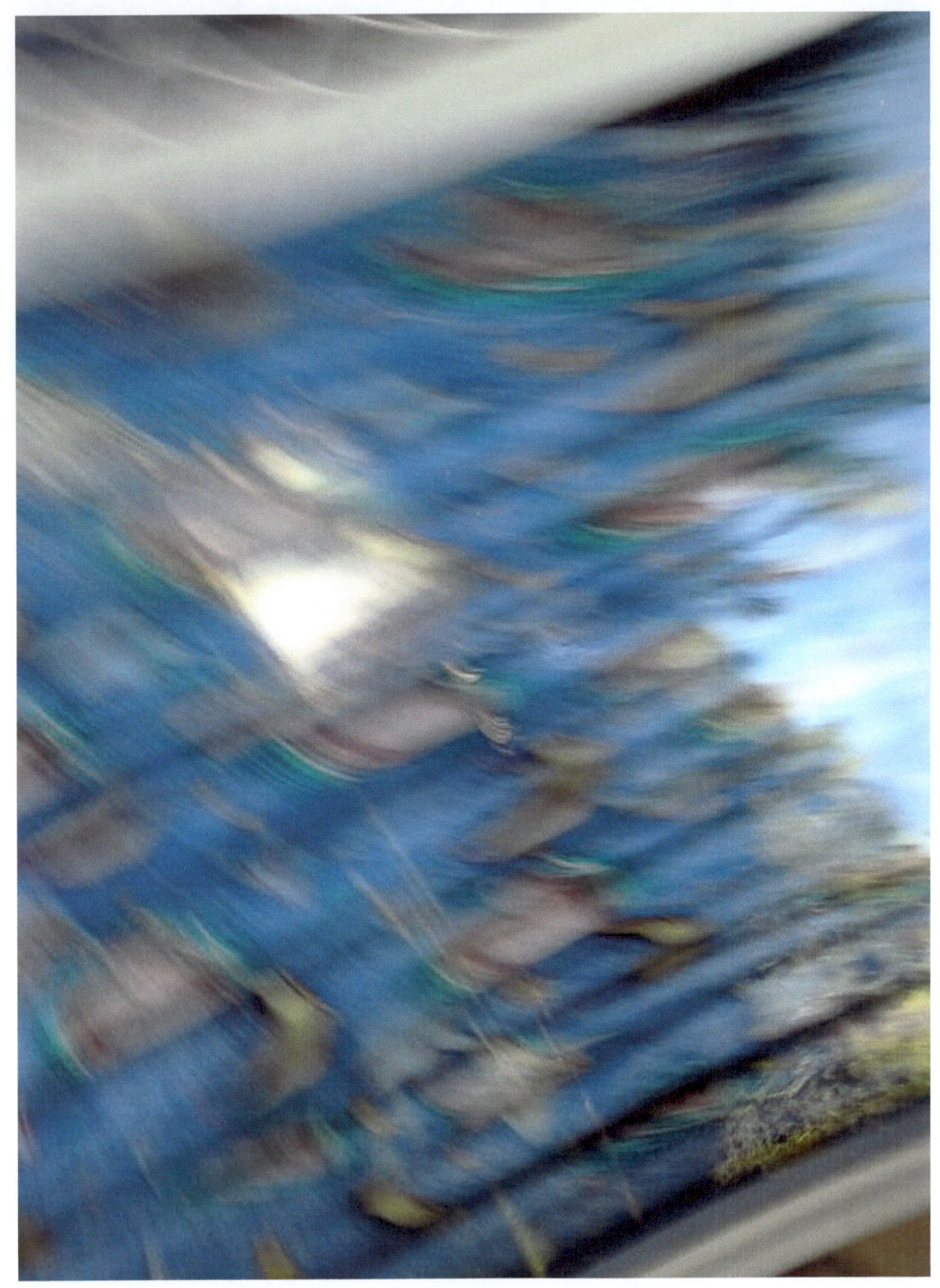

Patterns of stars and moons in rotation.

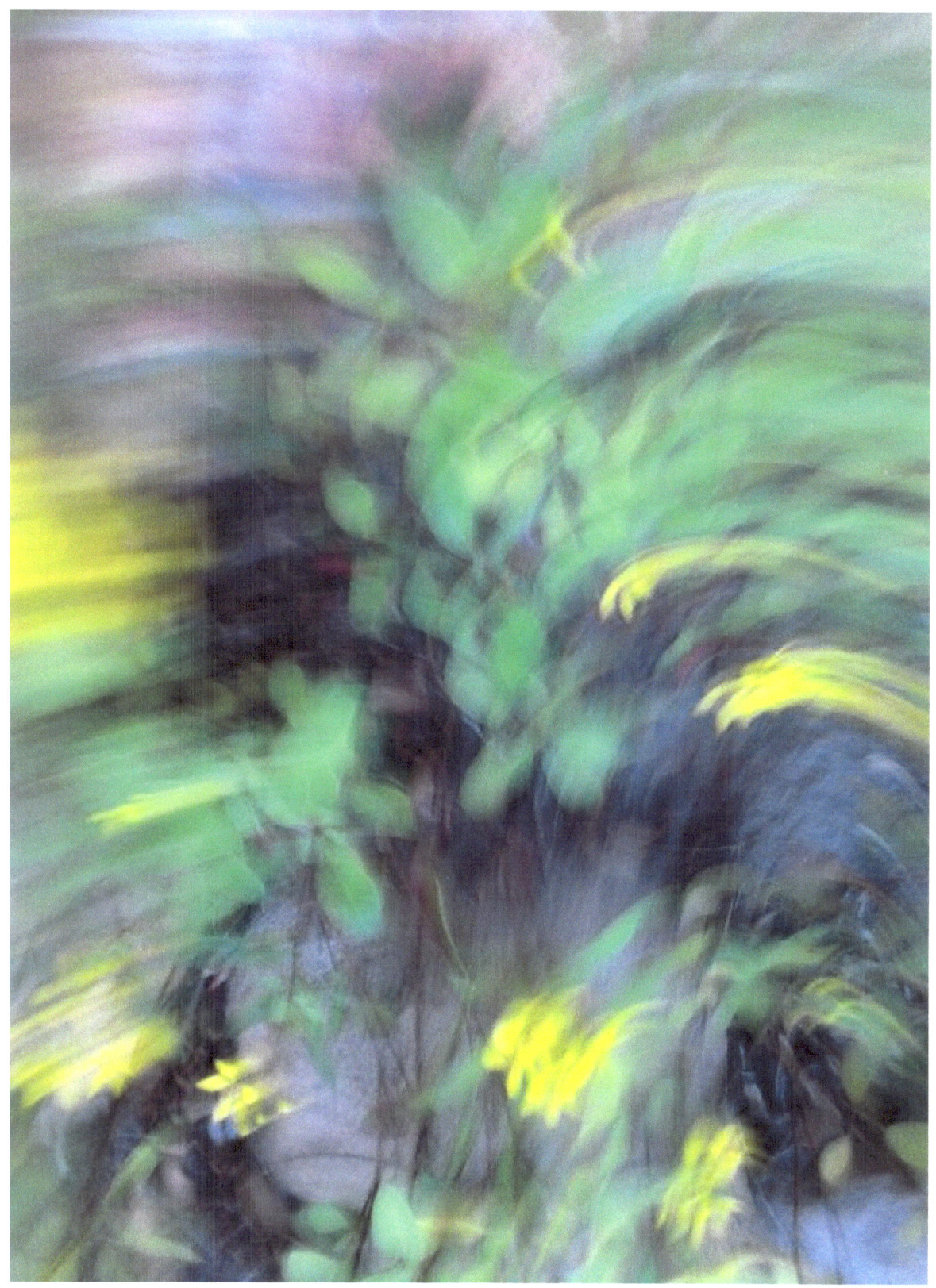

Flower movements and leaf movements in rotation.

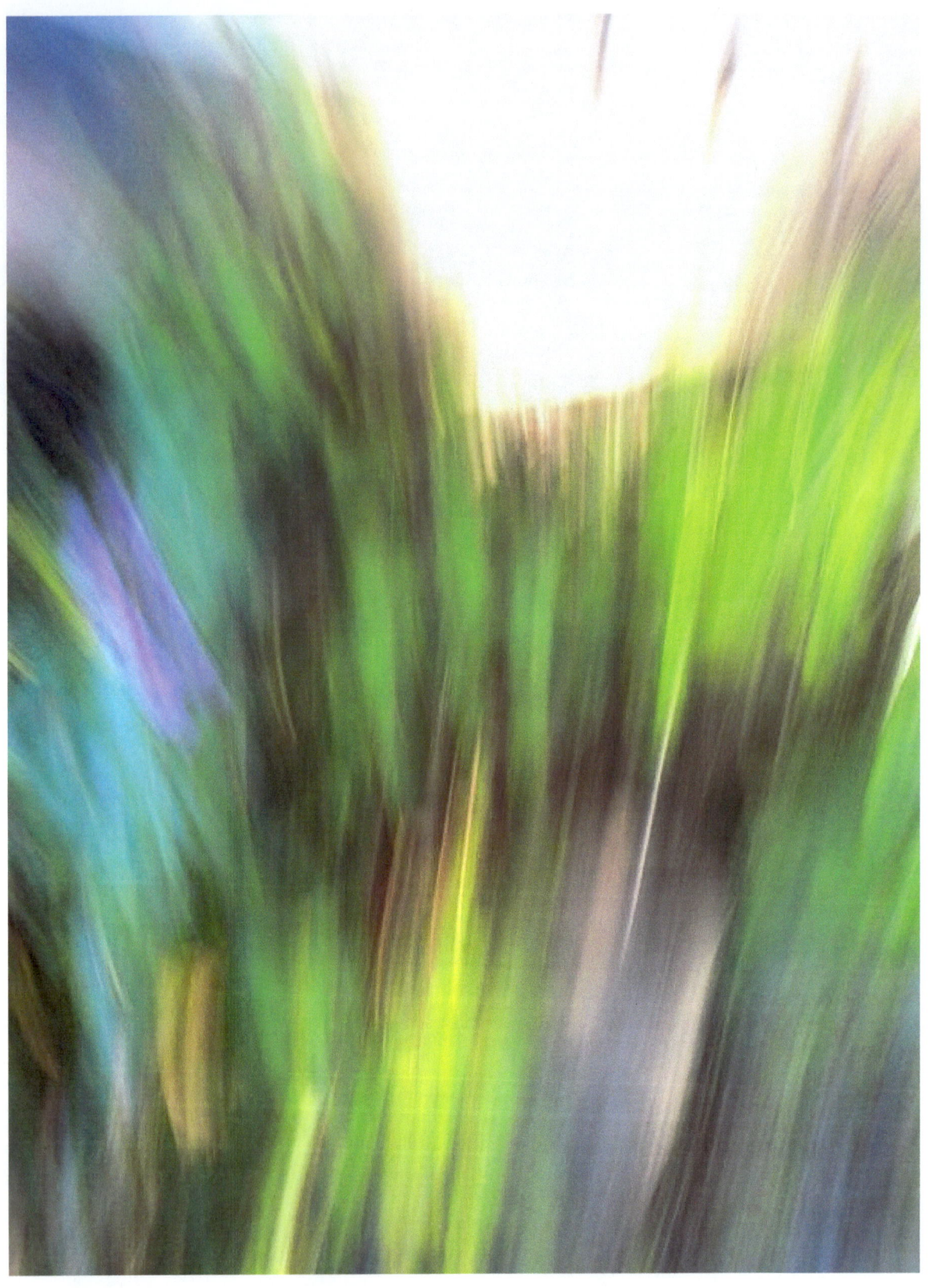

High levels of reflective light becomes luminous on the photograph.

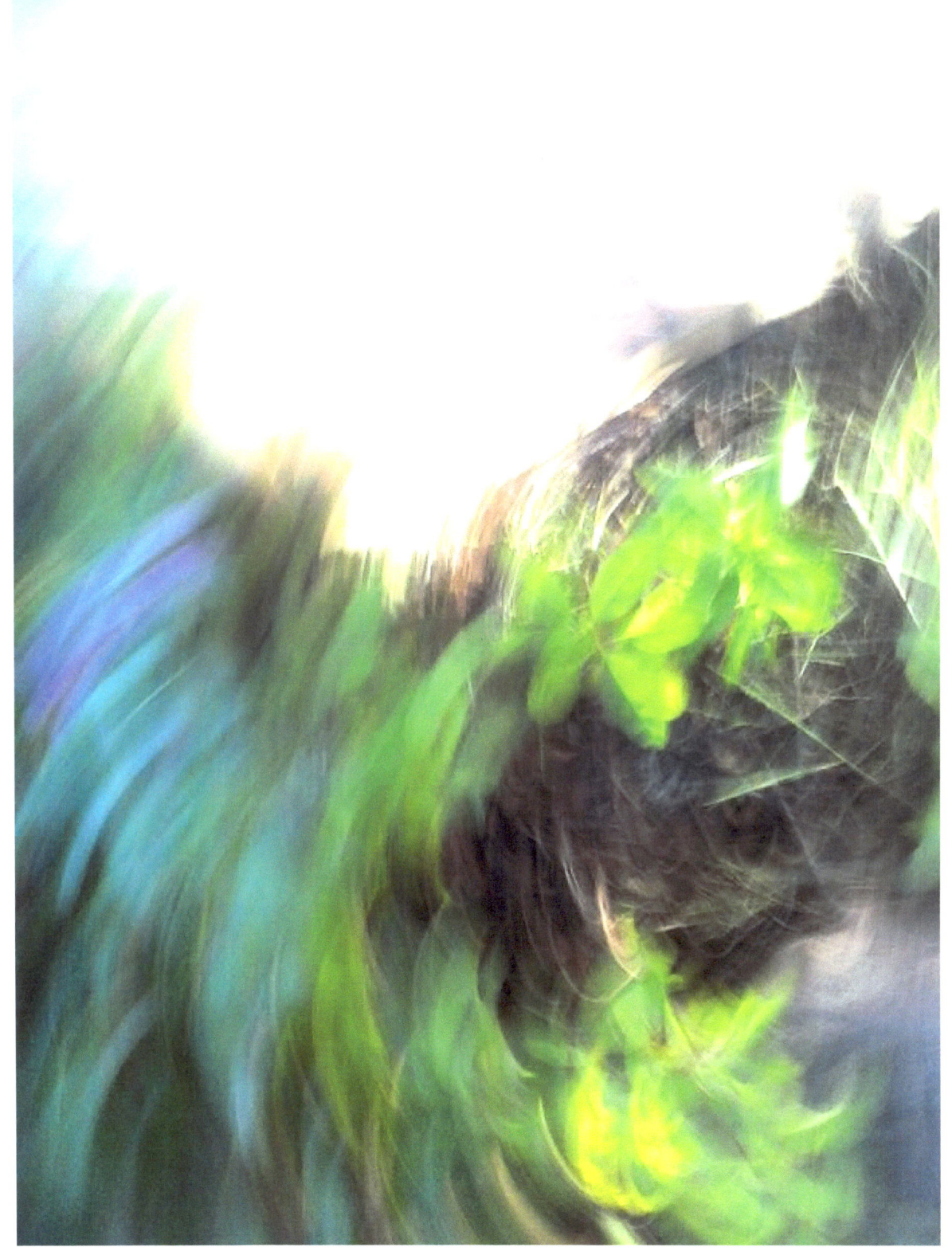

Light and the plant area mixing in rotation.

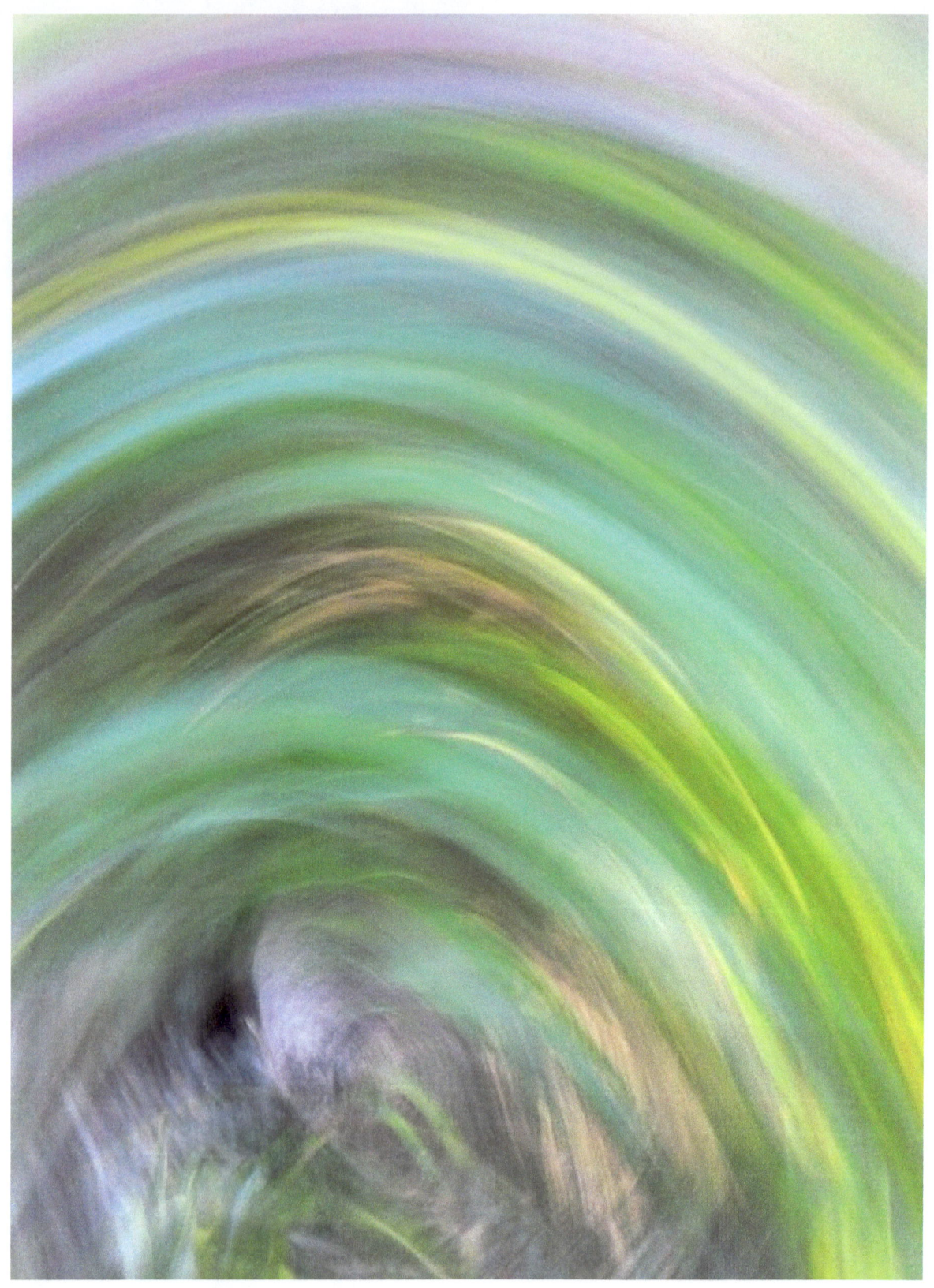

Rotation creating a mid-point.

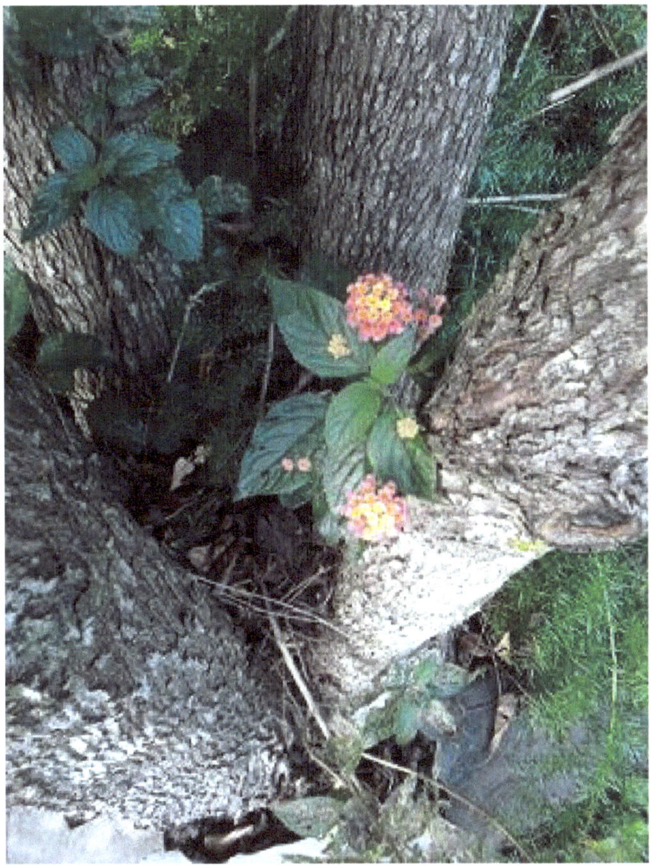

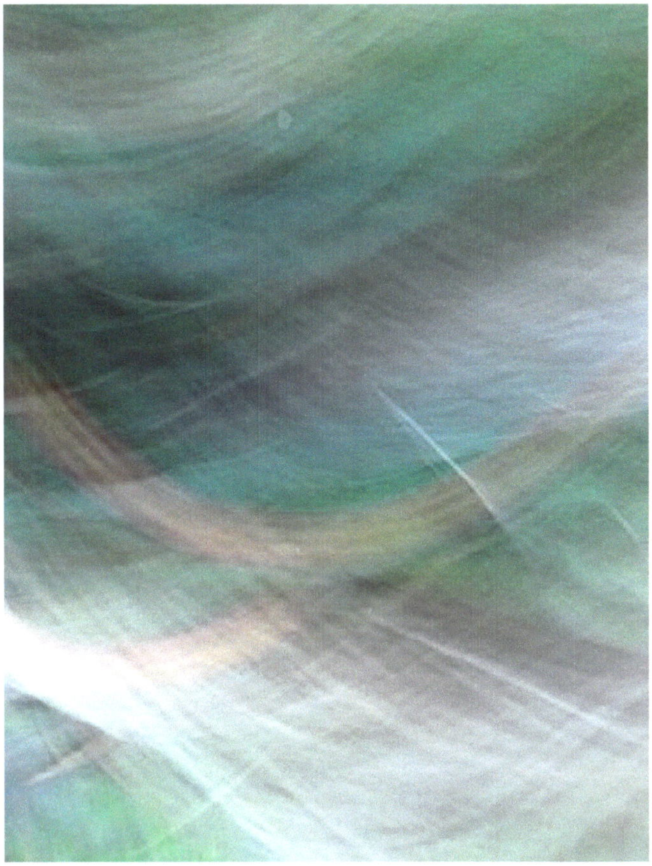

The original photograph on the left and the flowers moving in curves on the photograph on the right while the camera was in transit. Images also can change in human brain according to pressure and light movements and create an abstract form of images.

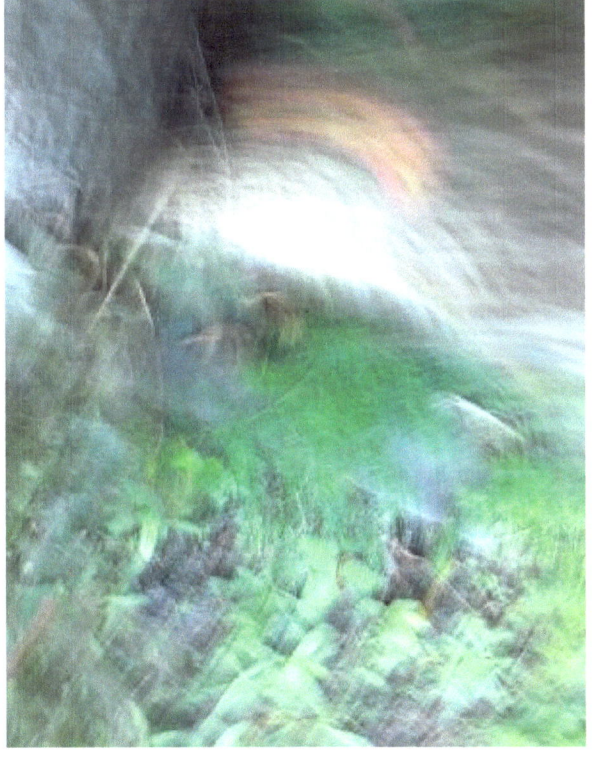

Short movements of flowers make a smaller curve.

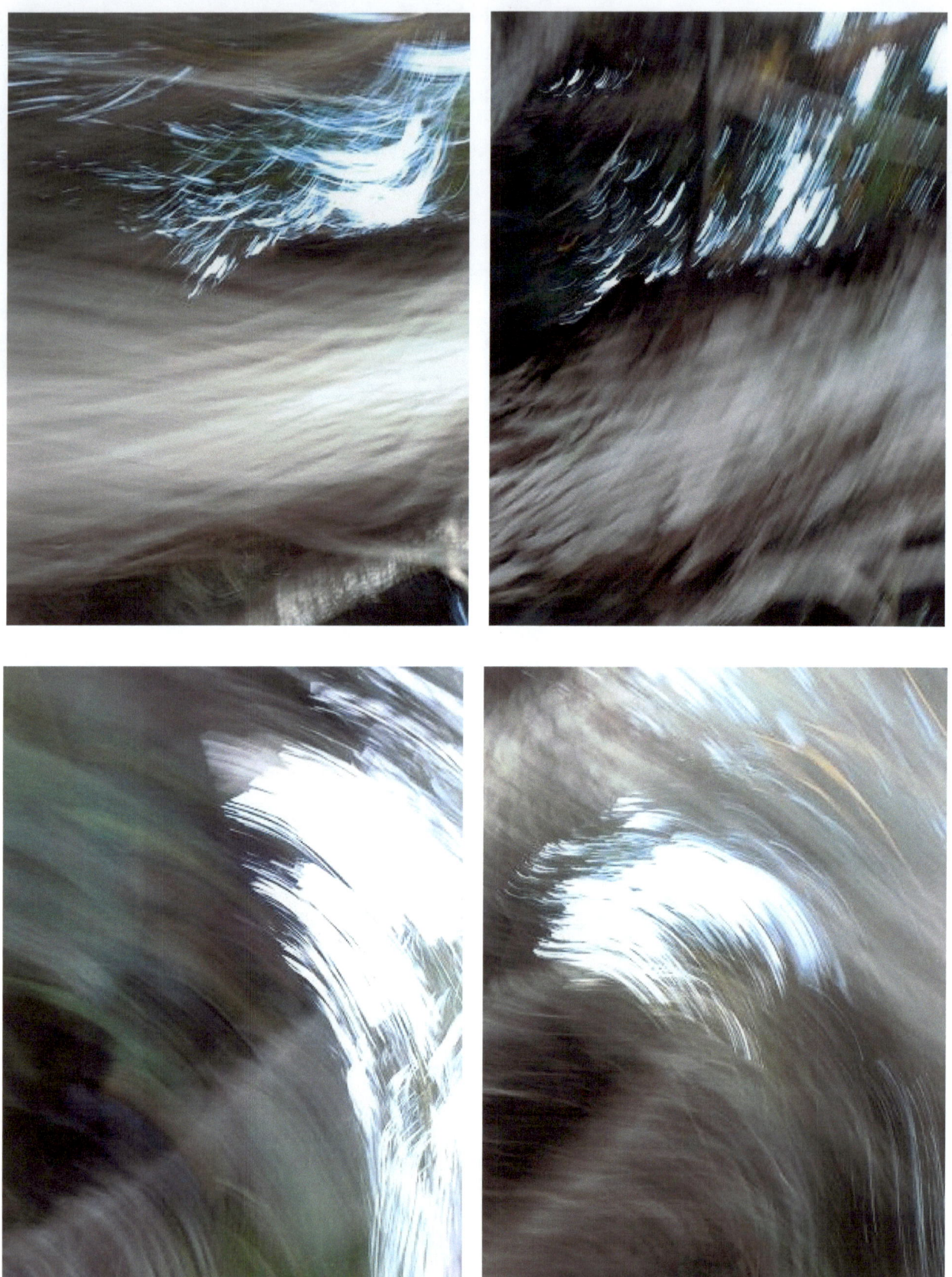

Pulling the light from the atmosphere by taking the photographs with a camera in transit.

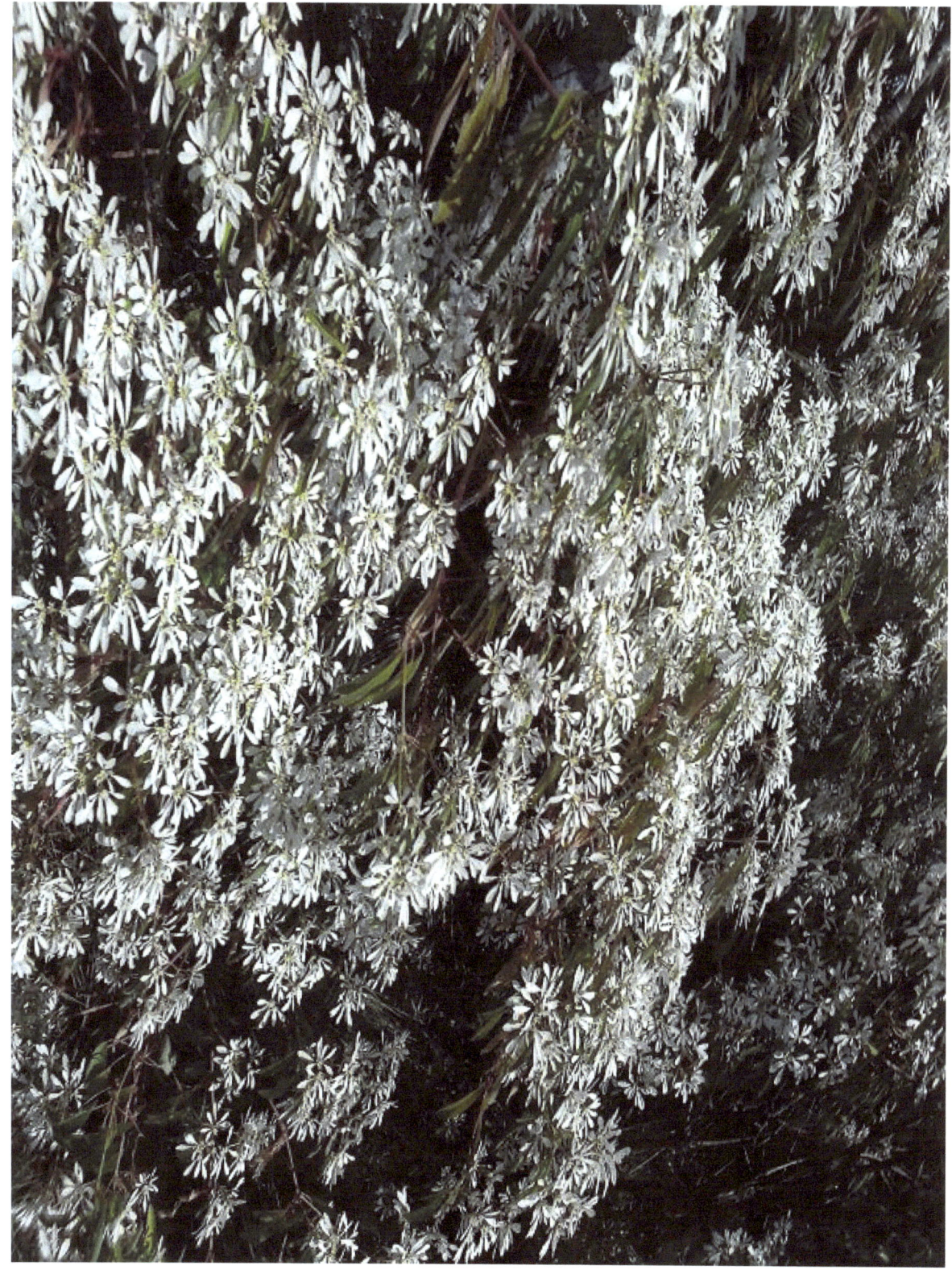

Original photograph taken without moving the camera and same plant taken a photograph in transit is on the next page.

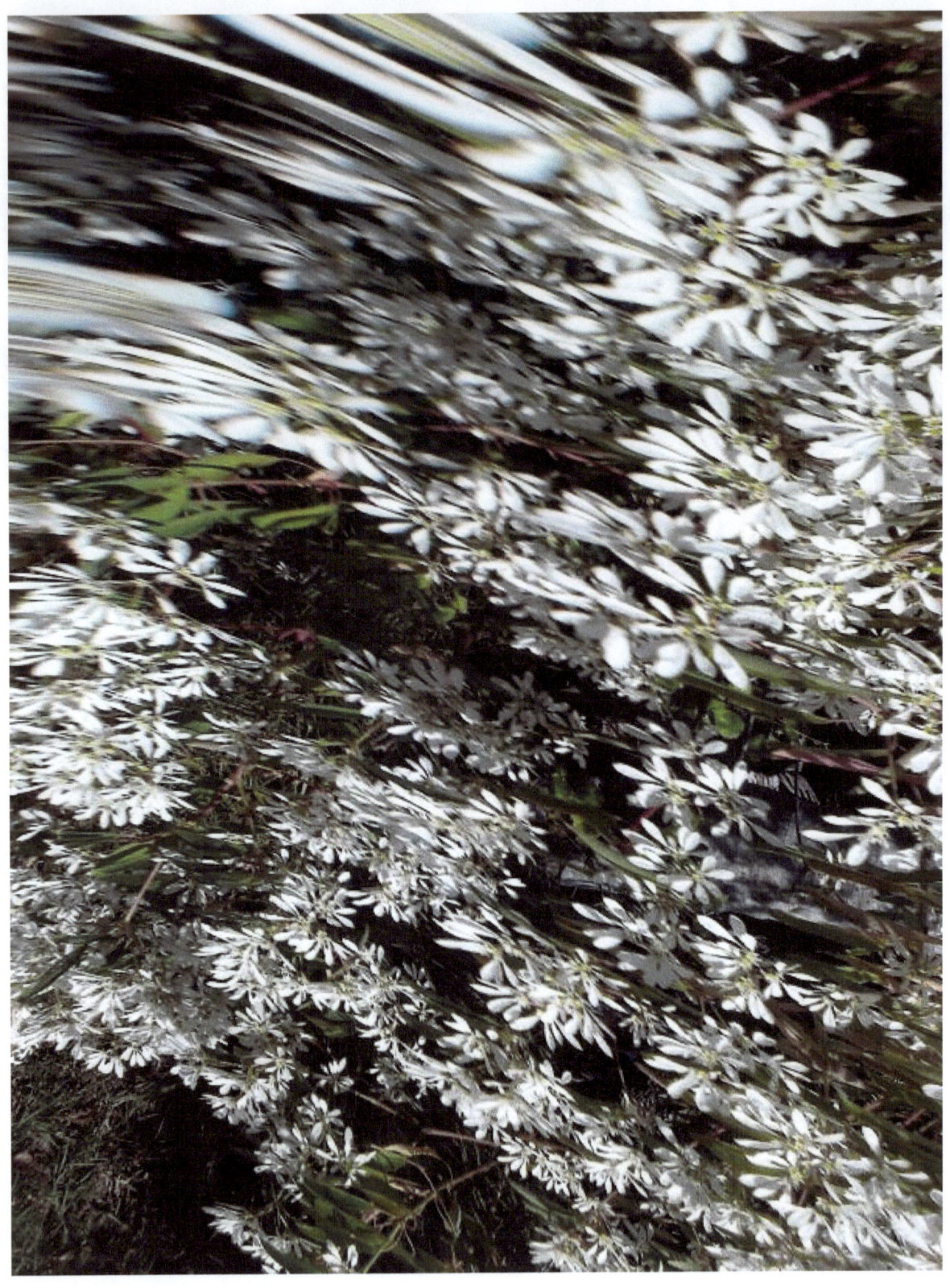

When photograph was taken in transit it will move the colour and the plant shapes with the camera movements.

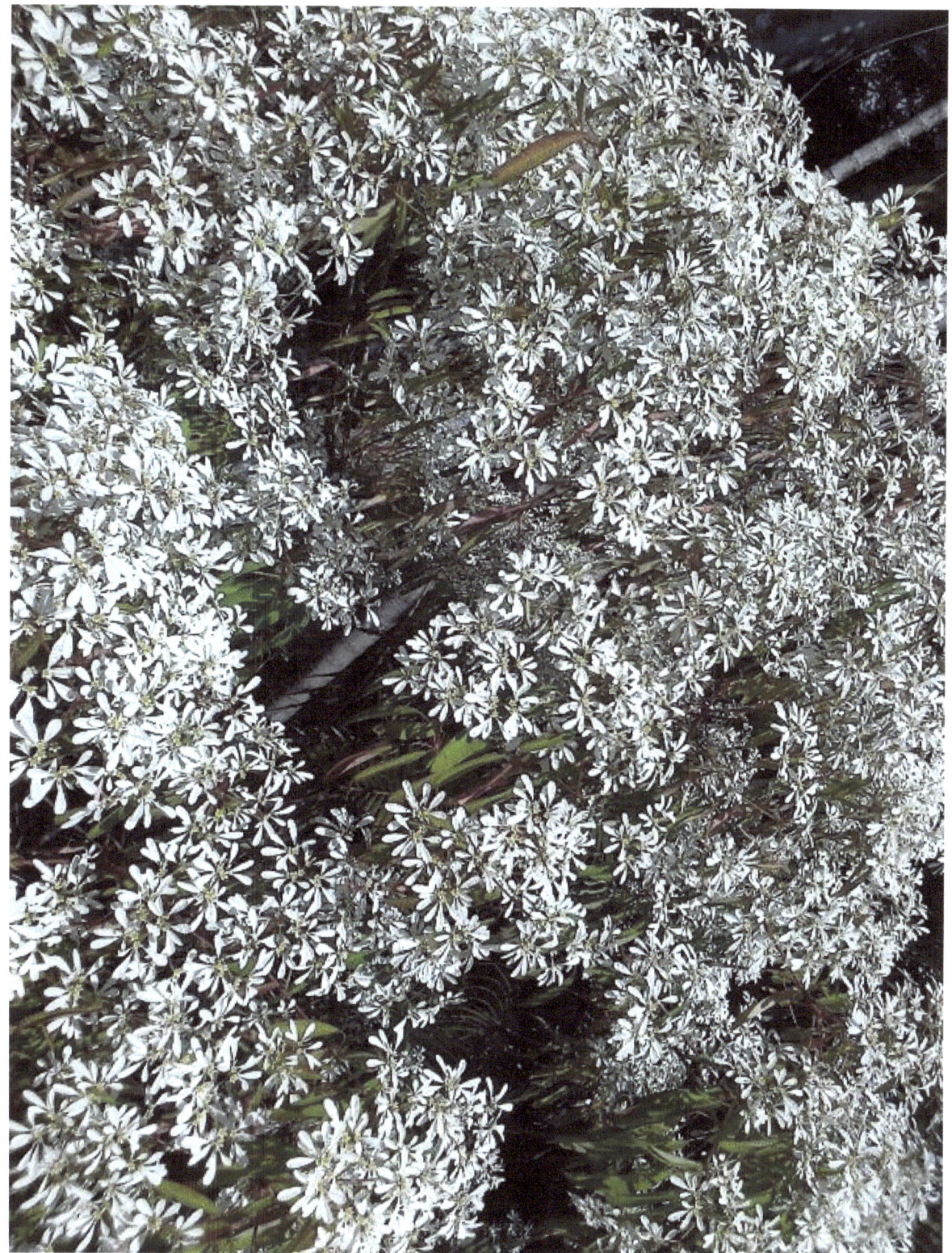

Original photograph without any movements of camera. On the next page same plant taken photograph when the camera was in transit. This tells us that light is connected to everything and we can move as light.

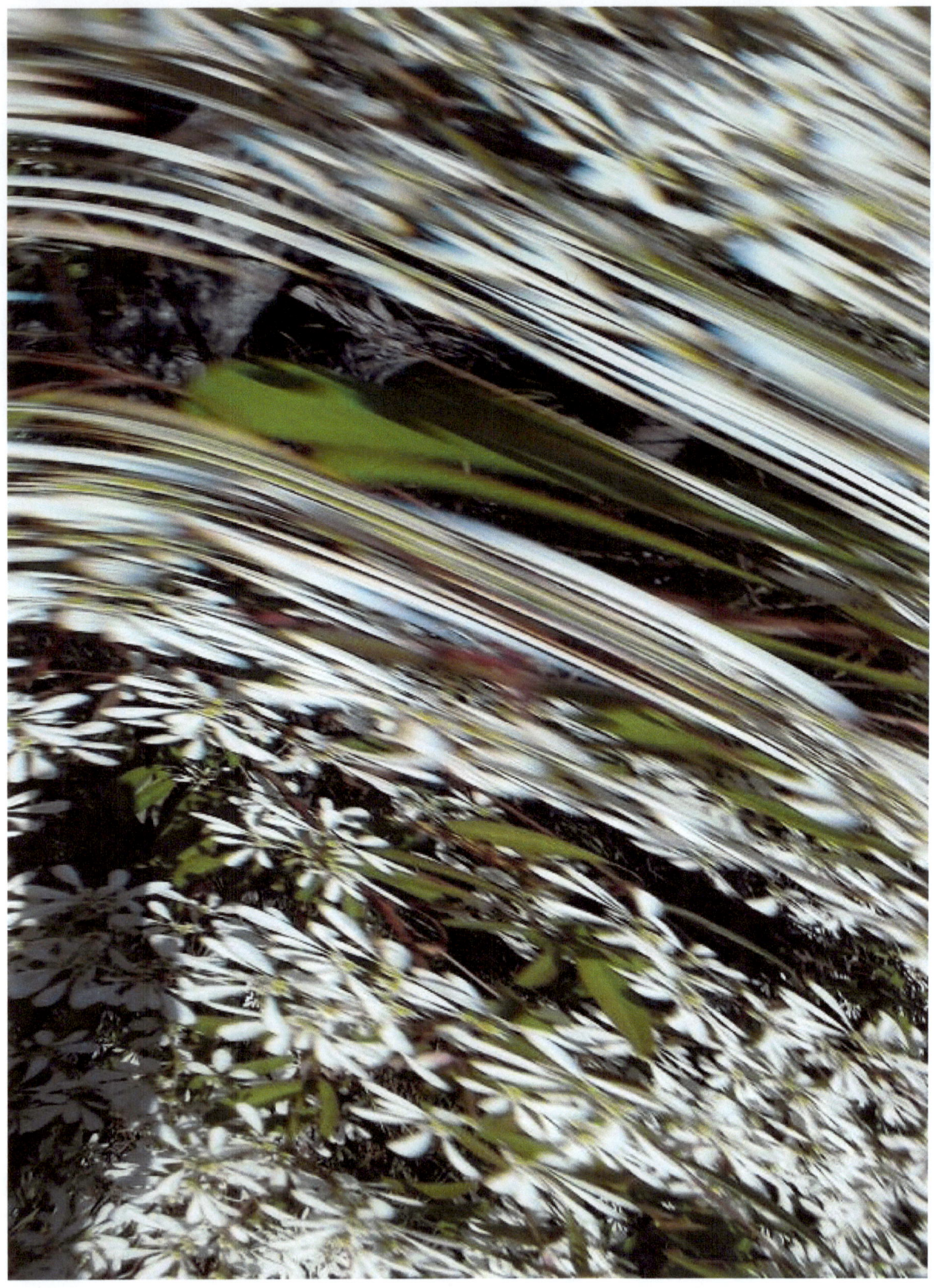

Movements of the camera totally lost the shapes of flowers and leaves and moving as light.

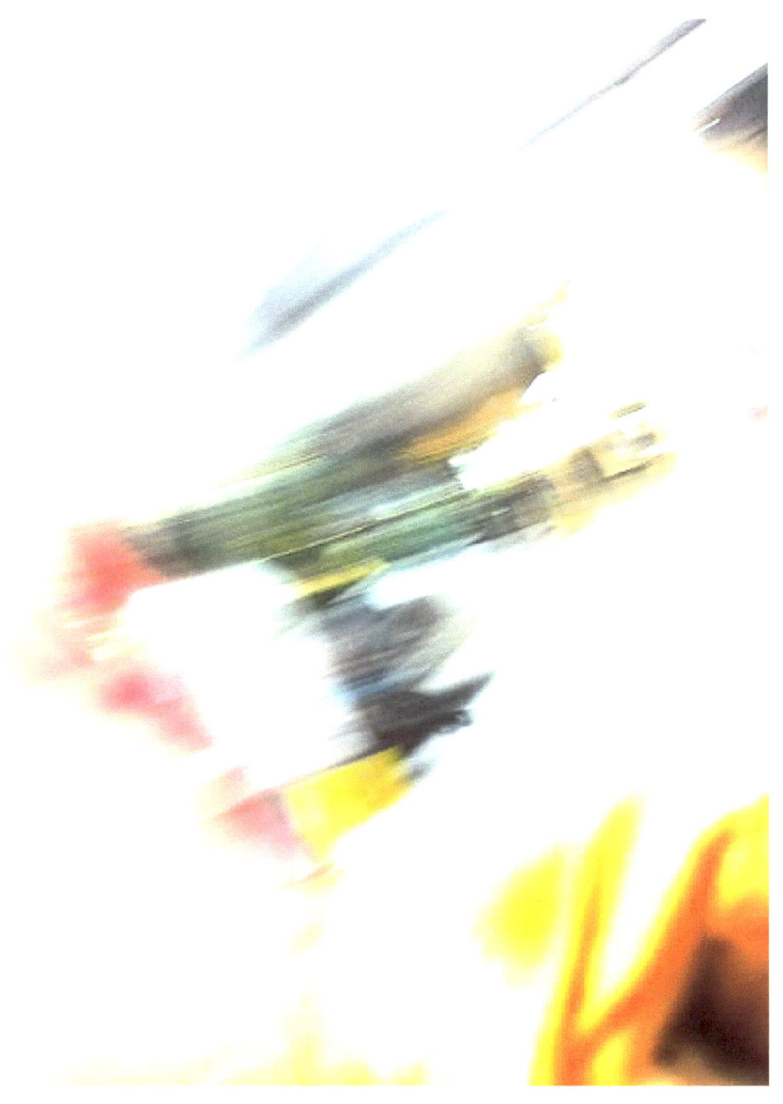

A moving camera picked up spots of colours.

This is a photograph of sun I took. It looks like a burnt sun spot. Why this happened is, the phone I used had the camera lens on the bottom. I took the photograph from an angle with clouds blocking the sun light. This reflective clouds somehow made the sun look black. Now I am beginning to wonder about the sun spots on the sun. Are they real or a photographic illusion. Black hole in space becomes questionable also, whether it is real or some cloud or pressure blocking the flow of sunlight and photographing through cloud layers may makes the sun look black. Black spots like the photograph also may happen on human skin and burnt like the above black spot. Even though the sun is black on the photograph it has orange fire like light around it like the sun spots on the sun.

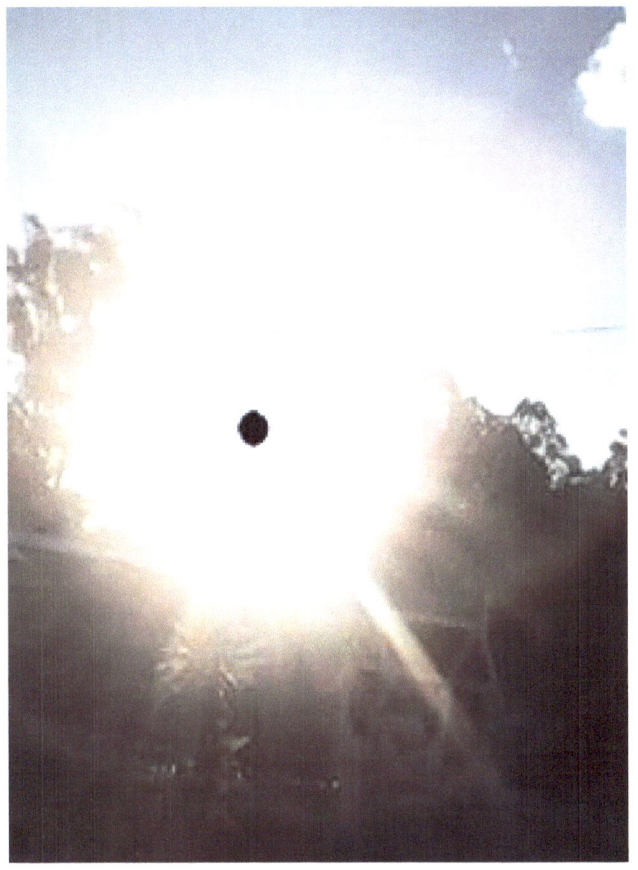

Black spot in the middle and the light around it. These photographic illusion spots we may see it on the sun and call it dead black spots on the sun.

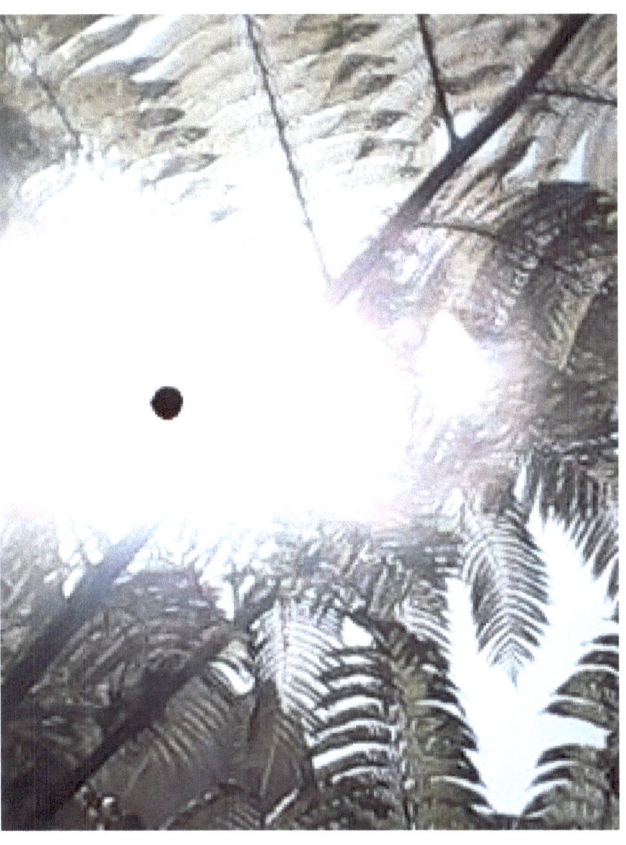

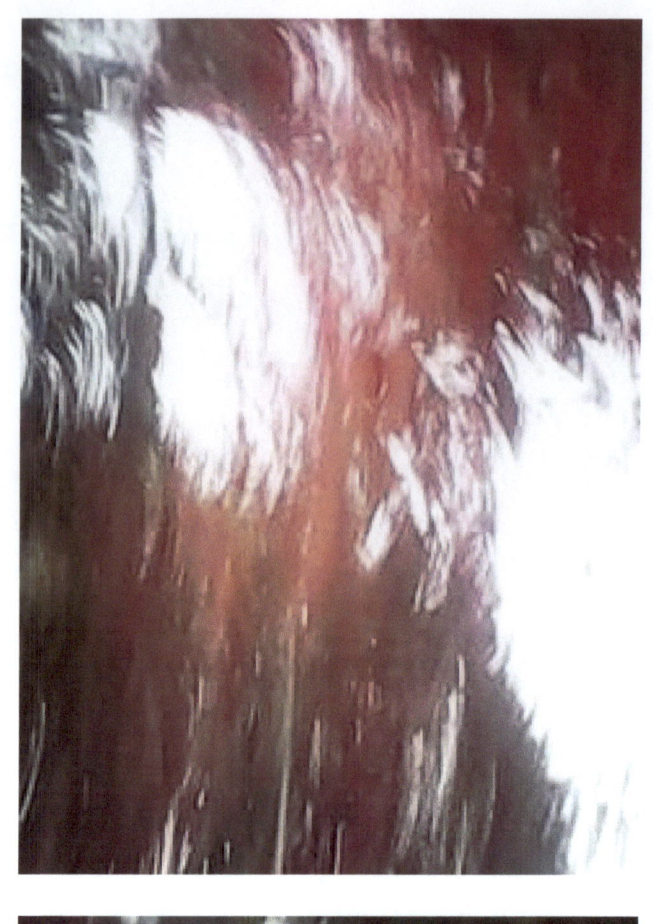

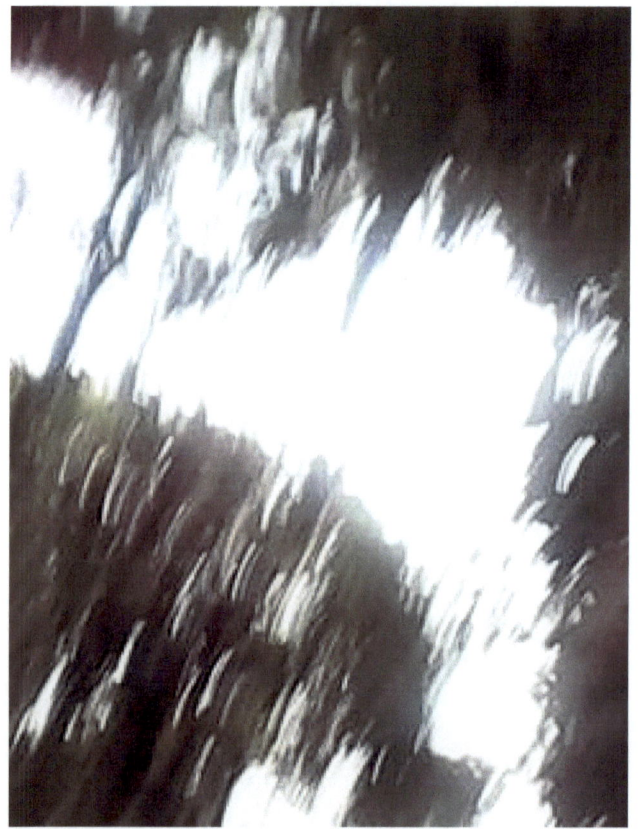

Light movements when camera was in transit.

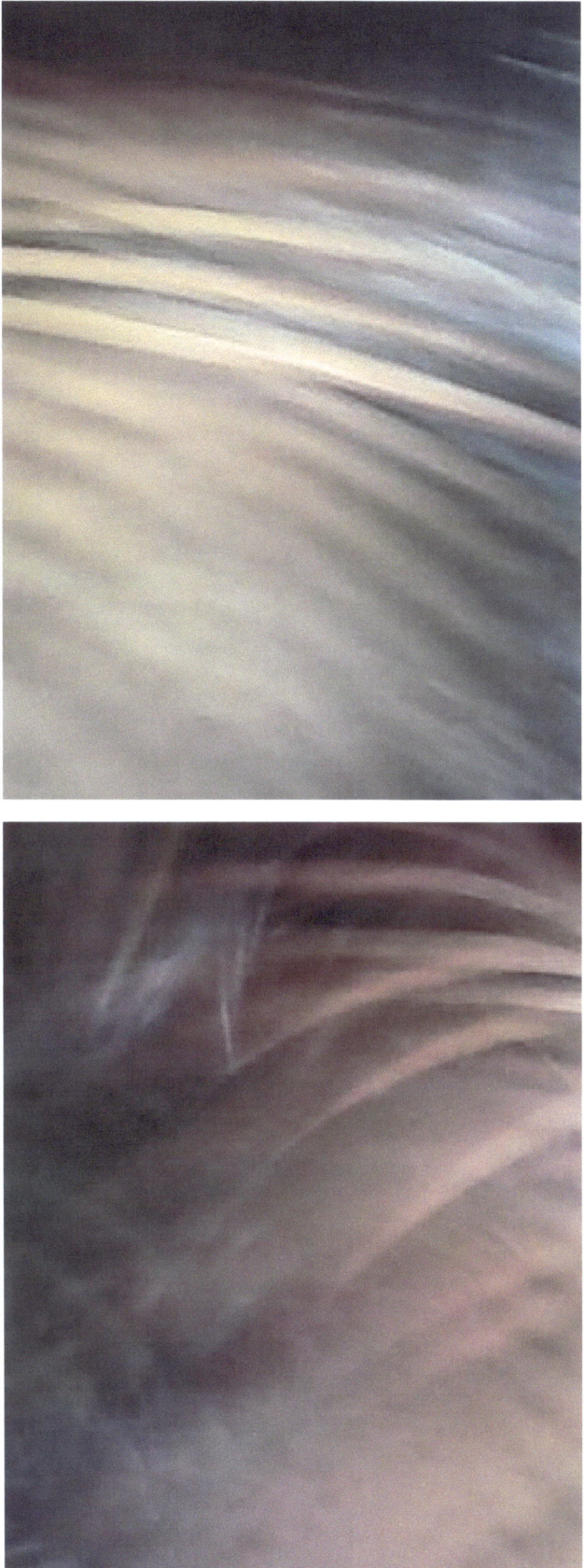

Palm leaves photographed when camera was in transit.

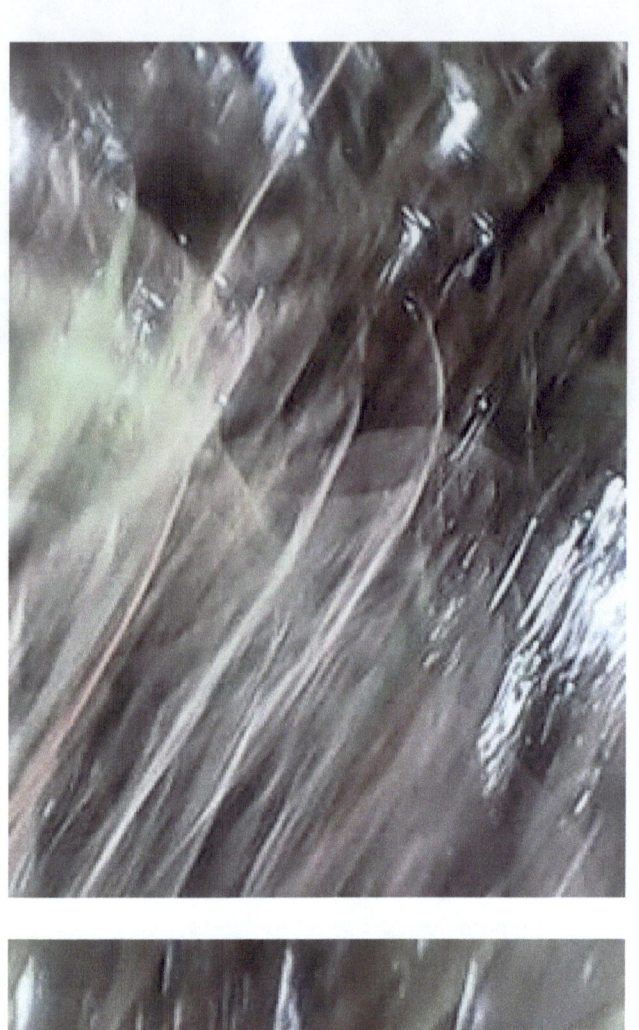

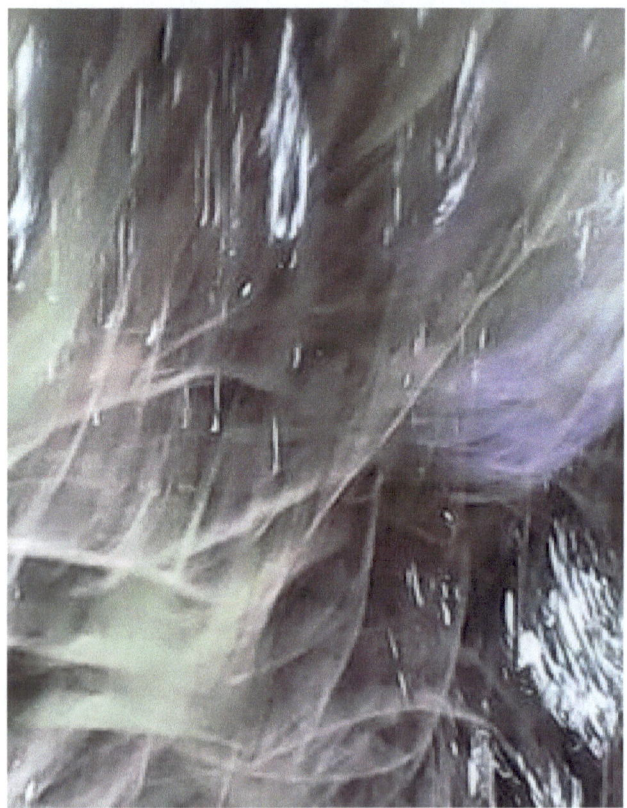

Plants in movements when photographed while the camera was in transit.

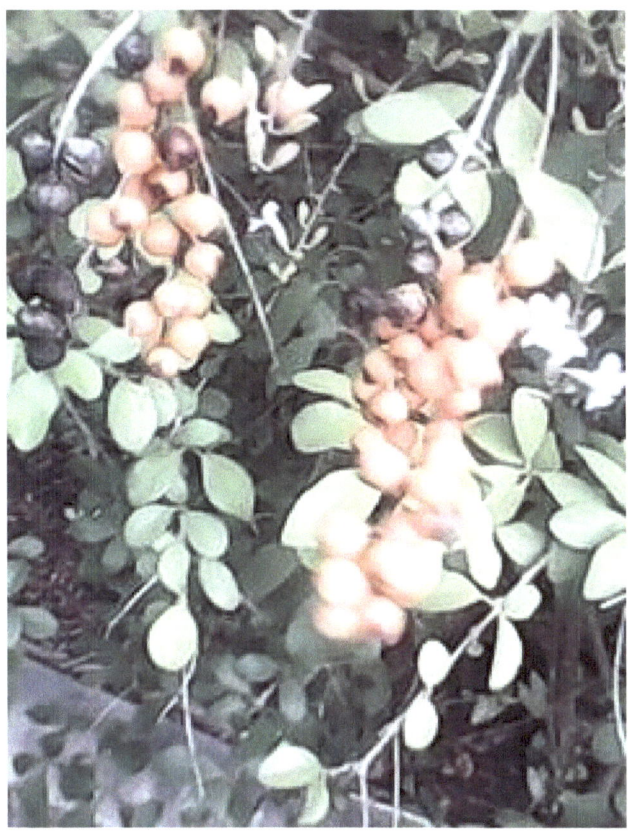
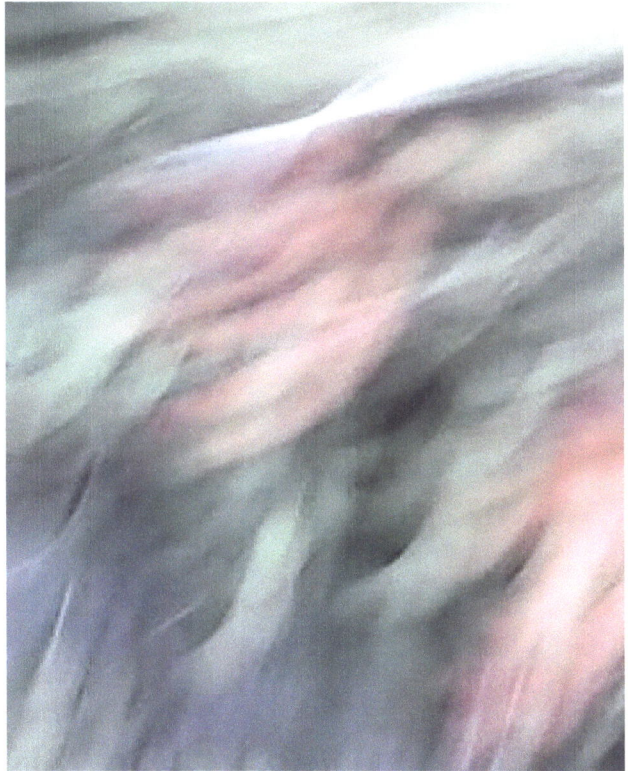

Original photograph of a plant above and the photograph below was taken while the camera was in transit.

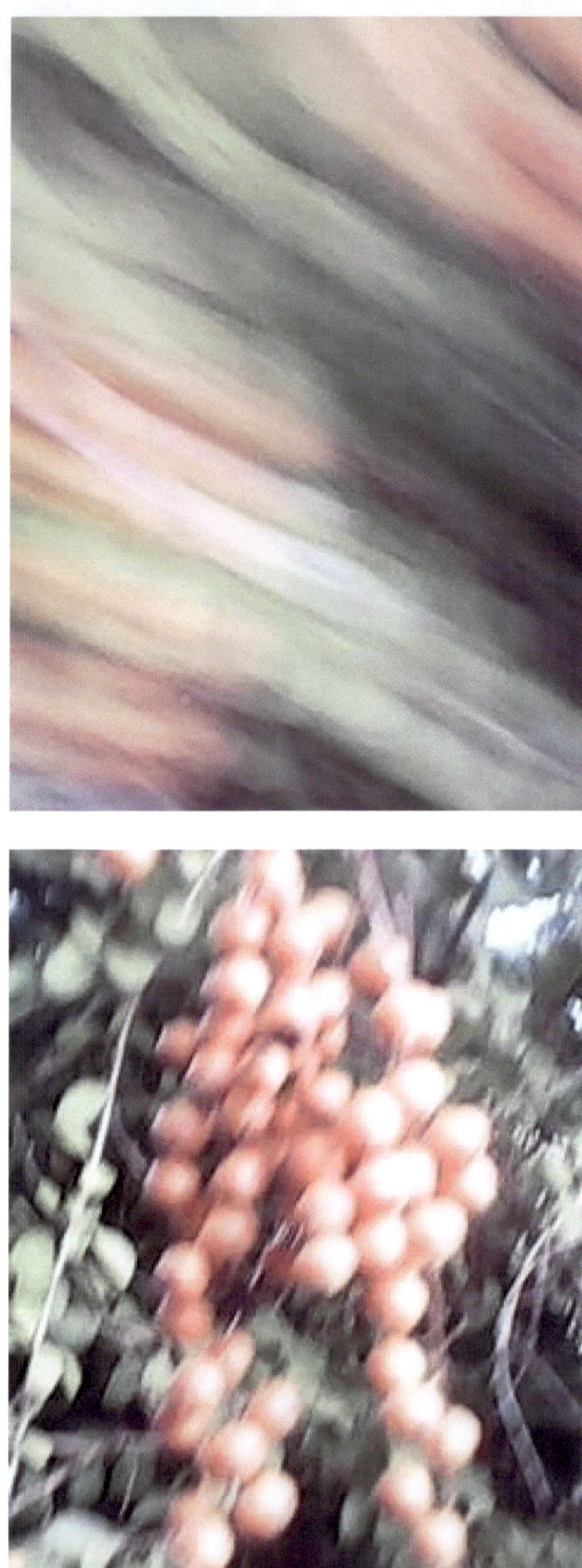

Original photo of a plant and the same plant photographed while the camera was in transit.

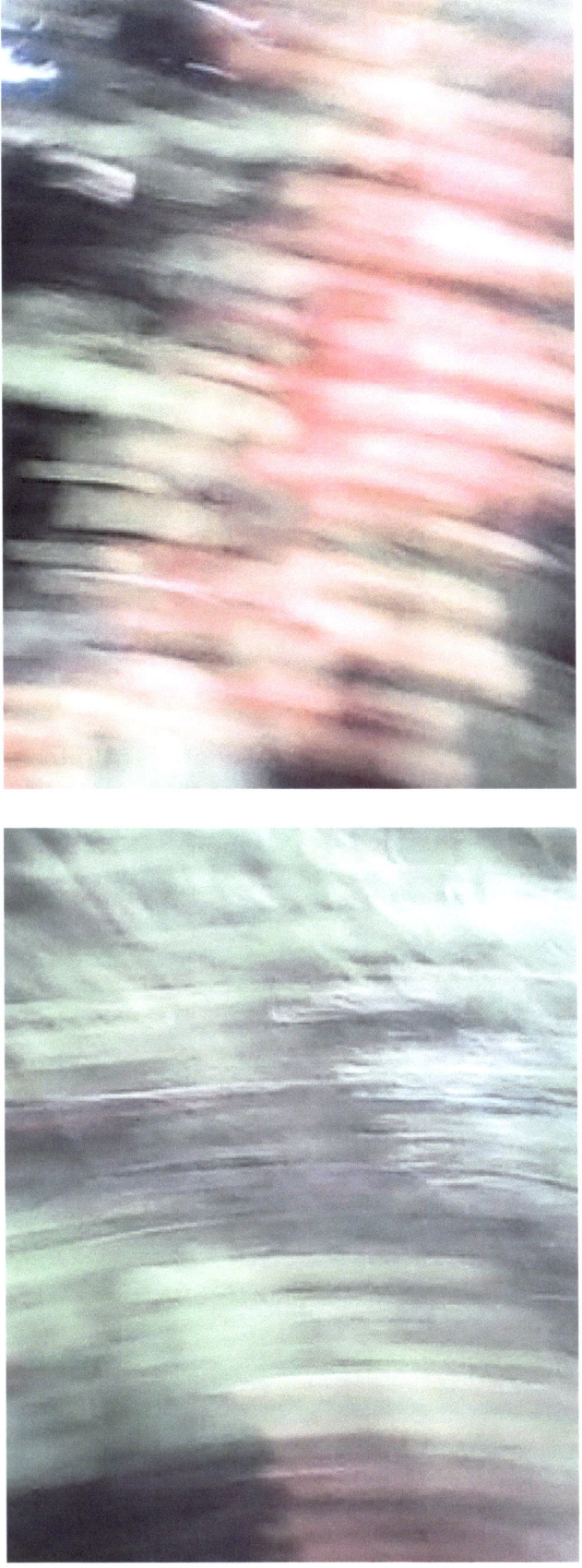

Photographs taken of plants while the camera was in transit.

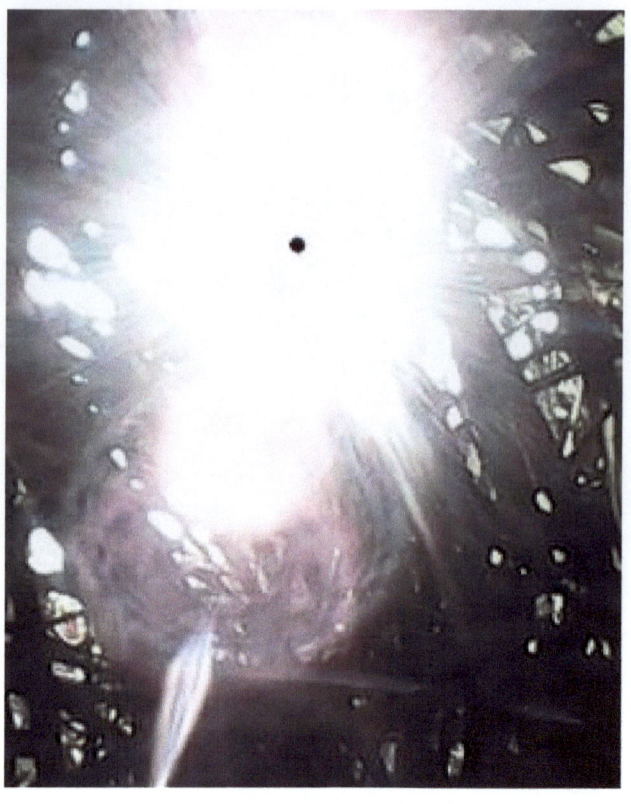

Light pulling from globe to a disc to a funnel and a bud like feature in pressure.

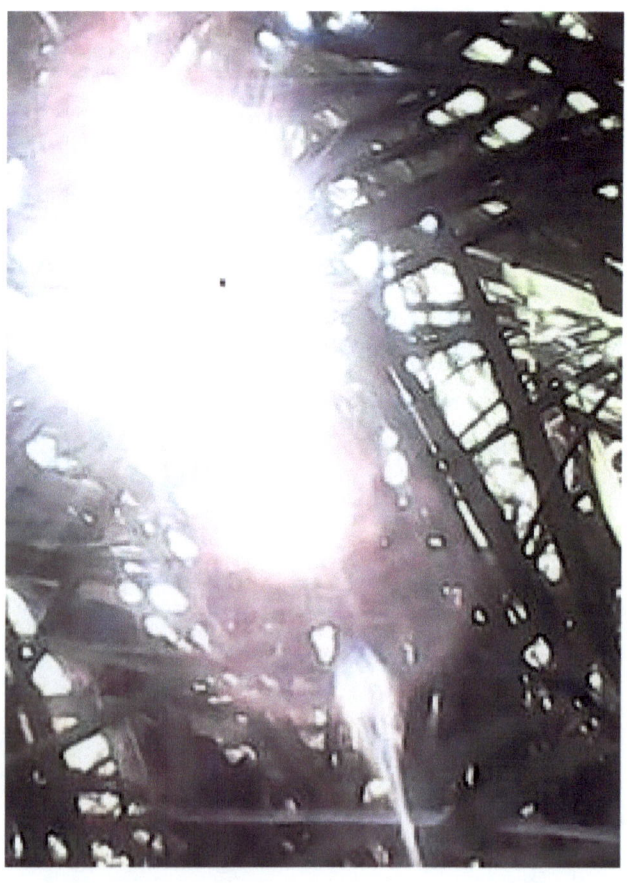

How flowers, fruits and leaves form in these patterns in pressure.